Drive Around

Florida

Thomas Cook

YOUR G RIVES

Titles in this series include:

• Andalucía and the Costa del Sol
• Bavaria and the Austrian Tyrol
• Brittany and Normandy
• Burgundy and the Rhône Valley
• California
• Catalonia and the Spanish Pyrenees
• Dordogne and Western France
• England and Wales
• Florida
• Ireland
• Italian Lakes and Mountains with Venice and Florence
• Languedoc and Southwest France
• Loire Valley
• Provence and the Côte d'Azur
• Scotland
• Tuscany and Umbria
• Vancouver and British Columbia
  and

• Selected Bed and Breakfast in France (annual edition)

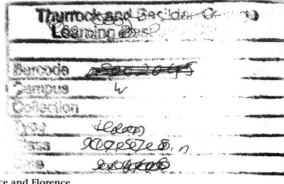

For further information about these and other Thomas Cook publications, write to Thomas Cook Publishing, PO Box 227, The Thomas Cook Business Park, 15–16 Coningsby Road, Peterborough PE3 8SB, United Kingdom.

Drive Around

Florida

The best of Florida's stunning
beaches and wildlife havens, plus
a full guide to the theme parks
of Orlando, the art deco buildings
of Miami Beach, the wilderness of
the Everglades and the relaxed
ambience of the Florida Keys

Mick Sinclair

Thomas Cook
Publishing
www.thomascookpublishing.com

Published by Thomas Cook Publishing,
a division of Thomas Cook Tour Operations Limited
PO Box 227,
The Thomas Cook Business Park
15–16 Coningsby Road
Peterborough PE3 8SB
United Kingdom

Telephone: +44 (0)1733 416477
Fax: +44 (0)1733 416688
E-mail: books@thomascookpublishing.com

For further information about
Thomas Cook Publishing, visit our website:
www.thomascookpublishing.com

ISBN 1-841574-66-X

Text: © 2005 Thomas Cook Publishing
Maps and diagrams:
City maps: © Thomas Cook Publishing
City maps supplied by RJS Associates
Road maps: Supplied and designed by Lovell Johns Ltd, OX8 8LH;
© MapQuest.com Inc., Mountville, PA 17554

Head of Publishing: Chris Young
Series Editor: Charlotte Christensen
Production/DTP Editor: Steven Collins
Project Administrator: Michelle Warrington
Written, researched and updated by: Mick Sinclair

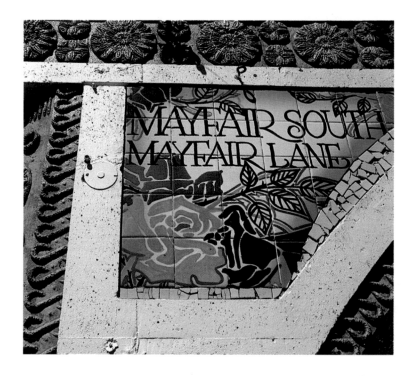

About the author

Mick Sinclair first visited Florida when Miami was more synonymous with retirement homes than art deco architecture and Mickey Mouse was still a recent arrival. Since then, he has witnessed Miami's transformation into a trendsetting modern city, Orlando's evolution into a theme park capital, and Florida itself becoming one of the world's most-visited but least-understood regions.

Intimately familiar with the state's top tourist attractions, best beaches and most scenic roads, Mick is also an initiate of rural Florida. He knows the wayside towns and villages, has canoed rivers and lakes, and hiked through prairies and swamps.

Between trips to the Sunshine State, Mick has written guidebooks to California, Chicago, New York, San Francisco and Scandinavia. His writing career began in 1980 with reviews and features on music, film, books and contemporary culture. Such work continues to appear in newspapers, magazines and books, and on websites, throughout the world.

Contents

About Drive Around Guides

Thomas Cook's Drive Around Guides are designed to provide you with a comprehensive but flexible reference source to guide you as you tour a country or region by car. This guide divides Florida into touring areas – one per chapter. Major cultural centres or cities form chapters in their own right. Each chapter contains enough attractions to provide at least a day's worth of activities – often more.

Star ratings

To make it easier for you to plan your time and decide what to see, the main sights and attractions are given star ratings. A three-star rating indicates an outstanding sight or major attraction. Often these can be worth at least half a day of your time. A two-star attraction is worth an hour or so of your time, and a one-star attraction indicates a site that is good, but often of specialist interest. The stars are intended to help you set priorities, so that travellers with limited time can quickly find the most rewarding sights.

Chapter contents

Every chapter has an introduction summing up the main attractions of the area, and a ratings box, which will highlight the area's strengths and weaknesses – some areas may be more attractive to families travelling with children, others to wine-lovers visiting vineyards, and others to people interested in finding castles, churches, nature reserves, or good beaches.

Each chapter is then divided into an alphabetical gazetteer, and a suggested tour. You can select whether you just want to visit a particular sight or attraction, choosing from those described in the gazetteer, or whether you want to tour the area comprehensively. If the latter, you can construct your own itinerary, or follow the author's suggested tour, which comes at the end of every area chapter.

The gazetteer

The gazetteer section describes all the major attractions in the area – the villages, towns, historic sites, nature reserves, parks or museums that you are most likely to want to see. Maps of the area highlight all the places mentioned in the text. Using this comprehensive overview of the area, you may choose just to visit one or two sights.

One way to use the guide is simply to find individual sights that interest you, using the index, overview map or star ratings, and read what our authors have to say about them. This will help you decide whether to visit the sight. If you do, you will find plenty of practical

Symbol key

- ❶ Tourist Information Centre
- Ⓦ Website
- ❷ Advice on arriving or departing
- ❿ Parking locations
- ❶ Advice on getting around
- ❸ Directions
- ❶ Sights and attractions
- ❶ Accommodation
- ❶ Eating
- ❍ Shopping
- ❾ Sport
- ❷ Entertainment

Practical information

The practical information in the page margins, or sidebar, will help you locate the services you need as an independent traveller – including the tourist information centre, car parks and public transport facilities. You will also find the opening times of sights, museums, churches and other attractions, as well as useful tips on shopping, market days, cultural events, entertainment, festivals and sports facilities.

information, such as the street address, the telephone number for enquiries and opening times.

Alternatively, you can choose a hotel, perhaps with the help of the accommodation recommendations contained in this guide. You can then turn to the overall map on page 10 to help you work out which chapters in the book describe those cities and regions that lie closest to your chosen touring base.

Driving tours

The suggested tour is just that – a suggestion, with plenty of optional detours and one or two ideas for making your own discoveries, under the heading *Also worth exploring*. The routes are designed to link the attractions described in the gazetteer section, and to cover outstandingly scenic coastal, mountain and rural landscapes. The total distance is given for each tour, as is the time it will take you to drive the complete route, but bear in mind that this indication is just for the driving time: you will need to add on extra time for visiting attractions along the way.

Many of the routes are circular, so that you can join them at any point. Where the nature of the terrain dictates that the route has to be linear, the route can either be followed out and back, or you can use it as a link route, to get from one area in the book to another.

As you follow the route descriptions, you will find names picked out in bold capital letters – this means that the place is described fully in the gazetteer. Other names picked out in bold indicate additional villages or attractions worth a brief stop along the route.

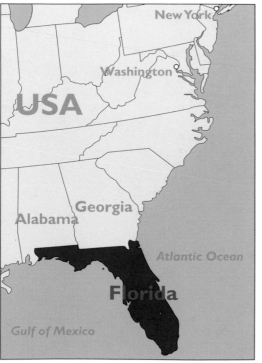

Accommodation and food

In every chapter you will find lodging and eating recommendations for individual towns, or for the area as a whole. These are designed to cover a range of price brackets and concentrate on more characterful small or individualistic hotels and restaurants. In addition, you will find information in the *Travel facts* chapter on chain hotels, with an address to which you can write for a guide, map or directory. The price indications used in the guide have the following meanings:

$	budget level
$$	typical/average prices
$$$	de luxe.

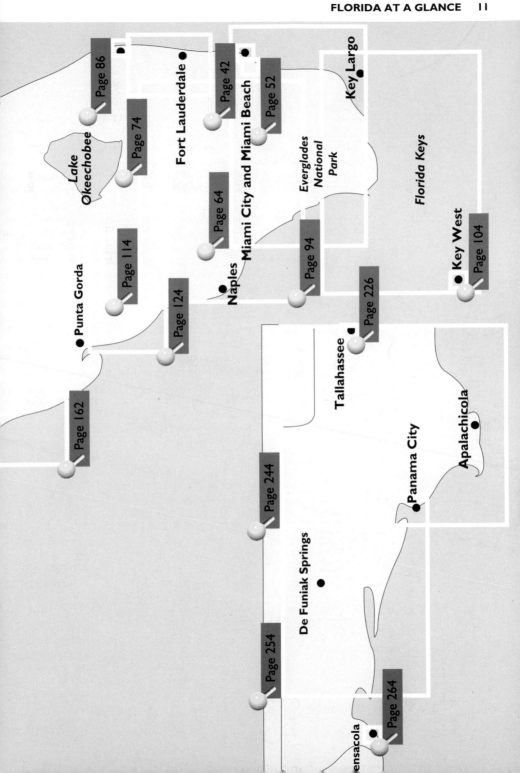

Page 86

Page 74

Lake Okeechobee

Fort Lauderdale ●

Page 42

Page 52

Key Largo ●

Everglades National Park

Florida Keys

Page 64

Miami City and Miami Beach

Page 114

● Punta Gorda

Page 124

Naples ●

Page 94

Key West ●

Page 104

Page 162

Page 226

Tallahassee

Page 244

Panama City ●

Apalachicola ●

De Funiak Springs ●

Page 254

Page 264

● Pensacola

Introduction

Subtropical sunshine, a thousand miles of beaches and the best theme parks human ingenuity can devise make Florida one of the world's greatest tourist destinations. Seventy-five million people come here each year and very few leave disappointed. Not many among them, however, really make the most of what this extremely varied and rewarding state has to offer.

At the heart of Florida is Orlando, the state's tourism linchpin. The major theme park complexes of Walt Disney World and Universal Studios are based here, as is every other conceivable attraction from 'haunted' houses to crazy golf courses. Yet small towns and historic communities also lie well within Orlando's sway, as do immense stretches of coast where deservedly popular areas such as Daytona Beach and Clearwater Beach lie alongside isolated tourist-free strands lining pine-fringed barrier islands.

Orlando's sprawling form denies it the character that many Florida cities possess. A large Latin-American population brings vibrancy to Miami, where Cuban restaurants delight the culinary adventurous and the Art Deco District is one of the state's architectural treasures. Miami Beach draws the young, fashionable and affluent to its smartest hotels, but no Florida city is more conspicuously wealthy than the long-time millionaire's playground of Palm Beach.

Different again is Florida's homely capital, Tallahassee, nestling amid the oak-filled hillsides of the Panhandle. And at the end of the Florida Keys, few places combine history, relaxation and scenic splendour – notably intensely dramatic sunsets – as effortlessly as Key West.

While tourism underpins the Florida economy, efforts are under way to ensure that visitor numbers, and a continually expanding permanent population, do not destroy the state's many unique environments. With its sawgrass prairies and cypress swamps, the Everglades are the best known of the many natural areas that come as a revelation to Florida first-timers. State parks and wildlife refuges are common, providing user-friendly introductions to denizens such as alligators and manatees. Even Florida's plants and trees can be stunning; many wild areas harbour glorious stashes of wild flowers while the state can also claim vast pine forests and several hundred species of palm.

Natural Florida also includes beaches, quickly revealed as much more than merely places to laze in the sun. Ranging in colour from golden brown to dazzling white, the sands might be favoured by surfers, prized for their shells, provide a venue for weekend barbecues or romantic escapes, or enable sea turtles to creep shyly ashore after dark to lay their eggs.

Despite its strong links with theme parks, it was not Walt Disney who discovered Florida but 16th-century Spaniards, who encountered a Floridian population established for tens of thousands of years. Although major pre-European remains tend to be confined to museums, plenty survives of Florida's colonial past. Spanish-founded St Augustine is one of the oldest cities in the US, while Pensacola was fought over by the British, Spanish and French before becoming a strategically important US base.

Florida's diverse cultural strands are evident throughout the state. The Cross Creek cottage of writer Marjorie Kinnan Rawlings reveals the deprivations of 1930s Florida as well as the landscapes that inspired the writer. The Koreshan State Historic Site, near Fort Myers, recalls a time when Florida, for some, represented the earthly Garden of Eden. And the Cuban presence, past and present, is strongly felt in Miami, Tampa and Key West.

Perhaps the most remarkable aspect of Florida is how much can be seen and enjoyed so effortlessly. The quality and comfort of American cars, the relatively low cost of petrol and an excellent and easily navigated road system with frequent scenic stretches makes getting around simple and pleasurable. Each of the 25 driving, walking and city tours in this book is designed to maximise time and minimise effort in discovering the best of Florida in all its forms.

Sleeping and eating are also good news. Hotels, motels and evocative bed-and-breakfast inns are found at every turn in all price ranges, as are the restaurants that suit all tastes and budgets. Whether ordering American staples such as milk shakes and burgers or Florida specialities like conch fritter, heart-of-palm salad, grilled mahi-mahi or fried catfish, you can rest assured that it will be served fresh and with a smile.

Right
The Biltmore Hotel, Miami

Travel facts

Useful addresses

Florida Bed and Breakfast Inns c/o AMS, PO Box 2147, Stafford, TX 77497; tel: (800) 524-1880; www.florida-inns.com

Florida Hotel & Motel Association 200 W College Avenue, Tallahassee, FL 32301; tel: (850) 224-2888; www.flahotel.com

Several websites detail specific bed-and-breakfast inns throughout the US and beyond including **International Bed & Breakfast Pages** (www.ippb.com) and **Bed and Breakfast Online** (www.bbonline.com).

Most tourist offices will have details of accommodation in their area.

Accommodation

From luxury hotels with in-room Jacuzzis to simple motels beside the Interstate, Florida is well served by accommodation of all kinds in all price ranges. National hotel chains such as Best Western and Holiday Inn (typically $70–$95 per room) are prevalent, as are motel chains such as Days Inn and Super 8 (usually $50–$75 per room). Most provide clean rooms with bathrooms and TV (usually with a range of cable channels to complement the nationally networked channels). Some offer rooms with kitchenettes, known as 'efficiencies', usually adding $15–$25 to the room price. In general, the more you pay, the bigger the room and more plentiful the facilities will be. Increasingly, many hotels and motels offer a rudimentary free breakfast.

Usually with much more charm than the chains are the many independently run hotels and motels, such as the art deco hotels of Miami Beach (likely to charge $90–$150) and those beside rivers and lakes catering primarily to boating and fishing enthusiasts (typically $45–$75).

Reservations are easily made by phone (most chains have a toll-free number) or fax and in many cases by email, ahead of arrival. Only during peak periods (this may mean a local sports event or festival, a national holiday or simply the main tourist season) is space likely to be in short supply.

More individual lodgings are offered by bed-and-breakfast inns (usually $90–$150), often century-old homes with a handful of guest rooms liberally filled with antiques and scented with potpourri. The hosts usually provide a full breakfast; some also offer afternoon snacks and complimentary wine or sherry. The hosts are well acquainted with local points of interest and driving and dining details. Many inns are booked well ahead for weekends, and there may be a minimum two-night stay over busy periods.

All accommodation is usually paid for by credit card, which can also be used to secure a reservation confirmation (be sure to acquire a reference number) ahead of arrival and not debited if you cancel the booking with reasonable notice. A reservation without confirmation will usually be held until 1600 or 1800 on the day of arrival. Sales tax and any local accommodation taxes are rarely part of the quoted price.

Above
Nassau Hotel, Miami Beach

Airports

See pages 32–3.

Children

With theme parks, zoos, wildlife parks, beaches and many kid-orientated museums and attractions, Florida could be designed for children. Most obviously, Orlando's theme parks are the stuff of youngsters' dreams, even though only Disney's Magic Kingdom really has a lot to appeal to younger ones.

Theme parks are large and often crowded, and it is very easy to become lost and separated. Most have a supervised Lost Kids Area, a mini playground with sufficient amusements for them to forget that they are lost until their parents show up to reclaim them. It is a good idea for kids to be given ID bearing their name so that park staff can contact parents over the PA system. For children old enough to explore on their own, parents should fix a time and place to meet later. At all parks, pushchairs ('strollers') can be rented for the day.

Along with theme parks, Florida also has over a hundred state parks. These are well-managed natural areas, most with walking trails and picnic tables, some with swimming and canoeing facilities. The park visitors' centre arranges park ranger-guided activities, many of them intended to introduce youngsters to the joys of wild Florida. Most activities take place at weekends and during US holidays.

Miami's Metrozoo (see page 58) boasts white Bengal tigers and komodo dragons among several hundred species spread over 300 acres of replicated habitats. Near Palm Beach, Lion Country Safari (see page 81) is a drive-through, 500-acre park holding not just lions but elephants, rhinos, antelopes, giraffes, chimpanzees and a host of other creatures.

In many towns and cities, museums encourage young visitors with hands-on, interactive exhibits designed to entertain as they educate. Two of the biggest are Tampa's Museum of Science and Industry (see page 138) and Fort Lauderdale's Museum of Discovery and Science (see page 80).

In all but the most formal restaurants, children are not only welcome but presented with their own menu as soon as they sit down, together with assorted small toys, colouring sets and picture books. Kids' menus are likely to feature burgers, hot dogs, pizzas and French fries in child-sized portions at parent-pleasing prices. Most restaurants have high chairs and kids' seats readily available.

Florida does have its pitfalls for children, though. Young skin is especially susceptible to sunburn, while heat and humidity (most intense during the south Florida summer) can quickly cause irritability. Long car drives bring problems, too, although roadside amusements, be it crazy golf or a stand selling boiled peanuts, can provide a welcome diversion.

Right
Miami Beach sunbathers

Climate

South and much of central Florida have a subtropical climate. The region has mild winters and hot and humid summers with frequent short but severe thunderstorms.

Winter is the peak tourist season. In northern Florida, summer is the busiest tourist period with hot, sunny days but usually much less humidity than experienced in the south. Winter days range from mild to cool, with occasional freezing night-time temperatures. The high moisture content of Florida's air can cause heavy morning and evening fogs from late autumn to early spring. The Panhandle very occasionally sees snow in winter.

Hurricanes may strike from June to November, though these are closely tracked and warnings are issued.

Currency

There are 100 cents to the dollar. Most commonly used are the $1, $5, $10 and $20 notes, and the 1 cent, 5 cent, 10 cent and 25 cent coins (respectively known as a penny, nickel, dime and quarter). A dollar coin is also in circulation and is infuriatingly similar to a 25 cent coin.

Visitors are strongly advised to carry the bulk of their money as US dollar traveller's cheques. In most transactions, such as paying a restaurant bill, these may be used as cash (ID is rarely required in this situation, but should always be carried). The most useful cheque sizes are $10, $20 and $50; anything larger used to pay a relatively small bill will not be appreciated.

It is common, and expected where large sums are concerned, for bills to be paid by credit card. Credit card holders who know their PIN numbers may also be able to get cash (for a fee added to the

Left
Art Deco District, Miami

Festivals

Festivals occur throughout
Florida at the slightest
excuse. A day of special
events may mark anything
of local interest – such as
seashells, arts and crafts,
sandcastle-building or
seafood – or be major film
and book festivals of the
kind staged annually in
Miami. Local tourist
information centres will
have full details.

next statement) from a cash dispenser (ATM) usually outside banks.
Most are part of the Cirrus or Plus networks accepting MasterCard and
Visa.

Customs regulations

Customs allowances for visitors aged 21 or over include one litre of
alcohol and 200 cigarettes. Prohibited items include lottery tickets,
chocolate liqueurs and fresh fruit. Check with customs officials at
home for returning duty-free allowances, but don't buy duty-free.
Alcohol, tobacco, perfume and similar items are cheaper at
supermarkets and department stores than at airport and downtown
duty-free shops.

Drinking

Whether you are driving, walking or doing anything else in the Florida
heat, bottled drinking water (readily available in shops and petrol
stations) is always useful and in some situations essential to
avoid dehydration. Many public areas also have drinking water
fountains, invariably safe and refreshing. Soft drinks are also readily
obtainable, as are various flavoured iced-teas and iced-coffee in bottles
and cans. As in the rest of the US, most diners serve (hot) coffee with
limitless refills.

Eating out

Simple diners and coffee shops that Americans take for granted but
which overseas visitors relish for their good value and attentive service
(especially towards children) are plentiful throughout Florida. Some,
such as Denny's and Waffle House, are ubiquitous national chains.
Alongside them are many local independents. Some establishments are
open around the clock; nearly all serve breakfast (rarely provided by
hotels and motels), lunch and, in many cases, dinner.

As well as internationally known burger outlets and pizzerias, every
town has a number of ethnic restaurants – Italian and Thai being
particularly plentiful – and coastal regions in particular have many
eateries specialising in seafood. Also widely found are buffet
restaurants, such as Shoney's, which may not offer the world's best
food but do offer it in unlimited amounts.

For top-class dining, most towns have a sprinkling of French
restaurants and others, especially common in Miami Beach, where
ground-breaking chefs explore the various avenues of new American
cuisine. In general, prices in an ordinary restaurant will range from
$6–$10 for breakfast, $8–$15 for lunch and $12–$20 for dinner. An
evening meal in the leading local restaurant will usually be $25–$40
per person, without drinks.

Electricity

America uses 110-volt 60-hertz current with two- or three-prong plugs. Power and plug converters are seldom available.

Beware of buying electrical equipment – it probably won't operate on your voltage at home. Exceptions are battery-operated items such as radios, cameras and portable computers.

Entry formalities

Citizens of most European countries and Australia, provided they have a full passport valid for more than six months, their trip is for less than 90 days' duration and they hold a return ticket, do not require a visa to visit the US, but must complete the visa waiver form provided on the plane.

Food

Traditional Florida rural fare includes gator tail (the only edible part of the alligator), frog's legs and turtle, though these dishes (especially the latter) are relatively hard to find. Much more plentiful is beef from the state's farms and the produce of its rivers and coast such as grouper, tuna, mahi-mahi (also called dolphin, but the fish, *not* the mammal), mullet, trout, catfish, oysters, shrimps and crab.

Eagerly devoured by locals during their April to October season are the creamy claws of stone crabs, usually served as an expensive appetiser. Less costly and available year-round is the sea snail known as the conch, frequently served as a chowder and, particularly in the Florida Keys, as deep-fried fritters.

As a result of its large Cuban population, Miami has many Cuban restaurants serving pork, beef, chicken and seafood dishes in traditional Cuban styles, accompanied by black beans, rice and plantains. Stands offering Cuban sandwiches – large rolls generously stuffed with meat, cheese and various pickles – and thimble-sized cups of potent Cuban coffee, are another Miami speciality. Cuban fare also inspired the nuevo-Cuban cuisine that was the talk of the city during the early 1990s.

Traditional dishes of the Southern US appear throughout Florida and especially in the Panhandle, where common side-dishes are grits (ground corn) and hush puppies (fried corn balls). Other regional fare includes heart-of-palm salad, using the vegetable at the centre of Florida's official state tree, and Key Lime Pie, a dessert common in the Florida Keys.

Health

Travellers are unlikely to encounter any unusual health problems in Florida. However, the strength of the sun should not be underestimated. Spend only a few minutes on the beach or beside the hotel pool during your first few days, and increase this time gradually. Always apply a strong sunscreen (SPF 25 at least). Remember that kids are especially vulnerable. Wear lightweight, light-coloured clothing, always carry a sun-reflecting hat and good-quality sunglasses. Avoid dehydration by drinking plenty of water: bottled water is easy to find and there are safe drinking fountains in many public places.

Conversion tables

Distances

Metric	Imperial/US
1m	3ft 3in
5m	16ft 6in
10m	33ft
50m	164ft
100m	330ft
1km	0.75 mile
2km	1.5 miles
5km	3 miles
10km	6 miles
20km	12.5 miles
50km	31 miles
100km	62 miles

Weight

Kg	Lbs
1	2
2	4.5
5	11
10	22
20	45
50	110
75	165
100	220

Fluid measures
(1 US gal. = 0.8 Imp. gal.)

Litres	US gal.
5	1.3
10	2.6
20	5.2
50	13

Area
1 hectare = 2.471 acres
1 acre = 0.4 hectares

Information

Leaflets, brochures and maps of all kinds are freely available from Florida's many Welcome Centers, Chambers of Commerce and Convention and Visitor Bureaux. Many hotels and motels also have racks of local and statewide tourist literature. Further details are given in the local sections of the book.

Insurance

For overseas visitors in particular, travel insurance is an important consideration. Besides covering lost items, delayed travel and other possible expenses, insurance is an essential safeguard against potentially astronomical medical bills in the event of illness or injury. A reasonable policy from a specialist insurer (identical policies offered by travel companies are usually much more expensive) should cost around £30–£40 for two weeks per person.

Maps

The grandly titled Official Transportation Map, issued by the Florida Department of Transport, is free from many tourist information centres and provides a good general overview of the state and its road system. Local tourist information centres also offer free maps of their area, but these are of variable quality and not always as useful as they first appear. The most detailed road maps are those of DeLorme's *Florida Atlas & Gazetteer*.

Museums

Florida might be known as the home of Walt Disney World but it does have some remarkably good cultural museums. They include a major collection of the work of Spanish surrealist Salvador Dalí (in St Petersburg), a noted Rubens stash (in Sarasota) and commendable museums of state history in Tallahassee and Miami. Smaller museums devoted to local history often reveal fascinating insights into Native American and frontier-era life. The largest of numerous child-friendly museums with interactive exhibits are in Miami, Fort Lauderdale and Tampa.

National and state parks

Much of Florida's distinctive scenery and the wildlife that lives in it is protected by several national (*www.nps.gov*) and over a hundred state parks (*www.floridastateparks.org*). The former include Everglades National Park which protects a section of the Everglades – a remarkable area of sawgrass and swamp occupying almost all of south

Left
Seven Mile Bridge, Florida Keys

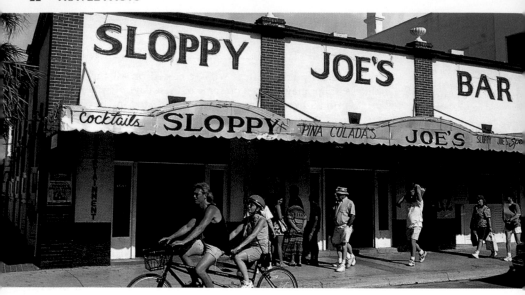

Above
Sloppy Joe's Bar, Key West

Packing

Be sure to pack lightweight cotton clothing that includes a hat, swimwear, sunscreen, good quality sunglasses, a jacket or sweater for possibly cool evenings and winter mornings, travel documents, including driving licence, currency as US dollar traveller's cheques and a small amount of cash.

central Florida – and the Canaveral National Seashore area close to the Kennedy Space Center. State parks tend to be less dramatic but offer tremendous wildlife-watching, walking trails and hiking routes, canoeing, swimming and much more. Almost all parks have informative visitors' centres and operate ranger-led activities such as guided walks and canoe rides.

Opening times

Regular shop opening times are weekdays 1000–1800, but many keep longer hours and open on weekends. Some, including many supermarkets, never close. A number of restaurants are open around the clock but most that serve breakfast do so from 0600 and typically stay open until 2200 or 2300. Some restaurants serve only breakfast and lunch but do not close in between; up-market establishments usually open only for lunch and dinner, from 1100–1400 and 1600–2300 respectively. Major theme parks are open every day of the year, usually from 0900 or 1000. Theme park closing times are adjusted seasonally with longer hours, sometimes until midnight or later, over holiday periods and many weekends.

Postal services

Stamps are sold by post offices, usually open 0900–1630/1700 on weekdays; major branches also open on Saturday. Stamps are also sold through vending machines in some hotels, supermarkets, shopping malls and petrol stations. Post boxes are blue and sited on street corners.

Reading

The ups and downs of modern Florida and its tourist industry have been ably and entertainingly chronicled by Carl Hiassen in a series of novels that includes *Double Whammy*, *Tourist Season* and *Native Tongue*. Alexander Stuart captured the ascent of Miami's South Beach into one of the world's trendiest places in *Life on Mars*, while from an earlier period, *Cross Creek* found Marjorie Kinnan Rawlings (better known for *The Yearling*) describing everyday life in 1930s rural Florida.

Architecture buffs will enjoy Hap Hatton's *Tropical Splendor*, a spirited and lavishly illustrated tale of good and bad Florida buildings, while Barbara Beer Capitman's *Deco Delights* is a fine companion to viewing Miami Beach's Art Deco District from the person who did most to save it. Saving the Everglades, meanwhile, was the preoccupation of Marjory Stoneman Douglas whose *Everglades: River of Grass*, published in the 1940s, remains the most erudite eulogy to this amazing natural area.

Public holidays

Banks and all public offices will be closed on all the following holidays; shops may be open on some of these days: New Year's Day (1 Jan), Martin Luther King Jnr's Birthday (third Mon in Jan), Presidents' Day (third Mon in Feb), Memorial Day (last Mon in May), Independence Day (4 July), Labor Day (first Mon in Sept), Columbus Day (second Mon in Oct), Veterans' Day (11 Nov), Thanksgiving Day (fourth Thur in Nov), Christmas Day (25 Dec). Good Friday is a half-day holiday and Easter Monday is a full-day holiday. Actual dates may vary if the holiday falls on a weekend.

Public transport

Long-distance public transport is limited to Greyhound buses (*tel*: *(800) 229-9424; www.greyhound.com*) and Amtrak trains (*tel*: *(800) 872-7245*), both of which operate limited services within Florida. Although many cities and larger towns have a bus service, this is usually of little use to visitors and often closes down in the early evening with a skeletal service operating at weekends. Only in Miami, where buses are complemented by the elevated Metrorail and the Metromover serving the Downtown area, is public transport more comprehensive. Wherever you are, a rental car really is essential.

Safety and security

Crimes against Florida's tourists have received far greater publicity than their frequency deserves but there are a number of safety tips that should be observed to ensure you leave the Sunshine State with nothing but good memories.

Do not open your hotel door to strangers. Leave valuables in the hotel safe when you go out. In crowd situations, be alert for pickpockets and in cities avoid walking on dimly lit streets. Be wary of discount tickets offered for major tourist attractions; some are genuine, many are fakes.

When driving, lock doors and keep windows closed. Stop only in populated, well-lit areas and do not stop to offer assistance to other drivers. Do not stop if flagged down by anyone other than a police officer: police cars use flashing blue and red lights to signal you to stop. Legally, you should stop if involved in an accident but do not do this if you are rammed from behind; instead continue to a well-lit, populated area. Always lock valuables in the boot.

Sales tax

A state sales tax of 6 per cent is added to the marked price of most purchases, with additional local taxes applied in some areas.

Above
Key Largo diving mural

Sport

Spectator sports

Florida claims three professional football teams – the Miami Dolphins, Tampa Bay Buccaneers and Jacksonville Jaguars. The Miami-based Florida Marlins brought professional baseball to the state in 1993, although other pro teams use Florida as a spring training centre, bringing many fans with them to watch pre-season matches. Professional basketball comes from the Miami Heat and Orlando Magic, and professional ice-hockey courtesy of the Miami-based Florida Panthers and Tampa Bay Lightning.

College sports, notably football, are highly popular. Matches featuring the Gators, from Gainesville's University of Florida, or their arch-rivals the Seminoles, from Tallahassee's Florida State University, often draw bigger crowds than their professional counterparts. Anyone wearing green and yellow in Miami is likely to be a fan of the Hurricanes, the nickname of all Miami University's sports teams.

Florida also hosts several major tennis and golf tournaments, top motor sports events such as the Daytona 500, and an important annual surfing competition at Sebastian Inlet.

Participant sports

Diving (a certificate is necessary; tuition is readily available) and snorkelling are immensely popular in the Florida Keys and wherever else conditions are suitable. State and national parks often have designated areas for canoeing and swimming. Horse riding is offered at several places, including on the sands of Amelia Island. With more than a thousand courses, a third of them open to the public, golf is played widely and avidly throughout Florida.

Information on spectator and participant sports is available from tourist offices, or from Florida Sports Foundation, *2930 Kerry Forest Parkway, Tallahassee, FL, 32309; tel: (850) 488-8347; www.flasports.com*

Stores

Many leading nationwide shops and department stores have outlets in Florida, usually gathered together on the outskirts of cities and towns

Travellers with disabilities

By law, public buildings must provide disabled access and designated parking spaces. This applies to most hotels and motels, museums and other places of visitor interest. Theme parks, too, are generally accessible to the disabled, as are sections of many national and state parks. Car-hire firms will provide hand-controlled cars if sufficient notice is given. Many local buses can accommodate wheelchairs. For further details, contact the tourism organisation for the area you are visiting and get broader info from one of the many relevant American organisations, such as SATH (Society for Accessible Travel and Hospitality), *347 Fifth Ave, Suite 610, New York, NY 10016; tel: (212) 447-7284; email: sathtravel@aol.com; www.sath.org*

into large shopping malls; Miami and Orlando each having a particularly large number. Factory outlet stores (and entire factory outlet malls) are also common, although increasingly these offer merchandise at little if any savings on regular retail prices. Around Orlando, especially, there are also many smaller roadside outlet malls, sometimes comprising no more than market stalls inside tents, selling assorted souvenirs and household items of variable quality at knock-down prices.

The latest Disney souvenirs are available from the shops at Disney West Side, part of Walt Disney World, as well as from the Disney parks.

Telephones

Public telephones are reliable and local calls are inexpensive. Hotel and motel lobbies, restaurants, petrol stations, shopping malls and many other places have public telephones and are usually safer and shadier places for making calls than public phones on the street. Hotel rooms are always equipped with telephones, though charges are higher than on public phones. Many tourist attractions have toll-free numbers prefixed 1/800, 877, 888 or 866, which require no money to be inserted, although these calls are often charged for if made from a hotel room. Card-operated public phones are increasingly common; phone cards are sold in many shops. Major credit cards can also be used to make phone calls.

Time

Most of Florida is on Eastern Standard Time (EST), five hours behind the UK and six behind the rest of Western Europe. The Panhandle west of the Apalachicola River uses Central Standard Time (CST), an hour behind the rest of the state.

Toilets

Most public buildings, museums, theme parks and tourist attractions, shopping malls, restaurants and petrol stations (where you will probably need to ask for the key) have free public toilets, usually maintained in good condition.

Tipping

Florida's service industry wages are notoriously low and most employees who serve the public rely on tips for a good proportion of their pay. In restaurants and taxis, tip 15–20 per cent of the bill; if a hotel porter carries your bags, tip at least $1 per piece.

Driver's guide

Automobile Clubs

There are no reciprocal agreements between the AA and RAC, and the equivalent AAA in the United States. You should ensure that you purchase sufficient insurance when you hire a car.

Autoroutes & Bridges

Florida has several toll roads, including Florida's Turnpike and the Bee Line Expressway. Most bridges charge a toll in one direction. Cash is fine, but no credit cards or traveller's cheques can be used. Florida has a SunPass system for commuters that deducts the toll automatically when an enrolled car passes through the tollbooth area.

Documents

A national driving licence is valid in Florida. An international one is not necessary. It must be in your possession at all times along with your photo ID. The minimum driving age, with driver training, is 16, but a driver is not permitted to drive without late-night restrictions until age 18. Provisional licences are not valid. Car rental companies require that all drivers be at least age 25. The vehicle registration, proof of liability and collision insurance cover, and rental car contract, must be in the car and accessible at all times.

Accidents

Legally, you must STOP after any accident and report it to the Florida Highway Patrol (FHP), County Sheriff's office or local police if there is an injury, death or property damage. You can be in serious trouble if you don't. If you are hit by another vehicle, particularly from behind, for your safety do not leave your vehicle but clearly indicate to the other driver to follow your car to a populated, well-lit area where the authorities can be contacted and damage inspected. Exchange information on who is involved, addresses, telephone numbers, make and model of car, licence number, vehicle registration and insurance details. If the accident renders your vehicle immobile, safeguard against a secondary accident by turning on hazard lights to signal to other traffic. Should the police investigate and prepare a written report of the accident and findings, you do not have to do so. But, if no police authority writes a report and property damage is over $100, within five days you must file a written collision report to the Department of Highway Safety and Motor Vehicles (offices are in the telephone book under Florida Government listings).

The universal emergency number is 911 to alert the police or to call an ambulance or the fire department. Dial FHP for the highway patrol. Show police your driving licence, vehicle registration and proof of insurance cover for car and collision damage. Remember to exchange the same details and your contact information with the other driver(s). Get the names of any witnesses. Note as many details as you can. Photographs can be helpful later. Most rental cars carry accident report forms that must be completed in the event of any accident.

If your vehicle collides with a parked vehicle, leave a note with your name, address and licence plate number securely affixed to the other vehicle. For a collision with an animal, do not try to move it, but call the nearest humane society, animal control department or police. With any accident, inform your insurers as soon as possible.

Breakdowns

If you have a breakdown, stop your vehicle on the hard shoulder, getting it as far to the right as possible, but where it can be seen for 200 feet in each direction. Tie a piece of white cotton on the left door handle or antenna, and (as long as it is safe) raise the bonnet. On ordinary roads, consider using the verge but beware of roadside ditches. Turn hazard lights on. Place one or more reflective warning triangles where other drivers driving in the same direction can see

Drinking and Driving

DUI, driving under the influence of alcohol (or any other drug), is illegal. The blood alcohol concentration (limit) is not to exceed .08 (.02 if under 21 years of age), and is strictly enforced. Drivers suspected of drunk driving have a choice of a breath, blood or urine test; police are also likely to ask any suspect to get out of the vehicle and walk in a straight line. Refusing a test is an admission of guilt. Penalties include imprisonment for up to six months, a large fine, 50 hours of mandatory community service, licence revocation, 12 hours of DUI school and the vehicle may be impounded.

Police establish random checkpoints, sometimes in unmarked vehicles and sometimes parked in less obvious places. Any alcoholic beverages must be carried in the trunk (boot). If you're driving, don't drink alcohol.

Essentials

You should travel with three red reflective warning triangles, road flares, a torch, a first aid kit and a jack for tyre repair. If the vehicle has a spare tyre, make sure that it is properly inflated.

them. (Remember, it can be very dangerous to walk on the hard shoulder of any expressway, turnpike or highway.) You and your passengers may be safer out of the vehicle and well up the verge away from the traffic, but for security, stay in the locked car if you are in an isolated area, it is night-time, or it is hard to see for any reason.

If you need assistance on a major road, you may use one of the free roadside telephones. You may call for a breakdown lorry, called a tow truck, usually dispatched from a local petrol (gas) station; on Florida's Turnpike, a Turnpike system contract garage must do the towing. Breakdown insurance is strongly recommended and one phone call is all it takes to hand the whole problem over to an operator who is expert in sorting things out. Your insurance company may call a towing service it has under contract for emergency roadside assistance repairs or towing to a repair garage. You are responsible for payment or for signing the form that affirms to your insurance company that you have had the service. Most car-hire companies either pay for repairs directly or reimburse the cost shown on repair receipts. If a rental car is going to be out of service for more than a few hours, the hire company will provide a replacement.

Caravans and camper vans (Trailers and RVs)

RVs are a popular way to move around the countryside and seek the best seasonal weather in Florida. They are favoured year-round by retired people, and may be ideal for those on a budget, planning to have some meals in, or not wanting to change lodging every night.

Woodall's (*www.woodalls.com*) is *the* reference for 14,000 camping spots, and publishes a comprehensive guide to the US as well as a guide to the South within this book's geographic scope. Many state parks have RV or trailer pitches (spaces) that should be reserved as far in advance as possible. Everglades National Park has two campgrounds with dump stations and fresh water but no electric, water or sewer hookups, while Gulf Islands National Seashore's two campgrounds have most services. Whether public or private, campsites may include a small barbecue grill and a picnic table with benches. Wherever you park along the side of a road or on city streets, the vehicle must always be pulled off the roadway and should only be parked in a safe well-lit place in view of passers-by. Thefts and break-ins are not unknown. Depending on local laws, it may *not be legal to occupy a vehicle parked overnight on the side of the road or on a city street*. Check with local tourism offices or the police authorities before parking. It is always safest to spend the night in an RV park or booked camping pitch. Official Florida Welcome Centers and Interstate highway rest areas permit stays of up to three hours, but overnighting is illegal.

Maintenance must be done; check the RV inside and out for its condition and understand its driving controls and systems upkeep before leaving the rental lot. For sanitary and environmental reasons, sewage system disposal must be done at authorised dump stations.

Fines

Drivers can be fined for moving violations like speeding, illegal turns or other infractions, for parking violations, and for DUI, Driving Under the Influence (of alcohol or illegal drugs). Police authorities or the highway patrol will issue a citation, commonly called a ticket, on the spot. The citation specifies the police authority, jurisdiction (city, town, county, state), legal code reference number, a short description of the violation, the vehicle reference, the police officer's badge (identification) number and name, your information if it is a moving violation, and where and how the ticket can be paid or challenged.

On-the-spot fine payments are *never* made, and anyone offering to pay a fine when cited may be assumed to be offering a bribe to a police officer, an extremely serious offence.

Citations are registered in a computer database by car licence that is linked to the vehicle identification number. The car or RV rental company will be notified of any citations issued to its vehicles.

Above
Key West milemarker

Motorhomes, towed vehicles and any vehicle with more than two axles pay more for bridge tolls. RVs and trailers are legally considered trucks and must observe truck speed limits and other road directions, including warnings on roads. RVs are blown about by wind more than cars and are more subject to drift or rollover in high winds. Taller and wider dimensions can create hazards at gas stations, tollbooths, car parks, and with over-hanging trees and signs.

Driving in Florida

Sightseers take to the roads on holidays and during the June–August school summer break, but Florida's mild climate means that visitors from colder climates will be on the road in winter, too.

Florida has several common types of road, and the common name for highways, Interstate Highways, Florida's Turnpike or faster routes within the state designed to speed traffic flow is 'Expressway'. Florida's Turnpike is the efficient, but expensive, toll route. State Roads have fewer traffic lanes than highways or freeways and are often a more scenic way to transit between areas. There are country roads or local roads that seldom have tourist attractions.

Generally, roads are numbered, with odd numbers running north–south and even numbers going east–west. Some roads are usually referred to by names like the South Dixie Highway (Highway 95 in southeast Miami); the Overseas Highway (Highway 1 along the Florida Keys); the Tamiami Trail (Highway 41, Tampa to Miami via the Everglades), and the Bee Line Expressway toll route (State Road 528, Orlando to Hwy A1A near Canaveral National Seashore).

In Florida, Interstate 10 (I-10) runs from Pensacola to Jacksonville. I-75 goes south from Georgia to central Florida before shifting south-west to Tampa. I-95 runs along the east side of the state to Miami. I-4 moves south-west from Daytona through Orlando to Tampa.

Despite being almost totally flat at sea level, Florida has some notable driving challenges. Tropical storms can bring high winds and hurricane warnings route people to shelters, marked with roadside signs. Ground fog can be a hazard almost anywhere. Fires create a thick curtain of smoke that can make for dangerous driving. Rain brings slippery road surfaces. Infrequently, parts of Florida freeze, adding to driving danger. Slow down and turn the headlamps on low beam for better visibility for you and oncoming drivers.

Driving rules

Traffic drives on the right in the United States. Florida traffic lights are hung above the centre of the road. Where streets meet and vehicles arrive at close to the same time, priority belongs to the vehicle on the right, and proceeds anti-clockwise. Traffic already on a roundabout (traffic circle or rotary), has the right-of-way, and those waiting launch into the curve whenever they can. Unless otherwise posted, a vehicle can turn right from the right-hand lane after a full stop. Before

Lights

All traffic must use headlights in rain, fog, smoke, or when visibility is poor or unclear ahead. Lights must be on from twilight before sunset to sunrise. Drive with lights lit on narrow country roads. Driving only with parking lights is illegal. Most motorcycles will have headlights on at all times and most bicycle riders will wear reflectors or have them on the bike.

Mobile phones

Mobile or cell(ular) phone use while driving is not illegal, but a hands-free device is recommended over one that requires dialling and distracts attention from the road. A cell phone can be useful to call 911 in an emergency or for breakdown assistance.

Road information

For Florida road conditions, including closures, listen to local radio or television for weather forecasts and road conditions. Two websites, *www.fhp.state.fl.us/traffic* and *www.fhwa.dot.gov/trafficinfo/fl.htm*, offer up-to-the-minute traffic reports.

Seat belts

The driver, front seat passenger and back seat passengers under 18 must wear seat belts. Children under the age of 5 must ride in National Highway Traffic Safety Administration-approved child safety seats (restraints).

turning, the driver signals the direction of the intended turn, although in practice, many drivers don't bother. When turning left, a green arrow gives right of way; a green light means you may turn but oncoming traffic has the right of way. Flashing amber lights indicate proceed, but with caution; flashing red lights mean stop and then proceed cautiously. Horns are seldom used.

Interstate highways, highways and freeway entrances are clearly marked with green and white signs. On city streets and occasionally on country roads, bicycle paths are marked as a separate lane on the right where bikes have the right-of-way. Buses stopping at the right side of the road and pulling out into traffic go first. A school bus stopped with flashing lights or signal lights at a railway crossing stop traffic as long as lights flash, and violations are serious.

Roadways are marked with a solid white line for 'do not pass', and with a broken line where passing another vehicle is permitted. Blind curves are not infrequent, dictating slower speeds. Police use radar, lasers and aeroplanes to track and stop speeding drivers. In Florida, pedestrians have the right-of-way at crossings and intersections.

Fuel

Petrol stations are plentiful on all but the most remote roads. Many are open around the clock with pumps equipped with credit card machines enabling payment to be made at the pump. Gas stations generally accept cash, credit cards, debit cards, and $20 traveller's cheques. Due to counterfeiting and safety concerns, gas station clerks will not accept $50 or $100 bills. Petrol (and diesel) is sold at gas stations in US gallons (about four litres per gallon). Most vehicles take unleaded gas that comes in regular, premium and super grades. Buy regular unless the car rental company or the vehicle operation manual specifies otherwise. Most stations are self-service, although some offer a higher-priced full-service alternative. Pump prices include all taxes. Fuel is cheapest at budget chains and at some discount stores and there is some competition, so prices can vary. Prices are reasonable off highways exits and highest in the cities where traffic flow is high. The cost is always shown with .9 at the end, as $239.9 or $198.9.

Information

The AAA has the widest map coverage in the USA, though local auto club map designs mean that maps are not consistent. Rand McNally publishes map series, and the DeLormé *Florida Atlas and Gazetteer* is best for detailed touring. Local Chambers of Commerce or Convention and Visitors Bureaux will have local maps of varying quality for free or for a small charge.

Florida road conditions, including closures, are listed on two websites, check: *www.fhp.state.fl.us/traffic* or *www.fhwa.dot.gov/trafficinfo/fl.htm*. Local radio stations broadcast weather and driving information.

An approved infant carrier must be used if the child is 3 years or younger. Safety seats can be hired with the car or purchased for under $100 at a discount store. In an RV, passengers riding behind the driver's seat need not wear belts, but should be safely seated when the vehicle is in motion.

Speed limits

Florida and the rest of the United States choose miles over metric. Kilometres appear alongside mileage on occasional highway and National Park signs.

Expressways: Interstate Highways, Highways, Freeways 55–70 mph (as posted); 40 mph min speed

In cities or towns 15–30mph unless posted otherwise

School zones 25mph

Poor driving conditions – keep to a safe speed

Road Signs

European-style road signs are widely used, but not universally. *Red* signs indicate stop, do not enter, or wrong way. *Yellow* signs are warnings or direction indictors. *Orange* means road repairs (road works) or detours (diversions). *White* shows speed limits and distances, almost always in miles. *Brown* indicates parks, camping and other recreation opportunities. *Blue* gives non-driving information such as services in a nearby town.

Parking

When parking during the day, look for a shaded area to prevent the car interior from becoming unbearably hot. If you are returning at night, for safety reasons, ensure that the car is parked in a well-lit area.

Theme parks and major tourist attractions have ample parking space, though many charge up to $10 per car. Make a note of where you are parked (Disney and some other parks provide a ticket with a tear-off segment for doing this) to help find the car later. In city centres during weekdays, street parking can be difficult although there is widespread metered parking (usually with a time limit) and public car parks. Parking is free at shopping malls, supermarkets, and national and state parks after an admission fee is first paid. Upscale restaurants will have fixed fee valet parking and major hotels levy a hefty daily parking fee. Kerbside parking time is usually limited, either by posted signs or coin-operated parking meters. Kerbs may be colour-coded: *red* means no stopping or parking at any time; *white* is for passenger loading/unloading only; *green* is limited parking, usually 10 minutes; *yellow* is a commercial loading zone; and *blue* is handicapped parking. Parking is not allowed by yellow kerbs or where no parking signs are posted, within 15 feet of a fire hydrant, 20 feet of an intersection, 30 feet of a flashing signal, stop sign or traffic signal, in bus stops, zebra crossings (crosswalks), on pavements, in front of driveways, or on highways. Fines vary from a few dollars to several hundred, depending on the infraction and jurisdiction. No police authority accepts cash on the spot to take care of the fine. Fines levied against rental cars are charged against the hirer's credit card.

Security

Sensible care should be taken, particularly where vehicles are left in vulnerable places such as tourist site car parks. Do not leave items on view inside the car. Even if you know they are of little or no value, a potential thief does not. Park in well-lit areas and double check that the vehicle is locked. Florida law requires the driver to take the keys upon exiting the vehicle. Lock car doors and keep windows closed while driving. Be sure that handbags, wallets, cameras, etc. are out of sight and reach and above all, never on a passenger's lap.

Park in accessible, well-lit areas. Check for intruders before getting in, especially at night and in an RV any time, and be suspicious of anyone lingering in a car park. Never leave the vehicle engine running when the driver isn't behind the wheel. Do not stop to offer assistance to any motorist who appears to have broken down and do not leave the vehicle if hit from behind. Stop only for marked police or Florida Highway Patrol vehicles that will flag you to a halt with blue and red flashing lights. Should you have the misfortune to become a victim of crime, your insurers will require you to report the circumstances to the police and to obtain a police report that you have done so.

Typical road signs in Florida

INSTRUCTIONS

Stop

Give way

Wrong way - often together
with 'No entry' sign

No right turn

No U-turn

One-way
traffic

Two-way left
turn lanes

Divided highway
(dual carriageway)
at junction ahead

Speed limit
signs: maximum
and maximum/
minimum limits

WARNINGS

Crossroads

Junction

Curve (bend)

Winding road

Stop ahead

Two-way traffic

Divided highway
(dual carriageway)

Road narrows
on right

Roadworks
ahead

Railway
crossing

No-overtaking
zone

Getting to Florida

Most visitors from outside the US, and many from within, arrive in Florida by air. None the less, the state is easily accessed by road from the southeastern US (the main Interstates routes being I-10 from Alabama, I-75 and I-95 from Georgia) and by rail with long-distance train services linking Orlando and Miami, and smaller Florida communities, with the major cites of the northeastern US.

Airports

Although almost every sizeable Florida community has an airport, the chief points of entry for airborne arrivals are Miami, Orlando and Tampa. Sanford (near Orlando) is the point of entry for many British charter operators. International visitors can often continue their journey on a domestic flight at little extra cost on the standard scheduled fare. All American and many major international scheduled airlines serve Florida, as do a number of charter companies.

Major car-hire companies are well represented at most airports and will transport pre-booked customers to their waiting cars. Alternatively, car hire can be arranged on the spot although this can be costlier and more troublesome than pre-booking (see *Driving*).

If arriving during rush hours or during the hours of darkness, it can be sensible to spend a night near the airport and collect your rental car the following day. This is especially true in Miami, where the road system can be confusing and some neighbourhoods are dangerous. Most companies will collect customers from airport area hotels free of charge; many airport hotels will collect guests free of charge from the airport.

Other than rental cars, transport from airports includes taxis and shuttle buses. Public bus services to and from airports are very limited.

Below
National Museum of Aviation, Pensacola

Miami International Airport
Seven miles west of Downtown and 14 miles west of Miami Beach, Miami International Airport (*tel: (305) 876-7000*) is Florida's major international airport and an important hub for routes between the US and South and Central

America. On arrival passengers may face lengthy queues to clear immigration. The airport is equipped with a wide range of restaurants and shops, including those offering duty-free sales for departing international passengers.

Super Shuttle (tel: (305) 871-2000) is one of several minibus companies operating between the airport and any destination in the city; fares are calculated according to the postal zip code of the destination and are displayed on notice boards. Public buses also serve the airport but are not recommended for passengers with luggage or anyone unfamiliar with Miami.

Taxis are plentiful and charge a fixed fee (not including tip) to specific destinations. All forms of ground transportation from the airport, including the courtesy buses of car-rental companies and major hotels, can be found directly outside the arrivals area.

Orlando International Airport

Approximately 9 miles east of International Drive, Orlando International Airport (tel: (407) 825-2001; www.orlandoairports.net) is also 13 miles northeast of Kissimmee and 14 miles east of Walt Disney World. Large, modern and exceptionally user-friendly with a full range of facilities, the airport's only drawback is the sheer numbers of passengers who pass through it.

The courtesy buses of car-rental companies and major hotels collect arrivals from the clearly indicated Ground Transportation area, which is also the place to find shuttle buses or taxis. A considerably cheaper (and safer) alternative are the local buses operated by Lynx (tel: (407) 841-8240) between the airport and International Drive, though this option is not well suited to passengers with bulky luggage.

Sanford International Airport

British charter flights are the only international arrivals at Sanford International Airport (tel: (407) 585-4000; orlandosandfordairport.com), 30 miles north of Orlando and 50 miles southwest of Daytona Beach. The small airport has been tailored to the needs of British holiday-makers. Alamo and Dollar car rental companies have a large reception area directly opposite the terminal; others collect their customers with courtesy buses.

Tampa International Airport

Tampa International Airport (tel: (813) 870-8700; tampaairport.com) is 6 miles north of Downtown Tampa and 13 miles from the Gulf beaches. A bright and modern airport, Tampa is generally less crowded than Miami and Orlando airports, receiving far fewer international flights.

The courtesy buses of car-rental companies and major hotels collect customers from outside the arrivals area, which is also the departure point for shuttle buses and taxis.

Above
A guard at the 1740 Castillo de
San Marcos, St Augustine

Setting the scene

A trendsetter in international tourism, with the world's most advanced theme parks and seemingly endless stretches of sunkissed beach, Florida is also a rapidly expanding and increasingly economically powerful state. It is fast losing its reputation as a retirement centre, and nowadays enjoys a reputation for the cosmopolitan lifestyles and dynamic multiculturalism epitomised by Miami.

Yet as it embraces the new, Florida also keeps much from the past. The state harbours some of the US's most precious natural areas, and many of the endangered creatures that are distant memories elsewhere are seen here in the wild. Florida history, too, is accessible – Native Americans, European explorers, frontiersmen, millionaires, architects, artists, writers, and all manner of eccentrics have left a mark on this beguiling region.

The first Floridians
Until they were devastated by European diseases to which they had no immunity, several diverse groups of native people inhabited the area from around 10,000 BC. Traditionally thought to have arrived from the north, recent theories suggest that at least some of these first Floridians originated in Central America and the Caribbean. By around 5000 BC, nomadic hunter-gatherer existence was giving way to semi-permanent settlements, and by the time Europeans arrived, Florida held an estimated 100,000 people split into four geographically distinct main groups – the Apalachee, the Tequesta, the Timucua and the Calusa. Evidence of their existence is provided by archaeological finds, shell mounds and the mysterious ceremonial stones near Crystal River.

European discovery
Although Florida had been sighted in 1498, it was not until 1513 that a Spaniard, Juan Ponce de León, former governor of Puerto Rico, made the first known European landing. Arriving on Easter Sunday, de León named the land 'La Florida' to mark the Spanish festival Pascua Florida. In search of the fabled 'fountain of youth' and to curry favour with the Spanish king, de León returned to Florida in 1521 with 200 would-be settlers intending to colonise it. The attempt was thwarted by strong native resistance, however, which drove the expedition back to Cuba where de León died from his wounds.

European exploration and settlement
Subsequent attempts at colonisation also ended dismally for the Spanish, due to native opposition and the treacherous nature of the

land. An expedition led by Hernando de Soto, lasting four years and beginning in 1539 with a landing on the west coast (the precise location is unknown but documented by a site at Bradenton), also ended in tragedy but did include the first European sighting of the Mississippi River and provided important written records of Florida at that time.

The arrival of a group of French Huguenots in 1562 and their building of Fort Caroline (near Jacksonville), encouraged the Spanish, fearful of losing their dominance of shipping routes, to renew their interest in Florida. The result was a Spanish massacre of the French and the creation of St Augustine, which became the base for a string of missions established by the Spanish across northern Florida, none of which were particularly successful and none of which survive.

British Florida

The already weak Spanish mission system in Florida was further undermined by native attack, often encouraged by the British who were now established in American colonies of their own. The British demonstrated their interest in Florida in 1568 when Sir Francis Drake led a bombardment of St Augustine. The 1763 Treaty of Paris, which was intended to end disputes over North America between Britain and France, forced Spain to cede Florida to Britain in return for Havana, Cuba.

US rule

Although the British began turning Florida into a productive colony, the Spanish regained control in 1783, largely through Britain's all-consuming involvement in the American War of Independence which led to the creation of the self-governing United States of America. Ostensibly to pursue Seminoles (*see below*) alleged to have attacked land owned by US citizens, General Andrew Jackson, later to become US president, made an illegal foray into Florida in 1818, sparking what became the First Seminole War and intentionally destabilising the region's colonial government. As a result, Florida formally become part of the US in 1821.

The Seminole and Miccosukee

Steadily pushed south from their traditional lands in Alabama, South Carolina and Georgia by European settlers, the Native American Seminole and Miccosukee people (sharing many cultural traits but speaking separate languages) began arriving in Florida during the 18th century. In Florida, too, came conflict between natives and white settlers, sometimes over the former's providing of sanctuary to the escaped slaves of the latter.

When Florida became part of the US, increasing white settlement heightened tensions, as did the US policy of enforced re-settlement of Native Americans to reservations in the American Midwest. Two further Seminole Wars followed. The capture of a celebrated Seminole chief, Osceola, in 1837 led to the Seminoles' surrender and the exodus of many Seminoles to Oklahoma. Several hundred, though, remained in Florida and moved into the uninhabited Everglades.

Around 14,000 Seminole and Miccosukee remain in Florida today, many on reservations in the south and central areas of the state. Some Miccosukee remain in the Everglades, living in the traditional open-sided, thatched-roof houses, raised on stilts from the ground, known as 'chickees'.

The Florida cracker

Some of the most evocative historic homes in Florida are 'cracker cottages', simple wood-framed structures of the mid-1800s to the early 1900s. Designed to make the most of breezes and often built with Dade County pine, a local wood resistant to the termites that ate many early Florida homes, the cottages were occupied by 'crackers', typically rugged and individualistic settlers who forged a living from the land or the sea, or a combination of both, in the days when Florida was still an isolated outpost of the US, barely penetrated by roads or rail. Sometimes used today as a term of abuse to denote an unsophisticated and usually racist white person, the term 'cracker' is of disputed origin but is thought by many to be derived from the crack of the cattle whip used by early settlers.

Railroads and developers

Apart from a few isolated settlers in the south, Florida's population was, by the late 1800s, concentrated in the north and northern central areas, and mostly concerned with cattle and citrus farming. A few rich tourists, however, were beginning to visit the state, largely for its natural springs. Seeking to turn this trickle into a flood were two millionaire entrepreneurs.

Standard Oil mogul Henry Flagler steadily extended his railroad from Jacksonville to Key West making the state's east coast accessible for the first time, building a series of luxury hotels, creating Palm Beach from scratch and stimulating the growth of Miami. Florida's west coast, meanwhile, was opened up by Henry Plant, who brought his railroad to Tampa, turning a sleepy town into a major port city and paving the way for a cigar industry that brought settlers from Cuba and Europe.

The advent of affordable cars found more Americans vacationing in Florida. In the 1920s, Carl Fisher turned an uninhabited island into Miami Beach, importing its sand and building the hotels that quickly become major tourist magnets, helping cement Miami's soaring reputation as the US's fun and sun capital.

Walt Disney's World

Florida's emergence as a modern pacesetter in global tourism is largely attributed to Walt Disney. The ground-breaking animator opened his first theme park, Disneyland, in Los Angeles in 1955 only to find that the park's success stymied its growth as non-Disney businesses quickly surrounded the park.

In the 1960s, the Disney Company began secretly purchasing plots of land close to the agricultural town of Orlando. By the time the Magic Kingdom opened in 1971, Walt Disney World, as the area was named, had its own roads, power supply and police force. It expanded with EPCOT Center in 1982, Disney-MGM Studios in 1990, Animal Kingdom in 1998 and a series of smaller recreational areas together with Disney-run hotels, restaurants, and shopping and entertainment areas.

As Walt Disney World put Orlando on the world tourism map, other major attractions such as SeaWorld and Universal Studios arrived, stimulating a statewide tourism boom.

Florida architecture

Many of Florida's older towns and cities, notably Key West and Fernandina Beach, have large numbers of well-preserved Victorian homes, the decorative carpentry of Queen Anne and Edwardian dwellings highlighting the break from the simplicity of the cracker era (*see opposite*) to reflect increased affluence.

Florida also found itself breaking new ground with luxury hotel architecture. Although put to new uses, those built by Henry Flagler in St Augustine and by Henry Plant in Tampa remain, as do 1920s resort hotels such as the Biltmore in Miami, the Don Cesar in St Petersburg Beach and the Breakers in Palm Beach. Miami Beach gained landmark hotels in the 1940s with the Eden Roc and Fontainbleau as part of the Florida hotel building tradition which continues into the present with the ever-more imaginative hotels of Walt Disney World.

From the 1910s Florida also became dotted with palatial millionaire's homes, often apeing the styles of the most lavish European palaces. Notable survivors include Henry Flagler's Whitehall in Palm Beach, the Ringling Estate in Sarasota and Villa Vizcaya in Miami.

A 1920s land boom encouraged the creation of entire towns in mock-Mediterranean Revival style, demonstrated by Palm Beach and Boca Raton. A decade later, when Miami Beach needed fast and cheap buildings, what is now the celebrated Art Deco District began taking shape.

The re-discovery of its art deco buildings, narrowly escaping demolition and, through the 1980s, given pastel colourings and accentuation of their period details, helped fuel Miami's emergence as a pacesetting style centre. Among Miami's modern landmark buildings was the Atlantis, a much-photographed bayside condominium built with a 'missing' central section occupied by a palm tree and red spiral staircase, designed by the local, world-famous firm of Arquitectonica.

Such innovation was rare, however, in a fast-growing state creating living space with tract housing and providing anodyne chain hotels for tourists. One coastal exception was Seaside, a town begun in 1981 using a mixture of old Florida and traditional New England styles to create wooden homes framed by picket fences and narrow walkways.

Florida people

The fourth most populous state in the US, Florida's population has been expanding since the 1920s. Of its 16 million people, 85 per cent live in urban areas. Revealing the shift in population from north to south, the state capital, Tallahassee, is located in the Panhandle with a population of just 150,000, while Florida's major city, Miami, holds two million in the state's heavily populated southeast corner.

Traditionally, Florida has attracted retirees, but while they once headed for Miami or St Petersburg they now tend to move to smaller towns in north and central Florida. A growth in white-collar job opportunities has brought many younger settlers from other parts of the US, serving to greatly reduce the average age of Florida residents and spicing up the state's previously staid image.

While most who settle in Florida are US citizens, the state has also gained sizeable ethnic groups, particularly from Central America and the Caribbean. In Miami, over half the population have a mother tongue other than English. Around 300,000 Cubans arrived in Miami during the early 1960s. They and their descendants are now highly influential in the city and beyond. Other Miami communities include significant numbers of Dominicans, Haitians, Jamaicans, Salvadorians and Nicaraguans.

Florida lifestyles range from the urban sophistication of multicultural Miami to the traditional Deep South mood and manners found in the Panhandle, geographically, historically and culturally linked to Alabama and Georgia. Central Florida possesses the state's major theme parks and is the dynamo that drives the state's tourist industry. Yet it also has small towns, some dominated by cattlemen working on the local farmlands and others, such as Micanopy, by the antiques shops in restored Victorian buildings that do most to draw visitors to otherwise forgotten communities.

Florida at work

With 75 million visitors yearly, tourism is the state's major source of revenue and directly or indirectly employs almost a third of the Florida work force. Other long-established industries include the state's 44,000 farms, predominantly in central Florida's grasslands which raise cattle and thoroughbred horses, and produce 70 per cent of all the citrus fruits sold in the US.

While fishing is a popular recreational pursuit throughout Florida, it is also a major employer in some areas. Shrimp, lobster, oyster, Spanish mackerel and grouper form just part of a catch worth $200 million annually.

Established ports and manufacturing cities such as Tampa and Jacksonville have thrived and evolved into important financial centres, while a knock-on effect of NASA's presence on the Space Coast has been the rise of electronic and high-tech engineering industries.

Florida's forests

Around 40 per cent of Florida is covered by forest. Although the state has over 300 tree species, it is various types of pine that predominate, particularly in north and central Florida, and which provide the raw material for the state's sizeable lumber industry. Live oaks are common throughout Florida, as in certain areas are various dogwoods, maples and palms such as cabbage palmetto, sable palm and the majestic royal palm.

Discovering unusual trees can be a highlight of a visit to a natural area. South Florida has the gumbo limbo, strangler fig and the swamp-dwelling bald cypress with its exposed root or 'knee' poking above water. South Florida coastal areas also have the hard-working mangrove, allowing new land to form by collecting debris around its tangle of exposed roots.

Florida's creatures

Among the immense variety of wildlife that inhabits the state's diverse terrain are several exotic species that are particularly loved, feared or simply fighting for survival as human impact upsets Florida's fragile ecosystems.

Florida's alligators have made a tremendous recovery since being hunted almost out of existence. An estimated two million now inhabit the state's rivers, lakes and swamps. Alligators rarely threaten without being provoked but are known to attack dogs and small children. While alligators are easily found, the same is not true of the Florida panther. Part of the cougar family, the Florida panther chiefly resides in the Everglades but hunts over wide areas. Though once prevalent, mercury contamination of wetlands is thought to have helped reduce numbers to around 100.

In the Florida Keys, Big Pine Key holds around 300 Key deer. This dwarf species of deer, usually reaching just 2ft in height, lives in pine woods but commonly appears in resident's back gardens looking for food. South Florida is the only part of the US where the snail kite survives. This small species of hawk lives only on apple snails, opening their shells with its pointed beak.

Between February and August, five species of sea turtle come ashore to lay their eggs on Florida beaches, the only time the creatures leave the security of the ocean. Just a few of the hundred or so eggs will produce a hatchling that survives to adulthood. Many eggs will be eaten by racoons while young turtles often become fatally disorientated when trying to find their way to the ocean. Guided tours lead visitors to watch the night-time egg-laying.

Florida's warm rivers and springs are ideally suited to the manatee (*see page 159*).

Highlights

Two days

Be it history, nature, scenery or theme parks, the drives and walks in this book cover many varied aspects of Florida. Some are especially suited to particular interests, however, and there are those that should not be missed if you only have two days to spare.

From Miami: **The Florida Keys, Key West**
From Orlando: **St Petersburg and its Beaches, The Space Coast**
In northern Florida: **St Augustine, Amelia Island and the Northeast Corner**

Beaches

The Space Coast (*see pages 200–209*)
The Culture Coast (*see pages 162–171*)
The Pensacola area and its beaches (*see pages 272–281*)
St Petersburg and its beaches (*see pages 144–153*)
From Orlando to Daytona Beach (*see pages 192–199*)

Theme parks and major attractions

Orlando and its theme parks (*see pages 180–191*)
The Space Coast (*see pages 200–209*)
Tampa (*see pages 134–143*)

History

St Augustine (*see pages 210–217*)
Pensacola (*see pages 264–271*)
Around Tallahassee: the Old South (*see pages 236–243*)

Nature

South Miami and Everglades National Park (*see pages 64–73*)
Coast to coast across the Everglades (*see pages 114–123*)
The Space Coast (*see pages 200–209*)
Fort Myers and the Lee County Islands (*see pages 124–133*)

Children

South Miami and Everglades National Park (*see pages 64–73*)
Orlando and its theme parks (*see pages 180–191*)
The Space Coast (*see pages 200–209*)

Homes of the rich and famous

Miami Beach (*see pages 42–51*)
Palm Beach (*see pages 86–93*)
The Gold Coast (*see pages 74–85*)
The Culture Coast (*see pages 162–171*)

Off the beaten track

The Nature Coast and rural Florida (*see pages 154–161*)
Between Tampa and Orlando (*see pages 172–179*)
Tallahassee to the Forgotten Coast (*see pages 244–253*)

Small towns

The Nature Coast and rural Florida (*see pages 154–161*)
Tallahassee to the Forgotten Coast (*see pages 244–253*)
Crossing the Panhandle (*see pages 254–263*)
From Orlando to Daytona Beach (*see pages 192–199*)

Below
Walt Disney World:
Magic Kingdom

Miami Beach

Ratings

Architecture	●●●●●
Beaches	●●●●●
Nightlife	●●●●●
Food	●●●●○
Outdoor activities	●●●●○
History	●●●○○
Museums	●●●○○
Art	●●○○○

Long and slender Miami Beach has 7 miles of beach and several distinctive neighbourhoods, but the place everybody wants to see is super-chic South Beach, home of the wonderful Art Deco District. The visual appeal of the art deco buildings made the area a venue for fashion shoots and TV commercials in the 1980s, stimulating the interest that quickly turned this once neglected quarter of Miami into a buzzing place-to-be, with recording studios, model agencies, trendy cafés and celebrity-owned nightclubs catering to the style-conscious rock, film and fashion superstars who arrived to sample the South Beach vibe.

Yet as trendy as it is, South Beach has plenty to offer even the most unfashionable visitor. Good-value hotels and restaurants abound, the beach and the art deco buildings really are stunning, there are several classy museums and the vibrant atmosphere is enhanced by warm ocean breezes rustling the palm trees.

Sights

ⓘ Art Deco Welcome Center
1001 Ocean Drive; tel: (305) 531-3484. Open daily 1100–2100.

Miami Beach Chamber of Commerce
1920 Meridian Avenue; tel: (305) 672-1270; www. miamibeachchamber.com. Open Mon–Fri 0900–1800, Sat 1000–1600.

Art Deco District✦✦✦

The 16 blocks of shops, apartments, single-storey homes and hotels in the heart of Miami Beach that display the distinctly American Streamline Moderne form of art deco design, based on the geometric ideas underpinning car, plane and ship design, were the result of fast and cheap building during the 1920s and 1930s. Narrowly escaping demolition in the late 1970s, many of the buildings acquired pastel colours and neon illumination through the 1980s and became the favoured backdrop for fashion photographers. Joined by a batch of new buildings in similar style, they became part of the unmistakable Miami Beach look.

Some of the best examples are the hotels on Ocean Drive, such as the **Breakwater**, the **Cardozo**, **Park Central** and **Waldorf Towers**, with its imitation lighthouse topping one corner. The **Leslie** is one of the more lauded attempts to turn an art deco original into an emblem

Bass Museum of Art

22nd Street

Boardwalk

The Boardwalk

Park Avenue

Alton Road

Bayshore
Golf
Course

Dade Boulevard

ns Canal

[i] Holocaust Memorial

Meridian Avenue

Washington Avenue

17th Street

Lincoln Road Mall

Ocean Beach

Lincoln Road Mall

Lenox Avenue

Michigan Avenue

ART DECO

15th Street

Collins Avenue

Espanola Way

Espanola Way

Flamingo
Park

13th Street

HISTORIC

Miami Beach Post Office

Washington Avenue

Ocean Drive

10th Street

The Wolfsonian

Atlantic
Ocean

Lenox Avenue

Michigan Avenue

DISTRICT

8th Street

6th Street

5th Street

Ocean Beach

Jewish Museum

Ocean Drive

3rd Street

Alton Road

iami
each
arina

Washington Avenue

Biscayne Street

0   300m

0   300 yards

South Pointe
Park

◉ Art Deco District tours Immensely informative 90-minute guided tours ($) of the Art Deco District begin at the Art Deco Welcome Center (see page 42) on Wed, Sat and Sun 1030 and Thur 1830. Bicycle tours ($) of the same area take place on the first and third Sun of the month from the Miami Beach Bicycle Center, 601 5th Street; tel: (305) 674-0150; email: info@mdpl.org; www.mdpl.org/weekend.html

◉ Art Deco Weekend A weekend each January is devoted to the celebration of the district's architecture with lectures and many other special events.

◉ Art deco landmark addresses

Bass Museum of Art $$ 2121 Park Avenue; tel: (305) 673-7530. Open Tue–Sat 1000–1700, Sun 1100–1700; www.bassmuseum.org

Breakwater 940 Ocean Drive; www.breakwater-hotel.com

Cameo Theater 1445 Washington Avenue.

Cardozo 1300 Ocean Drive; www.cardozohotel.com

Colony Theater 1040 Lincoln Road.

Delano 1685 Collins Avenue; www.ianschragerhotels.com

The Leslie 1244 Ocean Drive.

Lincoln Theater 555 Lincoln Road.

of 1990s Miami Beach. Along Collins Avenue are the towering **Delano** and **Shelbourne**, while Washington Avenue highlights include the **Cameo Theater** and the **Post Office** (see page 47).

Throughout the district, you need do no more than stroll to discover many art deco features such as porthole windows and imitation ships' funnels used to disguise rooftop storage tanks, and the Florida motifs such as sunburst friezes and pelican-decorated wrought-iron gates.

Bass Museum of Art✦✦

Among the more individual of Miami Beach's early art deco landmarks was the coral rock building adorned with Mayan motifs and bas-reliefs that once held the public library and is now the home of the Bass Museum of Art. The museum provides a welcome chance to escape the sun and ogle what is among the foremost art collections in the state, always bolstered by temporary exhibitions, usually on contemporary themes.

The museum's permanent holdings stem from a private collection of European art. While major names such as Rubens and Sir Thomas Lawrence are represented, the stand-out canvases tend to be from lesser-known names such as artist Marcellus Kofferman, notably with his *Holy Family*, and the Dutch artist Cornelis Cornelisz van Haarlem, whose intense *Crucifixion Triptych* occupies the centre of one gallery. *The Tournament*, a 16th-century tapestry created by the Flemish School, also captures the imagination.

Beaches✦✦✦

Some of the world's finest physiques can be seen tanning on the golden sands at Miami Beach. Seven miles long and in places 100yds wide, it is very much the focal point of daytime activity. Hit the sands shortly after dawn and you might also spot fashion-model photo shoots, commercials or music videos being filmed with the Art Deco District as a backdrop before the sunlight becomes too intense and the crowds too large.

It may be a surprise to learn that the beach is not natural but stemmed from an unlikely alliance between a Quaker farmer, who settled here in 1907, and developer Carl Fisher. They devised a scheme to plant palm trees and bring sand to what was then a swamp-filled island. Incredibly, Miami Beach became America's vacation capital by the 1920s.

The sand (often replaced following major storms) is pleasantly soft underfoot and uniformly yellow but the beach's social mixture is more varied. Around 1st Street would-be surfers lament the (usual) lack of suitable waves; the 21st Street area is predominantly gay; further north, is the rugged vegetated **Haulover Beach Park**.

Miami Beach as the world knows it, however, is between 5th and 18th streets, around **Lummus Park**. This is the place to work on your

Park Central 640 Ocean Drive; www.theparkcentral.com

Shelbourne 1801 Collins Avenue.

Sterling Building 810 Lincoln Road.

Waldorf Towers 850 Ocean Drive; www.waldorftowers.com

tan or simply admire everybody else's, take dips in the ocean watched by lifeguards from the historic art deco lifeguard station opposite 11th Street or simply laze in the sun as the music spills over from the bars across Ocean Drive. Incidentally, this is one of few places in the US where topless bathing is tolerated.

The Boardwalk❖❖

Formed of raised wooden planks and accessed from most adjoining streets, the Boardwalk lies between 21st and 46th streets carrying walkers and joggers along the beach's edge. There are rest points with shady seats and pathways providing access to several hotels noted for their architectural excesses, such as the Fontainebleau and the Eden Roc, and open-air bars tempting Boardwalk users with ice-cold drinks.

Española Way❖

Created in 1925, two-block-long Española Way has the barrel-tiled roofs, bell towers and striped awnings of a Mediterranean village that derive from the designer's plan to re-create a European artists' colony. In keeping with its would-be artistic heritage, Española Way has commercial art galleries and small apartments on its upper floors that property brokers describe as 'artists lofts' in the hope of selling them.

On the corner with Washington Avenue, the **Clay Hotel** was a popular nightspot during the 1930s. It was here that Cuban band leader Desi Arnaz helped create the rumba craze that spread across the US. Arnez is perhaps better remembered as the real-life husband of comedienne Lucille Ball, and her partner in the *I Love Lucy* TV series.

Below
Art deco landmark: The Leslie, at 1244 Ocean Drive

Holocaust Memorial**

Miami Beach has one of the world's largest communities of holocaust survivors and in 1990 gained a lasting memorial to the atrocities of the Nazi era with this affecting work by Kenneth Treister.

The memorial begins with a historical display on Jews in Europe, leading up to the rise of anti-Semitism in Germany. Visitors continue along the Lonely Path and through a tunnel, symbolising an individual's loss of identity and marked with the names of concentration camps, into the heart of the memorial. Here, a 42-ft-high bronze arm, etched with a concentration camp tattoo, reaches forever upward in a forlorn attempt to reach freedom. In the foreground many individual figures, contorted and bearing expressions of horror and torment, surround the visitor.

Although reactions to the memorial have been mixed, for many it is an emotionally draining experience. The final section, the Reflective Pool, provides an area of calmness, a chance to gather thoughts while gazing across a lily-decorated pond.

ⓗ Holocaust Memorial
1933–1945 Meridian Avenue; tel: (305) 538-1663; www.holocaust mmb.org. Open daily 0900–2100. Free.

South Florida Arts Center *810 Lincoln Road; tel: (305) 674-8278; www.artcentersf.org. See notice board in entrance for opening times. Free.*

Lincoln Road Mall*

Packed with clothing and jewellery stores, Lincoln Road was labelled the 'Fifth Avenue of the South', a comparison with the fashionable shopping strip of New York, during the booming 1950s. After years of decline, the area is again on the rise with a pedestrianised section that has become a thriving centre of creativity and culture.

Sidewalk restaurants give the area further appeal, as do the excellent restoration of art deco buildings such as the **Colony Theater** and the **Lincoln Cinema**, both performing arts venues, and the impossibly long and slender **Sterling Building**. The latter is partly occupied by the **South Florida Arts Center**, created in the 1980s to provide studios and exhibition space for contemporary artists, many of whom display their work during weekends and evenings.

Miami Beach Post Office /300 Washington Avenue. Open Mon–Fri 0600–1800, Sat 0600–1600.

Sanford L Ziff Jewish Museum of Florida $$ 301 Washington Avenue; tel: (305) 672-5044; www.jewishmuseum.com. Open Tue–Sun 1000–1700.

The Wolfsonian $$ (free Thur evenings) 1001 Washington Avenue; tel: (305) 531-1001; www.wolfsonian.org. Open Mon–Tue & Thur–Sat 1000–1800, Thur until 2100, Sun 1200–1700.

Miami Beach Post Office**

The 1939 Miami Beach Post Office is a splendidly restored example of deco federal, an architectural style that evolved during the federal-government building programme of the Depression. Classical motifs and subdued decoration distinguish the post office from the neighbouring art deco buildings. Within the rotunda, housing the public area, are original stamp tables and mail boxes; an eye-catching mural by Charles Hardin showing scenes of Cavalry and Indians fills one wall.

Sanford L Ziff Jewish Museum of Florida*

'Always a view, never a Jew' was one marketing slogan used by hotels in Miami Beach during the 1930s, a period when anti-Semitism forced local Jewish people to have homes only in the area south of 5th Street. Such prejudice is one issue documented by the exhibitions of this museum, housed in a 1936 synagogue designed by art deco luminary Harry Hohauser. The influx of European Jews into Miami Beach during the 1940s following the rise of Nazism and anti-Semitism led to the election of Miami Beach's first Jewish mayor in 1943.

The core exhibits are drawn from the Mosaic project, created in 1984 to travel through Florida charting the state's Jewish communities and gather items of historical interest. Objects such as a shell-covered dress made for a Purim party in Jacksonville in 1916, a Florida citrus label in Hebrew, items from Cuban Jews who arrived following the Castro-led revolution, and countless family and business photos make for engrossing browsing.

The building itself is a bonus. The loss of its congregation as the population moved north through the 1940s, and damage inflicted by Hurricane Andrew in 1992 led to a two-year restoration project that returned this art deco landmark to its former glory.

The Wolfsonian**

The son of the first Jewish mayor of Miami Beach, Mitchell Wolfson Jnr stored his expanding collection of items of design interest in a warehouse, until he decided to cut his losses on storage charges and buy the building. Now simply called the Wolfsonian, this fine museum is also a research centre devoted to the study of objects and their social and political context.

With ceramics, books, posters, paintings, industrial items and much more, the permanent collection includes 70,000 articles, mostly from the late-19th to mid-20th centuries. Selections are displayed to illustrate a particular theme and might feature anything from 1920s art deco ashtrays to 1960s experimental kitchens.

The first exhibit, however, is the 1927 Mediterranean-style building itself, its entrance decorated by Spanish-style bas-reliefs. Immediately inside are the stained-glass windows and green and gold terracotta façade salvaged from a 1929 theatre in Philadelphia.

Above left
Miami Beach Holocaust
Memorial

Above
Art deco architectural
details

Accommodation and food

Miami Beach's hotels range from fashion's cutting edge to simple rooms for those on a budget wishing to be near the action. Food is no less varied, with Cuban cuisine particularly worth sampling.

Clay Hotel $ *1438 Washington Avenue; tel: (305) 534-2988 or (800) 379-CLAY; www.clayhotel.com.* A landmark on the corner with Española Way, the Clay holds the local youth hostel and also offers private rooms at extremely good rates.

Delano $$$ *1685 Collins Avenue; tel: (305) 672-2000 or (800) 555-5001; www.ianschragerhotels.com.* Devilishly trendy and wickedly expensive, the Phillipe Starck-designed interiors draw ultra-fashionable faces from around the world.

Front Porch $–$$ *1418 Ocean Drive; tel: (305) 531-8300.* Healthy breakfasts and laid-back lunches are the stock-in-fare of this popular locals' haunt.

Indian Creek Hotel $$ *2727 Indian Creek Drive; tel: (305) 531-2727 or (800) 491-2772; email: indian2727@aol.com; www.indiancreekhotel.com.* Authentically restored to its 1936 appearance, the lobby makes a winning first impression; the inviting atmosphere and friendly staff make amends for the nice but slightly small rooms.

Larios on the Beach $$ *820 Ocean Drive; tel: (305) 532-9577.* Serves mouth-watering Cuban fare and, on Saturday nights, is enlivened by a Cuban band encouraging impromptu dancing.

News Café $ *800 Ocean Drive; tel: (305) 538-6397; www.newscafe.com.* With a few tables and a small menu of classy fare, this round-the-clock eatery has been the place to see and be seen for years.

Park Central $$ *640 Ocean Drive; tel: (305) 538-1611 or (800) 727-5236; www.parkcentral.com.* Once a favourite of gangster Al Capone, it has been renovated to bring out the best of its art deco features. Comfortable rooms, some with a fine view of the beach.

Publix $ *1045 Dade Boulevard; tel: (305) 534-4621; www.publix.com.* Small food shops are found all over Miami Beach but this enormous supermarket has the lowest prices and incredible 1960s architecture.

Raleigh $$$ *1775 Collins Avenue; tel: (305) 634-6300 or (800) 848-1775; www.raleighhotel.com.* Art deco landmark given a post-modern restyling to please a discerning, and very chic, clientele.

Van Dyke Café $ *846 Lincoln Road; tel: (305) 534-3600; www.thevandyke.com.* Excellent for people-watching while munching on king-sized sandwiches or other inexpensive dishes.

Yuca $$$ *501 Lincoln Road; tel: (305) 532-9822; www.yuca.com.* Nuevo-Cuban cuisine took off in Miami largely thanks to this restaurant which is still earning rave reviews after several years.

Nightlife

South Beach is the vibrant heart of Miami's nightlife, whether for Cuban music, trendy nightclubs or just bars with original art deco furniture. Read the free *New Times* for the latest happening places. The in-vogue spots may not operate a dress code but do have a simple fame code: if you lack it, you won't get in. The long-running bars and clubs listed below, however, generally have a more tolerant policy towards unknown faces.

Abbey Brewing Company *1115 16th Street; tel: (305) 538-8110.* Small, convivial bar with a variety of independently brewed ales.

Bash $$ *655 Washington Avenue; tel: (305) 538-2274; www.bashobe.com.* Local boy Mickey Rourke is one of the celebrities who co-own this perennially popular nightspot; much less trendy than it once was.

Clevelander *1020 Ocean Drive; tel: (305) 531-3485 or (800) 815-6829; www.clevelanderhotel.com.* Open-air hotel bar with regular live music at night and during weekend afternoons.

Club Deuce $$ *222 14th Street; tel: (305) 531-6200.* A bizarre mix of locals, tourists, drag queens and cops frequent this likeably scruffy neighbourhood bar.

Opium Garden $$ *136 Collins Avenue; tel: (305) 531-5535; email: info@opiummiami.com; www.opiummiami.com.* Merely getting into this ultra-cool nightspot might make you think you've arrived on the Miami scene but the really hip place to be is the roped-off VIP section called Prive.

Suggested tour

(P) Parking is difficult and expensive throughout Miami Beach, although there is metered parking along many streets. Traffic is particularly heavy at weekends. Many hotels have parking areas for guest use. If you are arriving from elsewhere in Miami, it is worth while checking local bus routes (mostly good) to avoid parking problems. As in the rest of Miami, buses have a flat-fare and correct change is necessary. If requested, drivers issue free transfers.

Length: Main tour 1 mile; with both detours, 4.5 miles. Buses are frequent along Washington Boulevard and can be used as a supplement to the walking tour.

Duration: Half a day is sufficient for a good sampling of the Art Deco District but allow a full day to cover the main tour and one or both detours, and to pause for meals and refreshments. Parking is difficult and traffic can be heavy, particularly at weekends.

Links: Using any of the causeways joining Miami Beach to mainland Miami, this route links easily with Miami (*see pages 52–63*). Heading north, the coastal Hwy-A1A continues for 23 miles and makes a scenic link to The Gold Coast (*see pages 74–85*).

The **ART DECO DISTRICT** ❶ is most impressively revealed by the hotels on Ocean Drive between 14th and 5th streets. While exploring these seductive few blocks, make a point of calling into the **Art Deco Welcome Center** ❷ on the beach facing 12th Street. From here, continue two blocks inland along 12th Street for the **MIAMI BEACH POST OFFICE** ❸ on Washington Avenue. The immediate area is lined with interesting shops and small restaurants and cafés. A short stroll north is **ESPAÑOLA WAY** ❹, between 14th and 15th streets. Continue north on Washington Avenue to **LINCOLN ROAD MALL** ❺ and another inviting spot for lunch or a snack.

Detour: Two blocks south on Washington Avenue from the Post Office, the imposing façade of the **WOLFSONIAN** ❻ marks the junction with 10th Street. Continuing south, crossing the major traffic artery of 5th Street, leads into a largely residential area and finds the **JEWISH MUSEUM** ❼ on the corner with 3rd Street.

Detour: While exploring Lincoln Road, turn northwards along Meridian Avenue for the **HOLOCAUST MEMORIAL** ❽, three blocks ahead just before the junction with the busy Dade Boulevard. Return to stroll the rest of Lincoln Road and turn north along Washington Avenue, noting the impressive profile of the Delano hotel beside the ocean at the eastern end of 17th Street. Passing the enormous Miami Beach Convention Center, Park Avenue forks to the right off Washington Boulevard to the **BASS MUSEUM OF ART** ❾. Cross the museum's sculpture-decorated gardens and turn right along 22nd Street for the southern end of the **BOARDWALK** ❿, continuing to 46th Street.

Also worth exploring

At the southern tip of Miami Beach, the well-kept trees and lawns of the 17-acre **South Pointe Park** provide a respite from the crowds that mill through much of South Beach. Here, the calm is usually disturbed only by the bluster of ocean breezes and the crashing of waves against the shoreline as cruise ships and cargo vessels move through the slender Government Cut, a channel dredged in the 1970s to provide smooth passage between the Port of Miami and the Atlantic.

Placed at intervals beside the winding pathways are benches perfect for picnics and ship-watching. Walk to the west edge of the park to admire the pricey private yachts moored at the marina. The park bandstand sometimes hosts concerts.

Miami: the City

Miami Beach steals the show but there is much more in this fast-growing city than art deco architecture, scantily clad roller-bladers and swathes of crowded beach. Scattered throughout are distinctive neighbourhoods, such as the sedate Mediterranean-style Coral Gables and fashionable Coconut Grove, that have long been cities in their own right. Meanwhile, even the briefest look around Little Havana reveals the strongly Latin-American element in a city where around half the population is Cuban or of Cuban descent.

For beach lovers, Key Biscayne has miles of tempting sand where tourists are usually outnumbered by locals and neither are much in evidence during the working week, making this a perfect retreat for beachcombers and hopeless romantics. One-of-a-kind sights include the immeasurably grand Vizcaya and a misplaced 12th-century Spanish monastery. More predictable but none the less excellent stops are the Metrozoo and Seaquarium. City driving on generally easily navigated freeways and local roads is simple if unspectacular.

Ratings

Architecture	●●●○
Children	●●●○
History	●●●○
Nature	●●●○○
Shopping	●●●○○
Beaches	●●○○○
Museums	●●○○○
Scenery	●●○○○

Sights

ℹ Greater Miami Convention & Visitors Bureau *701 Brickell Avenue, Suite 2700; tel: (305) 539-3000 or (800) 933-8448; www.miamiandbeaches.com. Open daily 0830–1700.*

ℹ The Barnacle $ *3485 Main Highway; tel: (305) 442-6866; www.floridastateparks.org/ thebarnacle. Tours Fri–Mon 1000, 1100, 1330, 1400.*

The Barnacle**

One of Miami's earliest and most ingeniously designed homes, the Barnacle was erected by Massachusetts-born yacht builder Ralph Middleton Monroe in 1891. Monroe purchased 40 acres of bayside land in Coconut Grove, which at that time lacked even a road link with the separate community of Miami, and created the Barnacle from wood salvaged from shipwrecks.

To improve air circulation and avoid flooding, he raised the house 8ft above ground, vented the roof and covered the porch to enable windows to be opened during storms. These and a host of other unique features made life bearable in the heat and humidity of the south Florida summer. Monroe continued to be inventive when his family expanded. He simply raised the Barnacle and slid in a new storey underneath.

The fine points are revealed on the guided tour, the only way to see inside the Barnacle and discover the wonderful collection of Monroe memorabilia, including photos of early Coconut Grove luminaries.

Palmetto Expresseway

North Miami Beach Bouleva

Dixie Highway

NW 135th Street

Red Road

NW 22nd Avenue

Biscayne Boulevard

NW 103rd Street

49th Street

441

27

North Bay Causew

Okeechobee Road

NW 27th Avenue

95

58th Street

Biscayne Bay

Hialeah Drive

Doral Blvd

Airport Expresseway

Biscayne Boulevard

195   Julia Tuttle Causeway

NW 25th Street

Palmetto Expresseway

Miami International Airport

SW 27th Avenue

MIA BEA

East West Expresseway

East West Expresseway

West Flagler Street

395

MacArthur Causeway

Little Havana

Bayside Marketplace

41   SW 8th Street (Calle O   )

41

(Tamiami Trail)

DOWNTOWN MIAMI

Historical Museum of South Florida

Merrick House

kell Avenue

Coral Highway

Venetian Pool

SW 22nd Street

Vizcaya

Coral Gables Congregational Church/ Biltmore Hotel

CORAL GABLES

COCONUT GROVE

Rickenbacker Causeway

Bird Road

Bird Road

Museum of Science and Planetarium

Bird Road

Douglas Road

Grand Ave

Seaquarium

y (toll)

Miller Drive

Main Hy

The Barnacle

Key Biscayne

Sunset Drive

Crandon Boulevard

Kendall Drive

Palmetto Expresseway

Dixie Highway

Dade Expresseway (toll)

Old Cutler Road

Red Road

Bill Baggs Cape Florida State Park

Killian Drive

1

Ludlam Road

Dixie Highway

Howard Drive

0   4km

0   2 miles

Coral Reef Drive

Miami Metrozoo

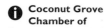

Bayside Marketplace
401 Biscayne Boulevard;
tel: (305) 577-3344;
www.baysidemarketplace.com.
Open Mon–Thur 1000–2200,
Fri–Sat 1000–2300, Sun
1100–2100.

The Biltmore *1200*
Anastasia Avenue; tel:
(305) 445-1926;
www.biltmorehotel.com.
Guided tours are free Sun
1330, 1430, 1530.

**Coconut Grove
Chamber of
Commerce** *Peacock Park,*
beside MacFarlane Road;
tel: (305) 444-7270;
www.coconutgrove.com.
Open Mon–Fri 0900–1700.

Miami City Hall *3500 Pan*
American Drive; tel: (305)
250-5300. Open Mon–Fri
0800–1700.

Bayside Marketplace*

Though no more than a collection of shops, Bayfront Marketplace is a surprisingly enjoyable place to pass an hour. Besides the obvious opportunities for buying and browsing – the stores sell everything from luggage and books to lingerie and gourmet chocolate – the walkways are pleasantly shady with views of the Downtown skyline and Biscayne Bay. Live music and other entertainment is common and there are several restaurants and a large food court.

The Biltmore**

Its elegant wings brought together by a 315-ft-tall tower, loosely modelled on the Giralda in Spain, and surrounded by palm trees, the Mediterranean-style Biltmore hotel oozes luxury from every stone. Architects Schultze & Weaver, better known for Manhattan's renowned Waldorf Astoria, gave the hotel crystal chandeliers, custom-loomed rugs and a lobby ceiling decorated with gold leaf to reflect the flames from over-sized fireplaces.

Completed in 1926, the Biltmore's first guests, including Judy Garland and the Duke and Duchess of Windsor, amused themselves in the hotel grounds with tennis, golf, fox-hunting or rides along mock-Venetian canals in mock-Venetian gondolas. Yet the Biltmore's glory days were short. A hurricane and financial disaster hit Miami just months after the hotel opened. It became a military hospital in 1942 and was empty for 20 years before undergoing a $55-million renovation and re-opening as a hotel in 1987.

Entering the lobby of the hotel, marketed as 'the last word in civilisation', reveals leering gargoyles above the staircases, the chirping of caged birds, and a terrace loggia with views across the restored Donald Ross designed championship golf course. Don't leave without seeing the pool where guests were once coached by Johnny Weissmuller, Olympic champion and future Hollywood *Tarzan*, who broke his first swimming record here in the 1920s.

Coconut Grove**

Smart art galleries, trendy shops and some of Miami's most expensive apartments are all features of Coconut Grove. One of Miami's oldest areas, it was settled in the 1840s by Bahamians who salvaged shipwrecks, and later by New Englanders, such as Charles and Isabel Peacock who opened Miami's first hotel on what is now Peacock Park.

The heart of Coconut Grove is around the junction of Main Highway and McFarlane Road, where the **CocoWalk** is a popular grouping of shops, cinemas and restaurants. The sloping, tree-lined **Peacock Park** is the venue of numerous well-attended festivals and brings views of the Dinner Key marina, where Coconut Grovers tether their yachts. The Streamline Moderne structure beside the key was once the terminal for PanAm's seaplane service to Latin America. The modest size of the building makes it hard to believe that it is now **Miami City Hall**.

Plymouth Congregational Church 3429 Devon Road; tel: (305) 444-6521; email: pccgrove@bellsouth.net; www.plymouthmiami.com. Open usually Mon–Fri 0830–1600.

Coral Gables City Hall 405 Biltmore Avenue; tel: (305) 446-6800; www.citybeautiful.net. Public areas open Mon–Fri 0800–1700. Closed holidays.

Coral Gables Chamber of Commerce 30 Greco Avenue; tel: (305) 446-1657; www.gableschamber.org. Open Mon–Fri 0830–1700.

Plymouth Congregational Church is another link with Coconut Grove's past. Built with mock medieval features and a 400-year-old door from a Pyrenean monastery, by a single Spanish mason, the church was completed in 1917.

Right
Coral Gables: the Biltmore Hotel

Coral Gables✦✦✦

Coral Gables is a 12-square-mile enclave of Miami with an appearance and character all its own. Dotted by Mediterranean-style fountains and plazas, bisected by quiet leafy streets lined by stucco-fronted homes and claiming some of Miami's most attractive buildings, Coral Gables was conceived in the 1920s by George Merrick, son of a local farmer, and marketed with the most expensive advertising campaign then known. It is a tribute to Merrick, and a 1970s conservation plan, that Coral Gables today probably looks as good as it ever did.

The commercial centrepiece is the **Miracle Mile**, lined by chic boutiques, and antiques and bridal shops. The western end is anchored by **Coral Gables City Hall**, with 12 columns fronting a semicircular rotunda topped by a three-tier clock tower. Inside, items from Coral Gables' history line narrow corridors while the interior of the dome carries a mural by Denman Fink, an artist who worked closely with Merrick.

Coral Gables Congregational Church
3010 De Soto Boulevard;
tel: (305) 448-7421;
www.coralgablescongregational.
org. Open by appointment.

Historical Museum of South Florida $ 101
W Flagler Street; tel: (305) 375-1492;
www.historical-museum.org.
Open Mon–Sat 1000–1700,
3rd Thur of month until
2100, Sun 1200–1700.

Coral Gables Congregational Church✦

This sturdy Mediterranean-Revival church stands on land donated by George Merrick (*see Coral Gables, page 55*) and was completed in 1924. It is claimed that some of the interior wood furnishings date from the 16th century and were recovered from shipwrecks.

Downtown Miami✦

Bustling by day and deserted by night, Downtown Miami has little to merit a lengthy stop save for the exhibits of the Historical Museum of Southern Florida (*see below*). The museum occupies one side of the 1980s Philip Johnson-designed **Miami-Dade Cultural Center**, facing the city's main library and the Center for Fine Arts. Much of the rest of Downtown is a conglomeration of jewellery and electrical shops, many of its customers on shopping trips from Latin America. One enjoyable way to view Downtown is from the **Metromover**, which navigates a circular route just above the rooftops.

Historical Museum of South Florida✦✦

This small museum does a fine job in weaving together the diverse strands that underpinned South Florida's rise from mosquito-infested outpost to the US's fastest-growing region inside 80 years.

Above
The Coral Gables
Congregational Church

Bill Baggs Cape Florida State Park
$ 1200 S Crandon Boulevard; tel: (305) 361-5811; www.floridastateparks.org/capeflorida/default.asp. Open daily 0800–sunset; lighthouse tours Thur–Mon 1000 & 1300.

Except for decimating the indigenous Tequesta people, the 16th-century Spanish who colonised other parts of Florida made little headway here. Not until the mid-19th century, when Key West boomed as a salvaging centre for shipwrecks and gained a cigar industry, was there major economic expansion. Displays and re-created buildings record the first boom era.

Another re-creation is of a 'chickee', a type of raised, open-sided hut used by Seminoles, a Native American group forced into the Everglades (where many still remain) by the 19th-century Seminole Wars. Inside are items describing traditional handicrafts and lifestyles.

Miami's inexorable rise, stimulated by oil tycoon Henry Flagler extending his east-coast railway to the newly emerging city in 1896, is charted by engrossing posters, photos and other artefacts, as is the 1920s property boom and the creation of Miami Beach. A segregated tram from 1925 provides a reminder of Miami's ethnic divisions.

The impact of Cubans in shaping Miami, of TV's *Miami Vice* in changing perceptions of it, the restoration of the Art Deco District and the devastation of 1992's Hurricane Andrew are among exhibits detailing more recent times.

Key Biscayne**

Key Biscayne is a desirable Miami address and the very tidy residential section is bordered by two of the city's most attractive natural areas. A 3-mile-long beach fringes **Crandon Beach Park**, lining a patch of shallow and very calm water. Until they were destroyed by Hurricane Andrew in 1992, rows of Australian pines added to the beauty of the setting. Despite the lack of shade, the park remains a popular venue for weekend barbecues.

Also much depleted by Hurricane Andrew, **Bill Baggs Cape Florida State Park** is crisscrossed by footpaths and has a boardwalk beside its inviting beach. Another draw is the **Cape Florida lighthouse**. Decommissioned in 1978, the lighthouse's fascinating history stretches back to the Civil and Seminole wars and is described on guided tours.

Little Havana**

Historically strong links between Florida and Cuba became firmer still when Miami became the point of arrival for approximately 300,000 Cubans fleeing the Caribbean island following the 1959 revolution. Many settled in what became Little Havana until their increasing prosperity financed a relocation to larger homes across the city. The humble dwellings here now accommodate 1970s and 1980s arrivals from strife-torn South and Central American countries.

Totems of Cuban culture predominate along **Calle Ocho** (SW 8th Street). Street counters dispense shots of sweet and strong *café Cubano*, Cuban men play dominoes in **Máximo Gómez Park**, and the eternal flame of the **Brigade 2056 Memorial** remembers those killed in the

🏠 Merrick House $
*907 Coral Way; tel
(305) 460-5361. Open Wed
& Sun 1300–1600; or by
appointment.*

Metrozoo $$ *12400 SW
152nd Street; tel: (305)
251-0400;
www.miamimetrozoo.com.
Open daily 0930–1730.*

**Museum of Science
and Planetarium $$**
*3280 S Miami Avenue;
tel: (305) 645-4200;
www.miamisci.org. Open
daily 1000–1800.*

Seaquarium $$ *4400
Rickenbacker Causeway;
tel: (305) 361-5705;
www.miamiseaquarium.com.
Open daily 0930–1800.*

1963 attempt to re-take Cuba by force which floundered at the Bay of Pigs. Close by are tributes to 19th-century Cuban heroes such as José Martí and Antonio Maceo.

Merrick House✤✤

Coral Gables (*see page 55*) took its name from the boyhood home of its creator George Merrick, so-named for the coral rock used in its construction and its gabled roof. The Merrick house stood at the heart of the 160-acre citrus and vegetable farm, developed by George's father, on which the city arose. An introductory video tells the extraordinary story of Merrick and the Coral Gables he created before the guided tour continues around the house, highlighting design features and oddities such as the amusingly amateurish paintings by George's mother.

Metrozoo✤✤

White Bengal tigers prowling a re-created Khymer temple and a pair of komodo dragons, the world's most powerful lizard and rarely seen outside its native Indonesia, are among the most photographed inhabitants of Miami's 290-acre Metrozoo. Moats rather than bars divide animals and humans, and a full circuit of the 3 miles of pathways (a monorail allows short cuts) should bring sightings of giraffes, zebras, gazelles, ostriches, rhinos, bears, and lots more.

Cleverly constructed artificial tunnels and caves enable many creatures to be observed at close quarters. The koalas and other cuddly creatures are perennial child pleasers, as are the elephant rides offered in PAWS, the children's section of the zoo.

Museum of Science and Planetarium✤✤

Entertaining, interactive, multimedia exhibits make this an enjoyable place for kids to experiment with perspective, gravity, light and other scientific fundamentals, while exhibits describe Everglades' wildlife and invite visitors to shoot cyber hoops on a virtual reality basketball court.

There is more to enjoy in the Wildlife Center, where owls, hawks and falcons are among the creatures being nursed after sustaining injuries in the wild. Other menagerie members include tortoises, tarantulas and turkey vultures. Mounted insects and butterflies can be seen in the Collection Gallery, arranged beneath several somewhat morbid rows of animal skulls.

Seaquarium✤

Touted as the home of TV's *Flipper*, the Seaquarium's shows demonstrate the abilities of dolphins and killer whales to respond to their trainers and entertain crowds. Elsewhere are pools of sharks, seals, sea lions, stingrays and manatees, an ungainly but much-loved creature found in Florida's waters. Alligators can also be seen, as can the much rarer American crocodile.

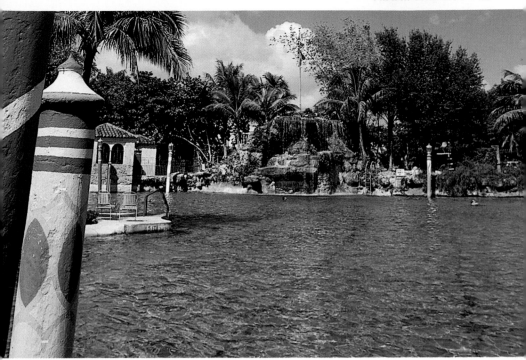

🅷 **Venetian Pool $**
*2701 De Soto
Boulevard; tel: (305)
460-5306;
www.venetianpool.com.
Open daily 1000 or
1100–1630 or 1730
according to season; until
1930 on weekdays in
summer.*

*Vizcaya $$ 3521 S Miami
Avenue; tel: (305) 250-
9133. Open daily
0930–1730.*

Above
The Venetian Pool,
Coral Gables

Venetian Pool✦✦

Few public swimming pools can match the grandeur of the 1924 Venetian Pool or provide an excuse to swim and sightsee at the same time. Ingeniously conceived to fill a quarry that provided the rock used in the building of Coral Gables, the pool maintains the Mediterranean theme of the neighbourhood with Venetian-style lampposts, tiled loggias and palm tree-lined walkways, and uses a limestone outcrop as a diving platform.

Vizcaya✦✦✦

Opulent homes are two-a-penny in Miami but none have the history or the grandeur to match Vizcaya, a pseudo-Italian villa costing $15 million, completed in 1916. With a fortune made from farm machinery, James Deering commissioned Vizcaya in what was then a jungle-like setting on the edge of Miami. Architect Paul Chalfin frequently exceeded the owner's expectations, causing Deering to lament 'must we be so grand' as yet more shipments of antiques arrived from Europe.

Intended to reflect 400 years of occupation, Vizcaya intentionally combines architecture and furnishings from the Renaissance, baroque, rococo and neo-classical periods, while contemporary domestic comforts, such as elevators and a bowling alley, were included but discreetly concealed.

Guided tours unravel a wealth of detail about Deering and the construction of Vizcaya as they pass through some of the 34 ground-floor rooms. These include a Robert Adams library, the beautiful rococo Music Room, and the Banquet Hall, decorated by two Ferrara tapestries that once belonged to English poet Robert Browning.

Visitors can wander at leisure around the upper floors, which include Deering's luxurious marble-walled bathroom, and stroll a few of the 25 miles of pathways that wind around the gardens, created over seven years using Italian and French formal landscaping methods.

Above
Vizcaya's opulent architecture

Accommodation and food

Miami Beach offers greater choice in accommodation than the rest of the city. None the less, there are hotels scattered all over and the pick of the bunch are in Coral Gables. Along with Coconut Grove and Little Havana, Coral Gables also holds some of the city's best dining options but, again, there is greater choice at Miami Beach.

The Biltmore $$$ *1200 Anastasia Avenue, Coral Gables; tel: (305) 445-1926 or (800) 727-1926.* The luxury evident in the public areas (*see page 54*) spreads to the rooms, although the ones to aspire to are on the upper storeys of the tower, costing up to $1800 nightly.

Cafe Tu Tu Tango $–$$ *CocoWalk, 3015 Grand Avenue, Coconut Grove; tel: (305) 592-2222; www.cafetututango.com.* Designed as an artist's garret, offering a tapas-style menu, daily specials and scrumptious pizzas.

Gables Inn $$ *730 S Dixie Highway; tel: (305) 661-7999; www.thegablesinn.net.* Outside of the academic year and college sports fixtures (the property is close to the University of Miami) this makes a reasonably-priced base in Coral Gables.

Hotel Place St Michel $$ *162 Alcazar Avenue, Coral Gables; tel: (305) 444-1666 or (800) 848-HOTEL; www.hotelplacestmichel.com.* Dating from 1927 and with just 27 rooms, this piece of neighbourhood history makes a wonderful romantic hideaway.

Restaurant St Michel $$$ *at the Hotel Place St Michel, 162 Alcazar Avenue, Coral Gables; tel: (305) 446-1666.* Coral Gables has many fine restaurants but this is the best bet for immaculately presented New American cuisine with a tropical twist.

Versailles $ *3555 SW 8th Street, Little Havana; tel: (305) 444-0240.* It's almost a crime to visit Little Havana and not eat at this long-running favourite of Miami Cubans, who come here for the festive mood as much as the Cuban food.

Suggested tour

Length: Main tour, 8 miles; Downtown and Little Havana detour, 6 miles; Key Biscayne detour 10 miles. Metrozoo is 15 miles from the main tour.

Duration: The main route can comfortably be covered inside a day but allow at least another half-day for one or more of the detours. Of these, Downtown Miami and Little Havana are worth seeing but dispensable if time is tight; Key Biscayne is ideal for a leisurely break and the Seaquarium is a good destination for kids, as is the Metrozoo. Vizcaya is less interesting for kids but adults might allocate two or three hours to it and could do so while the youngsters enjoy the nearby Museum of Science and Planetarium.

Links: Miami Beach (*see pages 42–51*), South Miami and Everglades National Park (*see pages 64–73*).

Take any route to Brickell Avenue. As it runs south from Downtown, this street is lined by sleek high-rise office buildings and on the left is the much-photographed Atlantis apartment building, a gap in its centre decorated by a palm tree. Just under a mile ahead, the entrances to **VIZCAYA ❶** and the **MUSEUM OF SCIENCE AND PLANETARIUM ❷** are on the left and right respectively.

Continuing south for 3 miles, the route becomes S Bayshore Drive and passes some of Miami's most exclusive homes (hidden behind effusive foliage) before reaching the driveway leading to **Miami City Hall ❸** and swinging right to become McFarlane Road and enter the heart of **COCONUT GROVE ❹**. Amid trendy boutiques and restaurants, a short footpath on the eastern side of Main Highway leads to the secluded **BARNACLE ❺**. Less than half a mile further on Main Highway is Devon Road and the **Plymouth Congregational Church ❻**.

Leave Coconut Grove headed west for 1.3 miles along Grand Avenue, passing through an undistinguished area until turning north on to Le Jeune Road (close to the busy junction with Dixie Highway). After 1.5 miles, the route reaches SW 22nd Street, locally called the Miracle Mile and the retail centre of **CORAL GABLES ❼**.

Ⓐ Ancient Spanish Monastery $
16711 W Dixie Highway;
tel: (305) 945-1461;
www.spanishmonastery.com.
Open Mon–Sat 1000–1600,
Sun 1200–1600.

Ⓜ The single-carriage Metromover runs on a loop circuit above Downtown Miami, an enjoyble break from exploring on foot and bringing elevated views of the skyline. Board from the Government Center terminal, adjacent to the Miami-Dade Cultural Center.

Ⓟ Coconut Grove and Coral Gables have limited metered street parking in their main areas and several well-signposted parking garages. The city's major attractions all have ample parking spaces for visitors' use. On weekdays, Downtown parking can be expensive; an incentive for using the centrally placed Metro-Dade Cultural Center parking garage is a discount at the Historical Museum of South Florida. Another option is to park at Bayside Marketplace. Crandon Beach Park and Bill Baggs Cape Florida State Park have their own car parks.

The immediate area is best explored on foot but return to the car to drive west to Coral Way and the **MERRICK HOUSE ❽**, then south along the curving De Soto Boulevard for the **VENETIAN POOL ❾** and **CORAL GABLES CONGREGATIONAL CHURCH ❿**, within sight of the splendid **BILTMORE ⓫** hotel.

Detour: At the meeting point of several freeways, **DOWNTOWN MIAMI ⓬** is an easy detour and the site of the **HISTORICAL MUSEUM OF SOUTH FLORIDA ⓭**. **BAYSIDE MARKETPLACE ⓮** is just north of Downtown beside Biscayne Boulevard, travelling between the two by foot is easy. By car, turn right along SW 8th Street, just south of Downtown, for **LITTLE HAVANA ⓯**, 2 miles west.

Detour: To reach **KEY BISCAYNE ⓰**, take the Rickenbacker Causeway (toll), the multi-laned approach to which is off Brickell Avenue between the Atlantis and Vizcaya. The causeway makes a 3.5-mile crossing of Biscayne Bay, passing the entrance to the **SEAQUARIUM ⓱** before reaching Key Biscayne itself. **Crandon Beach Park ⓲** is on the left and the road continues for 1.5 miles through the island's residential section before reaching the **Bill Baggs Cape Florida State Park ⓳**.

Detour: The **METROZOO ⓴** is 18 miles from Downtown Miami and most easily reached by taking any route to the Florida Turnpike (toll) and travelling south to the 152nd Street exit, from which the zoo is signposted.

Also worth exploring

On a trip to Spain in 1925, multimillionaire William Randolph Hearst so liked an abandoned 12th-century Cistercian monastery that he bought it for $500,000, had it dismantled and shipped to the US. With tax demands biting into the Hearst fortunes, the dismembered monastery stayed in a New York warehouse until the 1950s when two entrepreneurs decided it would make a perfect Florida tourist attraction.

The reassembled monastery, known as the **Ancient Spanish Monastery**, regained a religious function in 1964 when purchased by the Episcopalian church and makes an incongruous Gothic addition to an unprepossessing area in the northern part of Miami. Items such as a lambskin parchment hymn book, a walnut cabinet used by Pope Urban VII (1623–44) and a Christ the King statue believed to have been carved by one of the original monks are dotted about, and the peaceful gardens are a delight to stroll in.

The monastery is best reached from the centre of Miami with I-95, exiting on to North Miami Beach Boulevard and following the signs after crossing Biscayne Boulevard. The monastery is also simple to reach from Miami Beach, crossing from Sunny Isles.

Ancient
Spanish Monaste ■

North Miami Beach Bouleva

Dixie Highway

Palmetto Expresseway

Red Road

NW 135th Street

NW 22nd Avenue

NW 103rd Street

441

Biscayne Boulevard

49th Street

27

North Bay Causewa

NW 27th Avenue

95

58th Street

Hialeah Drive

Biscayne
Bay

Biscayne Boulevard

Doral Blvd

Okeechobee Road

Airport Expresseway

195

Julia Tuttle Causeway

NW 25th Street

Palmetto Expresseway

Miami
International Airport

SW 27th Avenue

MIA
BEA

East West Expresseway

East West Expresseway

395

MacArthur Causeway

Altonª

East West Expresseway

West Flagler Street

41

Little Havana ⑮

⑭ Bayside Marketplace

⑬

(Tamiami Trail)

SW 8th Street (Calle Ocho)

Brickell Avenue

Historical Museum
of South Florida

DOWNTOWN
MIAMI

Merrick House ⑧

Coral Highway

⑫

Coral Gables Congregational Church/ ⑩
Biltmore Hotel

⑨ Venetian Pool

SW 22nd Street

② ① Vizcaya

Rickenbacker Causewa

⑦ CORAL
GABLES

Bird Roa

Bird Road

⑪

Museum of
Science and
Planetarium

Seaquarium

⑰ (toll)

COCONUT
GROVE

④

Douglas Road

Miller Drive

Grand Ave

③

Main Hwy

Key Biscayne

⑯

⑤

The Barnacle

Sunset Drive

⑥

Palmetto Expresseway

Dixie Highway

Old Cutler Road

Red Road

Crandon Boulevard

⑱

Dade Expresseway (toll)

Ludlam Road

⑲

Bill Baggs
Cape Florida State Park

Killian Drive

1

0   4km

Howard Drive

Dixie Highway

0   -   2 miles

Coral Reef Drive

⓪ Miami Metrozoo

South Miami and Everglades National Park

Ratings

Diving and snorkelling	●●●●●
Nature	●●●●●
Boating	●●●●○
Children	●●●●○
Scenery	●●●●○
Photography	●●●○○
History	●●○○○

Petrol stations, supermarkets and motels quickly give way to sawgrass prairies, alligators and beautifully plumaged birds as the suburban sprawl of South Miami becomes the wide-open natural expanse of Everglades National Park.

The section covered on this route is just one of the park's main areas (others are covered on pages 114–23) but it does provide a representative sample of the area's many diverse features and offers canoeing and boating opportunities. The natural world of the Everglades is matched by the coral reefs and tropical fish of Biscayne National Park, best enjoyed by snorkelling or scuba-diving but also accessible by glass-bottomed boat. The route also includes one of Miami's quirkiest sights, the Coral Castle.

Think twice about visiting the Everglades during the hot, humid and mosquito-infested summer, when much of the park is flooded. In winter temperatures are milder, mosquitoes fewer and park wildlife is at its most abundant.

ANHINGA TRAIL❖❖❖

This simple half-mile trail begins as paved track before becoming a boardwalk traversing part of a sawgrass marsh. During winter, this is a particularly good place to spot birdlife – herons, great and snowy egrets (spot the latter by their yellow feet) and the characterful anhingas. Sometimes called the 'snakebird' for its style of swimming with only its neck exposed, the anhinga spears fish on its pointed beak before breaking surface and tossing the fish upwards to catch it in its mouth. After feeding, the anhinga can often be seen drying itself perched on a rock with its white-tipped wings at full stretch. Alligators, turkeys, marsh rabbits and various other creatures may also be viewed on this popular route.

BISCAYNE NATIONAL PARK❖❖❖

Few places in Florida are better able to reveal the wonder of coral reefs than Biscayne National Park, 95 per cent of its 275 square miles being

ⓘ Tropical Everglades Visitors Center

160 Hwy-1, close to the junction of Hwy-1 and 344th Street (Palm Drive), Florida City; tel: (305) 245-9180 or (800) 388-9669; www.tropicaleverglades.com. Open Mon–Sat 0800–1645. Run by local chambers of commerce, with a knowledgeable staff, this large and very informative stop is packed with brochures, leaflets and discount coupons for local services. More specific Everglades National Park information is provided by the visitor centres within the park (*see page 68*).

beneath the waves. Clear, clean waters make this a perfect spot for scuba-diving and snorkelling, or simply staying dry and enjoying the aquatic splendour from a glass-bottomed boat.

About 10 miles offshore, the coral reefs provide a home for turtles, lobsters, sponges, crabs and an array of other creatures, such as the stoplight parrotfish, the goosehead scorpion fish, the princess venus and the peppermint goby whose names are almost as exuberant as their colouring. The coral itself might look like a large lump of rock but is actually composed of billions of polyps, small soft living creatures that spend their days inside hard, rock-like skeletons and emerge at night to feed on plankton.

The park also holds 15th- and 16th-century Spanish shipwrecks, the target of many divers, and 44 small islands. The most northerly of the Florida Keys chain, the islands appear as vivid dots of green in this otherwise azure expanse of sea and sky. The islands' dense vegetation supports bald eagles, egrets, herons and other birds, and two are protected as nesting areas. Another, Elliot Island, which can be reached by boat, beckons visitors with hiking trails and the promise of utter tranquillity.

The reefs are the highlight of the park but don't overlook the mangrove forest that marks the shoreline. Blurring the distinctions between land and ocean, it protects the shore from extreme weather and forms a barrier to prevent pollutants entering the ocean. As the unwanted material trapped around the mangrove roots decomposes, it provides food for marine life and birdlife. The surprisingly fascinating life of the mangrove is described on the glass-bottomed boat tours.

CORAL CASTLE❖❖

Coral Castle $
28655 S Dixie Highway;
tel: (305) 248-6344;
www.coralcastle.com. Open
daily 0700–2100.

One of Miami's greatest mysteries, the Coral Castle was created by Latvian émigré Edward Leedskalnin, using coral rock dug from the ground on an acre of land he bought in 1918 for $12. Working alone with rudimentary hand tools, the uneducated Leedskalnin not only managed to move chunks of rock weighing several tons without assistance but created rock sculptures, many resembling pieces of furniture, to exact dimensions (the Florida-shaped table, for example, is a precise scale model of the state) seemingly using advanced mathematics to do so.

Twenty years in construction, the Coral Castle provided a home for Leedskalnin until his death in 1951. His visitors would enter by the Three Ton Gate, a rock that did indeed weigh 3 tons but which, due to Leedskalnin's mechanical skills, could be opened by finger pressure. The entrance used today is less interesting but the 1000-pound armchairs, the 25-ft-long telescope and the photogenic crescent moon, and many other objects, remain as curious to visitors now as when they first appeared. Still nobody can explain how or why Leedskalnin created them.

FLAMINGO❖

**Flamingo Visitor
Center** Located 38
miles from the main entrance,
at the southern end of the
park.

Flamingo, the last stop on the road through Everglades National Park, once held a community of smugglers, fishermen and hunters, many of them making a living by killing roseate spoonbills and selling their feathers. Like many present-day tourists, the settlers thought the spoonbills were flamingos and named their community accordingly.

A hundred years on, Flamingo's sole permanent residents are a handful of official personnel who organise the only food and accommodation (other than camping) available in this section of the park. They also run the boat, canoe, walking and tram tours originating here. All the details can be found at the Flamingo Visitor Center alongside exhibits on local ecology. Among several trails in the vicinity is the easy route to **Eco Pond**, an artificial freshwater pond overlooked by an observation platform. During winter, early mornings and late afternoon egrets, woodstorks and many other birds are likely to be seen.

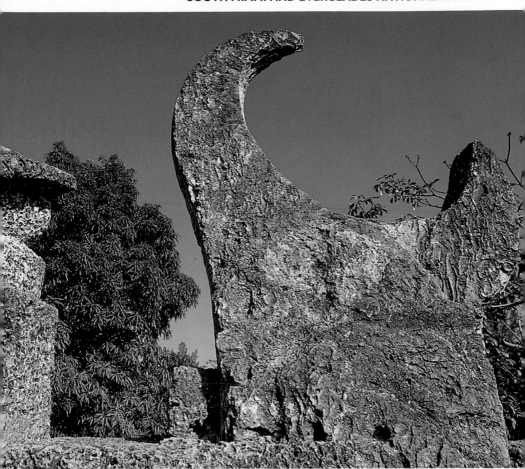

Gumbo Limbo Trail❖❖

Above
Coral Castle

A half-mile round-trip trail on a paved road, this begins close to the Royal Palm Visitor Center and weaves through what was, before being ravaged by Hurricane Andrew in 1992, a very shady hardwood forest. Many of the gumbo limbo and royal palm trees support epiphytes, such as orchids, that grow on other plants without damaging them, taking water and nutrients from the air. By contrast, the strangler fig, also seen here, usually begins as a wind-carried seed and steadily wraps itself around a host tree until the latter, deprived of light and water, dies.

Popularly known in Florida as the 'tourist tree' because its peeling red bark resembles sunburnt skin, the gumbo limbo tree sometimes plays host to the rare liguus tree snail, distinguished by the intense colouring of its shell, anything from deep orange or yellow to green and blue.

Right
The Mahogany Hammock
Trail

MAHOGANY HAMMOCK TRAIL✧

A hardwood hammock similar to but much denser than the Gumbo Limbo Trail (*see page 67*), the Mahogany Hammock Trail passes an observation tower giving views over many miles of sawgrass prairie, before disappearing into the cave-like interior of the forest. The damp conditions are ideal for ferns and epiphytes, many of which are found amid palms and gumbo limbo trees. Also here are the mahogany trees that give the trail its name, including the largest example in the US. Brittle mahogany wood, however, is particularly susceptible to hurricanes: these were badly affected by Hurricane Andrew in 1992.

MAIN VISITOR CENTER✧✧✧

Everglades National Park $ tel: (305) 242-7700; www.nps.gov/ever. Main Visitor Center daily 0900–1700; Flamingo Visitor Center Nov–Apr, daily 0730–1700.

The first and largest of several visitors' centres in the park, this is an essential stop for the latest weather and mosquito information, and for listings of the day's park activities; any guided tour is well worth joining. Also here are park maps and exhibits and displays on the Everglades' unique ecology, grasping even a little of which will greatly enhance your visit.

Pa-Hay-Okee Overlook❖❖❖

A celebrated naturalist and writer, Marjorie Stoneman Douglas did much to encourage conservation of the Everglades and bestowed it with a lasting epithet: 'river of grass'. The description seems entirely apt from the 12-ft-high observation tower on this short trail which overlooks a sawgrass swamp stretching to the horizon.

Covering 8 million acres of the Everglades, the sawgrass plain is flooded each year as summer storms bring water spilling south from the vast Lake Okeechoobee. The shallow waters (average depth is around 6ins) move imperceptibly slowly through the sawgrass towards the sea. The stillness of the setting and knowledge that everything in the Everglades depends on this natural cycle (greatly affected over the years by human attempts at drainage and demands for drinking water) help make this an awesome sight.

Pinelands Trail❖

Formed by limestone ridges, the highest elevations in the Everglades are between 3 and 7ft above sea level. Height keeps the ridges dry while sufficient soil gathers in their hollows to enable slash pine to grow. Also called Dade County pine, these trees have a strong and durable wood with a resistance to termites that made them the preferred building material for many early Florida homes.

During the wet season, the pinelands provide shelter for wildlife usually not seen elsewhere in the park, such as racoons, reef geckos, the cotton mouse and the five-lined skink, a type of lizard. The sharp edges of the limestone ridges generally make pineland exploration tricky, but this trail provides a safe way to explore this branch of the Everglades' ecosystem. A further bonus is the wonderful array of wild flowers.

Alligators: the keepers of the Everglades

Widely misunderstood and often unreasonably feared, alligators are prevalent throughout Florida and are nicknamed 'the keepers of the Everglades' for the crucial part they play in sustaining wildlife during the Everglades' dry winter months.

During the winter, alligators are able to locate the water hidden beneath ground following the subsiding of the summer floods, digging with their powerful tails to create small ponds or 'gator holes'. Besides providing a habitat for the alligator, these holes allow fish, snails and turtles to survive, and provide sustenance to bobcats, otters, the occasional deer and other creatures. Everglades' birdlife depends on the gator holes' provision of food as part of their reproductive cycle.

When the summer rains return, the pathway worn by the alligator between the pond and its nest becomes a creek, speeding the flow of water and easing the movement of wildlife from the gator holes across the quickly flooded Everglades.

Accommodation and food

Besides camping at three sites (*tel: (800) 365-2267*), accommodation within Everglades National Park is limited to the hotel at Flamingo. There are many motels in and around Homestead and Florida City, within a few minutes' drive of the park entrance, which make a feasible base if you are taking this route between staying in Miami and crossing the state to the Gulf coast. Food in the park is similarly limited to the winter-only restaurant and café at Flamingo (the marina store is open year-round and sells provisions). Again, there is more choice around Homestead and Florida City.

Capri Restaurant $–$$ *935 S Krome Avenue, Florida City; tel: (305) 247-1542; www.the-capri.com.* Full menu of American and American–Italian fare; often has good seafood. Closed Sun.

El Toro Taco $ *1 S Krome Avenue, Homestead; tel: (305) 245-8182.* Embarrassingly inexpensive Mexican food in a friendly setting; some of the ingredients are home grown.

Below
Sunset over mangroves

Flamingo Lodge $$ *Flamingo; tel: (800) 600-3813 or (941) 695-3101; email: info-flamingo@xanterra.com; www.flamingolodge.com.* Open year-round with comfortable rooms and a few cottages with cooking facilities. During summer the hotel restaurant is closed and guests need to provide their own supplies.

Flamingo Restaurant and Café $–$$ *Flamingo; tel: (941) 695-3101 or (800) 600-3813; www.flamingolodge.com.* The former has a full lunch and dinner service; the latter provides snacks. Both are open only during the winter.

Hampton Inn $ *124 E Palm Drive; tel: (305) 247-8833.* Nationwide chain with expansive rooms and great location within an easy drive of Everglades National Park; morning coffee and internet access included.

Inn of Homestead $ *1020 Homestead Boulevard; tel: (305) 248-2121 or (800) 248-4656; email: Sales@joneshospitality.com; www.joneshospitality.com.* A former national chain hotel given a complete makeover by new owners.

Suggested tour

Length: The entrance to Everglades National Park is 42 miles from Downtown Miami; the distance from the park entrance to Flamingo is 38 miles.

Duration: Driving time from the park entrance to Flamingo and back is 2–3 hours. Biscayne National Park and the Coral Castle are each 20-minutes' drive from the park entrance.

Links: Miami: the City (*see pages 52–63*), the Florida Keys (*see pages 94–103*).

From Miami, take Hwy-1 (S Dixie Highway) southbound. This is a fairly uninspiring journey through the bland suburbia of South Miami. An alternative is to head west to link with the speedier, but no more interesting, Florida Turnpike (toll). Both roads meet south of Perrine at South Miami Heights.

On either route, turn right on to 344th Street (Palm Drive), taking Hwy-27, the well-signposted main route into **Everglades National Park**. Inside the park, Hwy-27 becomes known simply as Main Park Road and this is the route that continues for 38 miles to Flamingo. Stop first at the **MAIN VISITOR CENTER ❶** immediately to the right on entering the park to check the park conditions and daily events such as guided tours which may require advance booking.

Two miles ahead, a left turn leads to the Royal Palm Visitor Center and the start points of the **ANHINGA TRAIL ❷** and **GUMBO LIMBO TRAIL ❸**. Returning on the main route, 4.5 miles ahead is a left turn for Long Pine Key, the limestone ridge which holds the **PINELANDS TRAIL ❹**. From here, the flatness of the Everglades becomes apparent as Main Park Road passes through an immense expanse of sawgrass.

After a further 6 miles comes the right-hand turn for **PA-HAY-OKEE OVERLOOK ❺**, a chance to leave the car and absorb the dramatic sawgrass vista at first hand. The only disturbances to the pancake-flatness are the tree islands called hammocks; one of the densest lies 7 miles further on Main Park Road and can be explored on the **MAHOGANY HAMMOCK TRAIL ❻**, accessed by a signposted side road. Main Park Road continues for 20 miles to **FLAMINGO ❼**, the centre of visitor services in this section of the park and starting point for guided tours.

Detours: Two miles north of Homestead, turn off Hwy-1 heading east along SW 288th Street for the **CORAL CASTLE ❽**, close to the junction with 157th Avenue. Further south off Hwy-1, **BISCAYNE NATIONAL PARK ❾** can be reached by turning east on to SW 328 Street and continuing to the end of the route at Convoy Point, park headquarters and departure point for boat tours. Bear in mind that boat tours should be booked prior to arrival, particularly during the peak winter season.

Fruit and Spice Park $ *24801 SW 248th Street; tel: (305) 247-5727; www.floridaplants.com/fruit&spice. Open daily 1000–1700.*

Monkey Jungle $ *14805 SW 216th Street; tel: (305) 235-1611; www.monkeyjungle.com. Open daily 0930–1700.*

Also worth exploring

The Homestead area is very much a rural, agricultural counterpart to modernistic Miami. While many people spend a night in the plentiful motels, few take the trouble to explore a bit deeper and discover some of the low-key charms and nearby attractions. Krome Avenue is the commercial heart of Homestead, with a pleasant small-town America atmosphere. The area bore the brunt of Hurricane Andrew in 1992 and some of the scars are still visible. One of the worst affected spots was the **Fruit and Spice Park**, which lost many of its exotic herbs, spices, plants and trees but has made great efforts to restore its former glory; delights such as the panama candle tree remain. Slightly further north, **Monkey Jungle** gives various species of primates space to roam through replicated rainforest habitats as humans view them from caged walkways.

Ratings

Beaches	●●●●●
Scenery	●●●●○
Architecture	●●●○○
Museums	●●●○○
Nature	●●●○○
Sport	●●●○○
Children	●●○○○
History	●●○○○

The Gold Coast

Known as the Gold Coast supposedly for the sunken treasure lying offshore, the nickname commonly attached to this section of Southeast Florida also suggests the large amount of money needed to live in some of the state's most expensive coastal communities. Prized for their location within commuting distance of Miami as much as the proximity of superb beaches, Fort Lauderdale and Boca Raton, the former with a glorious shoreline and several excellent museums, the latter known for its Mediterranean Revival architecture, dominate the area.

Around these major towns, however, are many undeveloped beach tracts that make this route an attractive combination of unspoilt nature and stylish urban areas. Remnants of pioneer-era Florida are surprisingly easy to find as most communities here began as farming settlements – an unusual one is remembered by the Morikami Museum and Japanese Gardens – that battled the scrub and swamp that still asserts itself in the region's inland portions.

BOCA RATON✦✦✦

ℹ Boca Raton Chamber of Commerce *1800 N Dixie Highway; tel: (561) 395-4433; www.bocachamber.com. Open Mon–Thur 0830–1700, Fri 0830–1600.*

🅟 Mizner Park *400 N Federal Highway.*

Boca Raton Old Town Hall *71 N Federal Highway; tel: (561) 395-6766; www.bocahistory.org. Open daily 1000–1600. Free.*

Wealthy and conservative, and typically populated by boat-owning forty-somethings with a penchant for fine dining, Boca Raton is immediately recognisable for its Mediterranean appearance. Red barrel-tiled roofs, fake bell towers and tile-walled courtyards appear at every turn, a style originally introduced by legendary architect Addison Mizner in the 1920s.

Mizner's scheme to create an entire community on the 1600 acres he had purchased with the proceeds of his Palm Beach work (*see pages 86–93*) was ended by a collapse in the property market. None the less, a resurgence of interest in his work has led to new buildings in the same style in the Downtown area, such as the pink stucco open-air shopping mall, **Mizner Park** (which also holds the Museum of Art, *see page 76*).

One of the few Mizner-designed buildings that remain is the greatly restored 1927 **Old Town Hall**, now owned by the local historical society who operate a library and mount modest displays in the interior. Much more spectacular is the **Boca Raton Resort and Club**, originally the Cloister Inn, a luxury resort built by Mizner to lure

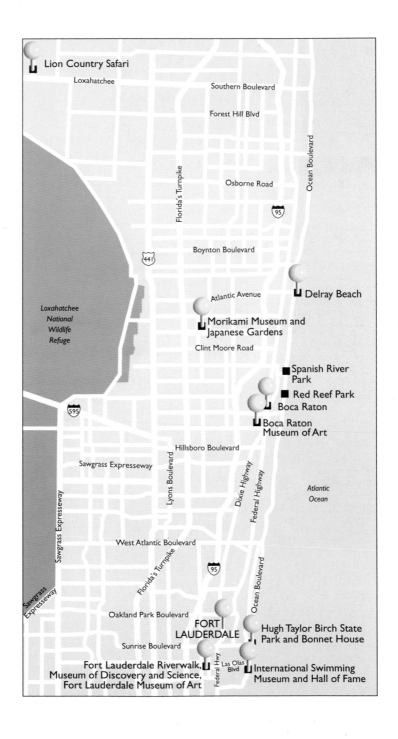

Lion Country Safari

Loxahatchee

Southern Boulevard

Forest Hill Blvd

Ocean Boulevard

Florida's Turnpike

Osborne Road

95

441

Boynton Boulevard

Loxahatchee
National
Wildlife
Refuge

Atlantic Avenue

Delray Beach

Morikami Museum and
Japanese Gardens

Clint Moore Road

Spanish River
Park

Red Reef Park

Boca Raton

Boca Raton
Museum of Art

Hillsboro Boulevard

595

Lyons Boulevard

Dixie Highway

Federal Highway

Atlantic
Ocean

Sawgrass Expresseway

Sawgrass Expresseway

Sawgrass Expresseway

West Atlantic Boulevard

Florida's Turnpike

95

Ocean Boulevard

Oakland Park Boulevard

FORT
LAUDERDALE

Hugh Taylor Birch State
Park and Bonnet House

Sunrise Boulevard

Fort Lauderdale Riverwalk,
Museum of Discovery and Science,
Fort Lauderdale Museum of Art

Federal Hwy

Las Olas
Blvd

International Swimming
Museum and Hall of Fame

Boca Raton Resort and Club *501 El Camino Real; tel: (561) 395-3000 or (888) 491-BOCA; www.bocaresort.com. Guided tour $ Wed 1330.*

Boca Raton Museum of Art $ *Mizner Park, 501 Plaza Real; tel: (561) 392-2500; www.bocamuseum.org. Open Tue, Thur–Fri 1000–1700; Wed 1000–2100; Sat–Sun 1200–1700.*

Gumbo Limbo Environmental Complex $ *1801 N Ocean Boulevard; tel: (561) 338-1473; email: info@gumbolimbo.org; www.gumbolimbo.org. Open Mon–Sat 0900–1600, Sun 1200–1600.*

Red Reef Park $ *1400 N Ocean Boulevard; tel: (561) 393-7989. Open daily 0800–2200.*

socialites to his intended city. Excellent guided tours weave through the hotel's cloisters and courtyards.

Boca Raton Museum of Art, one of Florida's best small art museums and rated highly enough to attract notable travelling exhibitions, grew from the Mayers Collection of late-19th and early 20th-century works, bequeathed in 1989 and including artists such as Braque, Modigliani, Léger, Degas, Matisse and Picasso, the latter remembered here with several interesting charcoal sketches.

With its excellent beach flanked by a boardwalk passing over coarsely vegetated sand dunes, **Red Reef Park** makes the most of its natural setting and is a justifiably popular place for swimming, sunbathing and weekend barbecues. It is also a noted spot for snorkelling, its piers providing access to an artificial reef that attracts myriad species of brightly coloured tropical fish. The park extends across Hwy-A1A to include the **Gumbo Limbo Environmental Complex**, where an informative visitors' centre provides the inside info on the complexities of Florida's coastal ecosystems. A boardwalk trail plots a course over coastal dunes and mangrove wetlands and through hammocks of hardwood and sable palm. A 40-ft-high observation tower offers a scintillating view of the park.

Accommodation and food in Boca Raton

Boca Diner $–$$ *2801 Federal Highway; tel: (561) 416-6060.* Tempting range of American diner fare served around the clock, from high-rise stacks of pancakes to burgers and milkshakes.

Boca Raton Resort and Club $$$ *501 E Camino Real; tel: (561) 395-3000 or (800) 327-0101; www.bocaresort.com.* The most luxurious place to stay along this section of the coast, and a major chapter in local history.

Ocean Lodge Motel $$ *531 N Ocean Boulevard; tel: (561) 395-7772.* Well-furnished rooms just across Hwy-A1A from the beach.

Red Star Tavern $$ *99 SE Mizner Boulevard; tel: (561) 391-3463.* Creative twists on familiar dishes, such as tempura fish and chips and barbecued meatloaf, plus an impressive array of cocktails.

DELRAY BEACH✦✦

Cason Cottage $ *5 NE 1st Street; tel: (561) 274-0223. Open Tue–Fri 1000–1600.*

Right
Fort Lauderdale beach wall

Quiet and welcoming Delray Beach grew from a struggling agricultural community into a winter resort boasting a very pleasant **beach**. The beach lies at the eastern end of **Atlantic Avenue**, the primary commercial artery lined by art galleries and antiques shops, and illuminated at night by imitation gas lamps. The restored 1910s and 1920s buildings of **Old School Square** (*www.oldschool.org*) provide a centre for cultural events and temporary exhibitions. At its heart is the

**⑪ Cornell Museum of
Art and History $**
*51 N Swinton Avenue; tel:
(561) 243-7922;
www.oldschool.org. Open
Tue–Sat 1300–1630,
May–Sept also open Sun
1300–1630.*

former elementary school building, dating from 1913 and now holding the **Cornell Museum of Art and History**. Diverse exhibitions, many focusing on Florida arts and artists, occupy the museum's four galleries while the archives of the local historical society on the second floor provide the basis for temporary exhibitions on aspects of the community's past. Among other events, the Entertainment Pavilion, occupying what was, until the 1950s, the local high school, hosts free Friday night open-air movies. Close by, the wood-framed **Cason Cottage**, built for a doctor in 1915, brings intriguing insights into pioneer-era Florida living.

Accommodation and food in Delray Beach

Bermuda Inn $$ *64 S Ocean Boulevard; tel: (561) 276-5288.* Friendly staff, good-sized rooms and within a few strides of the beach, as well as being ideally placed for exploring the rest of this enjoyable town.

Sundy House $–$$$ *106 S Swinton Avenue; tel: (561) 272-5678 or (877) 439-9601; email: info@sundyhouse.com; www.sundyhouse.com.* Top-rated Floridian cuisine served in one of the town's earliest homes, built in 1902.

FORT LAUDERDALE✧✧✧

One of the best-known vacation destinations in Florida and for years venue of a riotous Spring Break (the annual pre-exam invasion of American students), Fort Lauderdale is an instantly likeable place. The idyllic beach strip, where the lengthy white sands are shaded by palms, is sufficient allure for many. But since the 1980s the Downtown area, 3 miles inland, has undergone a complete facelift, gaining two excellent museums, restoring several historic homes and developing the commendable Riverwalk.

The core of Fort Lauderdale's **beach strip** runs for 2 miles along Atlantic Boulevard. Sunbathers and swimmers hit the sands by day and, by night, many of them can be found in adjacent cafés and restaurants cooled by ocean breezes. The 1960 film *Where the Boys Are* cemented Fort Lauderdale's reputation as a Spring Break destination but the annual six weeks of under-age drunkenness and general mayhem ended when Fort Lauderdale set about re-inventing itself as a classy resort town.

Immediately inland from the beach are the slender canals created from mangrove swamps during the

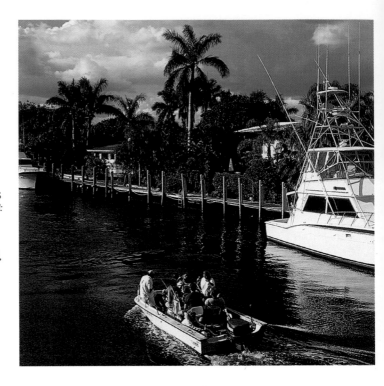

ⓘ Fort Lauderdale Convention & Visitors Bureau *100E, Broward Boulevard; tel: (954) 765-4466 or (800) 22-SUNNY; www.sunny.org. Open Mon–Fri 0830–1700.*

Greater Fort Lauderdale Chamber of Commerce *512 NE 3rd Avenue; tel: (954) 462-6000; www.ftlchamber.com. Open Mon–Fri 0830–1700.*

ⓗ Stranahan House $ *335 SE 6th Avenue; tel: (954) 524-4736; email: stranahan1@aol.com; www.stranahanhouse.com. Open Wed–Sat 1000–1500, Sun 1300–1500; tours on the hour.*

Old Fort Lauderdale Village & Museum $ *219 SW 2nd Avenue; tel: (954) 463-4431; www.oldfortlauderdale.org. Open Tue–Fri 1100–1700, Sat–Sun 1200–1700.*

Fort Lauderdale Museum of Art $ *1 E Las Olas Boulevard; tel: (954) 525-5500. Open daily 1100–1900, Thur until 2100.*

1920s that earned Fort Lauderdale the sobriquet 'Venice of America'. Private yachts tethered in backyards are a common sight in a well-heeled residential area that separates the beach strip from **Downtown Fort Lauderdale**. Local administrative hub and site of the Museum of Discovery and Science (*see page 80*) and Museum of Art (*see below*), Downtown Fort Lauderdale also provides a good impression of the town's history with the 1901 **Stranahan House**, a two-storey wood-framed home built for a settler from Ohio who operated a ferry service across the town's New River.

The 1.5-mile **Riverwalk**, a bricked footpath dotted with seats and picnic stops, meanders along the banks of the New River past a fine group of old buildings, including the 1907 **King-Cromartie House** and the reconstructed 1899 **Schoolhouse**, collectively known as **Old Fort Lauderdale Village & Museum** under the auspices of the **Fort Lauderdale Historical Society**, which also displays its own collection of memorabilia.

Fort Lauderdale Museum of Art✧✧✧

In an architecturally splendid 1980s building, designed by the renowned Edward Larrabee Barnes and a significant part of the

Hugh Taylor Birch State Recreation Park $ *3901 E Sunrise Boulevard; tel: (954) 564-4521; www.floridastateparks.org/ hughtaylorbirch. Open daily 0800–sunset.*

Bonnet House $
900 North Birch Road; tel: (954) 563-5393; www.bonnethouse.org. Open Wed–Fri 1000–1500, Sat–Sun 1200–1600, last tour 1430.

International Swimming Hall of Fame $ *1 Hall of Fame Drive; tel: (954) 462-6536; www.ishof.org. Open Mon–Fri 0900–1900, Sat–Sun 0900–1700.*

revitalisation of Downtown Fort Lauderdale, this museum holds a fine collection of mostly modern art including the largest collection of CoBrA work in the Americas. Founded in 1948 by artists from Denmark, Belgium and Holland and named with the initial letters of their capital cities (Copenhagen, Brussels, Amsterdam), CoBrA took inspiration from mythology and children's drawing. The Dane Asger Jorn, Dutchman Karel Appel and Belgian Pierre Alechinski are among the major contributors to the many bold paintings, ceramics, sculpture and graphics on display. With too many works to display as a whole, selections are made to illustrate particular aspects of the movement.

Also strongly represented is William Gluckens, an American realist painter and founder member of The Eight, also known as the Ashcan school for their warts-and-all image of modern society. Relatively minor works by major names such as Andy Warhol, Frank Stella and Larry Rivers are generally less impressive than the displays from Africa and the Pacific region, and Florida's largest collection of Pre-Columbian American art.

Hugh Taylor Birch State Park and Bonnet House**

An undeveloped oasis amid the wall-to-wall hotels and restaurants that dominate the coastal section of Fort Lauderdale, the Hugh Taylor Birch State Recreation Area has a long and narrow mangrove-lined freshwater lagoon and is fringed by tall Australian pines. Locals spend many weekend hours boating around this tranquil body of water before enjoying a barbecue at one of the two picnic pavilions. The area was donated to the state in 1942 by the 93-year-old former Chicago attorney Hugh Taylor Birch, who had acquired several hundred acres of oceanside land in 1893.

Directly across Sunrise Boulevard from the park, the Bonnet House is another reminder of times gone by. The house and the 35 acres it occupies was a 1921 wedding present from Hugh Taylor Birch to his son, muralist Frank Clay Bartlett. Touring the 30-room plantation-style dwelling, built in Dade County pine and coral rock, you will come across many of Bartlett's murals, plus the often whimsical art and objects gathered by him and his first and second wives. Bartlett's appreciation of nature is apparent throughout, and the grounds are still inhabited by the swans and monkeys introduced during his time.

International Swimming Hall of Fame*

Many diverse facets of watersports are celebrated, at the aptly named International Swimming Hall of Fame, where champions from around the world – though most are American – are remembered with displays, video clips and scores of cups, medals, shields and other trophies. Those honoured include Mark Spitz, winner of seven Olympic golds in 1972, and Johnny Weissmuller, the greatest

Museum of Discovery and Science $$ *401 SW 2nd Street; tel: (954) 467-6637; www.mods.org/home.htm. Open Mon–Sat 1000–1700, Sun 1200–1800.*

swimmer of the 1920s but better known for his Hollywood role as the first on-screen Tarzan.

Also featured are less mainstream aquatic sports such as water polo and synchronised swimming. Other entertaining displays recount the evolution of the swimming costume and future president Ronald Reagan's short career as a lifeguard. Outside the main hall, two Olympic-sized pools and sky-high diving boards are regularly used for competition events and training potential champions.

Museum of Discovery and Science**

The $30-million Museum of Discovery and Science is among the largest and most entertaining of its kind, providing an introduction to the wonders of the physical world that will keep grown-ups and kids amused for a couple of hours. Innovative and imaginative exhibits cover everything from the ecosystems of Florida, including a coral reef, a cave, and a walk-through beehive, to the workings of the human body.

The Gizmo City section allows access to the internet and the playing of virtual volleyball (less physical but much more cerebrally demanding than the real thing). Visitors can also try their hand at repairing a satellite in orbit and join a simulated space flight to the moon. The adjoining IMAX Theater screens spectacular films, some of them in 3D.

Accommodation and food in Fort Lauderdale

Beachcomber Hotel and Villas $$ *1200 S Ocean Boulevard; tel: (954) 941-7830 or (800) 231-2423; www.beachcomber-ftlaud.com.* Large rooms, two pools and a patio.

Ernie's BBQ Lounge $ *1843 S Federal Highway; tel: (954) 523-8636.* Unpretentious hole-in-the-wall spot renowned for its wonderful fresh chowder, served with sherry.

The Floridian $ *1410 E Las Olas Boulevard; tel: (954) 463-4041.* Simple coffee shop in the trendy heart of Downtown Fort Lauderdale.

Jackson's Steakhouse $$–$$$ *450 E Las Olas Boulevard; tel: (954) 522-5400.* Immense portions of exactly what its name suggests presented amid dark mahogany furnishings; do not come here for a snack.

Riverside Hotel $$$ *620 E Las Olas Boulevard; tel: (954) 467-0671 or (800) 325-3280; www.riversidehotel.com.* Built in the 1920s, this much modernised slice of local history has large rooms and makes an excellent base for Downtown Fort Lauderdale.

Try My Thai, Too $–$$ *1507 N Federal Highway; tel: (954) 630-0030.* Small and friendly spot for good value Thai food.

Waterfront Inn $ *521 North Atlantic Boulevard; tel: (954) 564-4341 or (866) 543-2006; www.waterfrontinns.com.* One of the best of many small accommodations adjacent to the beach.

LION COUNTRY SAFARI❖

Lion Country Safari $$ *State Road 80 W, Loxahatchee; tel: (561) 793-1084; www.lioncountrysafari.com. Open daily 0930–1630.*

Right
Tandem zebras at Lion Country Safari

An 8-mile road loops through the 500-acre Lion Country Safari, split into five areas of replicated wildlife habitats from Asia, Africa and the Americas. Visitors, who must stay inside their cars but can stop as often as they wish, are likely to spot lions, giraffes, rhinos, zebra, bison, elephants, chimpanzees and even Australian emus among the host of inmates who sometimes venture remarkably close, providing a tremendous though somewhat hair-raising photo opportunity. Many of the animals sleep through the hottest parts of the day so early morning is the best time to visit.

MORIKAMI MUSEUM AND JAPANESE GARDENS❖❖❖

Morikami Museum & Japanese Gardens $ *4000 Morikami Park Road; tel: (561) 495-0233; www.morikami.org. Open Tue–Sun 1000–1700.*

Established in the early 1900s, the Yamato Colony consisted of 50 young Japanese settlers who aimed to turn a patch of mosquito-infested wilderness into a thriving pineapple and winter vegetable farm. Eventually, only one settler remained, George Sukeji Morikami, whose success as a grapefruit wholesaler enabled him to become the owner of a sizeable plot of land. On his death this was bequeathed to the local authorities with the proviso that a memorial to the colony, and his home country, be established on it.

The result is the excellent Morikami Museum which explores diverse aspects of Japanese culture with a teahouse (venue of monthly tea ceremonies) and interactive exhibits on traditional arts and

⬛ The Gold Coast has several shopping hot spots plus the world's largest shopping mall.

Las Olas Boulevard is lined by pricey art galleries, boutiques and specialities stores, the clientele just as chic and up-market as the merchandise. *Los Olas Boulevard, Downtown Fort Lauderdale, mostly around the junction with SE 6th and 7th avenues.*

Sawgrass Mills is believably the world's largest discount shopping mall, with some 300 brand-name stores offering new goods at discounted prices. *12801 Sunrise Boulevard, 12 miles west of Downtown Fort Lauderdale; tel: (954) 046-2300; www.sawgrassmillsmall.com*

Boca Center Boca Raton is dotted by stylish shopping centres but none can compete with this conglomeration of clothing, home accessories, books, gifts and much more. *5050 Town Center Circle, off N Military Trail, just west of I-95 (Glades Road exit); tel: (561) 361-9804; www.bocacenter.com*

crafts. Just as the building reflects traditional Japanese architecture with its use of dark wood trim, shoji screens and tatami mats, so the Japanese Gardens outside are designed in formal style. Meditative trails lead through the gardens passing a bonsai display, koi carp- and turtle-filled ponds, and cross narrow bridges to delightful small waterfalls.

Also within the gardens is the villa-like Yamoto-kan where the Yamoto Colony is documented with photographs, grainy monochrome prints giving an impression of the forbidding terrain that the early settlers sought to tame.

Suggested tour

Length: Main tour 25 miles, 60 miles with detours.

Duration: Main tour driving time, 2 hours; 4–5 hours with detours. The quick way to tackle this route is to stick largely to I-95, scything north–south through the edge of the coastal communities. The slower and much more scenic alternative is Hwy-A1A, a two-lane route that sticks as close as possible to the ocean. Most of the tour is devised by using a combination of these routes, the two detours making the most of the coastal road.

Links: The coastal Hwy-A1A continues south for 23 miles to Miami Beach (*see pages 42–51*). Palm Beach (*see pages 86–93*) is a similar distance north on the same route and 15 miles east of Lion Country Safari on Route 80.

Take any route to **FORT LAUDERDALE** ❶. The heart of **Downtown Fort Lauderdale**, site of the **Riverwalk** and the **Museum of Art** and **Museum of Science and Discovery** is around the junction of Hwy-1 (Federal Highway) and Las Olas Boulevard. Take the latter for a scenically appealing 3-mile course to the ocean, passing trendy shops and million-dollar homes lining slender canals before crossing New River Sound to reach Hwy-A1A (Atlantic Boulevard) and **beachside Fort Lauderdale**.

From the Hwy-A1A junction, turning right leads into Seabreeze Boulevard and the signposted **International Swimming Hall of Fame**. Turning left takes you through the most popular section of Fort Lauderdale's palm-lined beach. The concentration of restaurants, motels and beach accessory shops suddenly thins as Hwy-A1A passes the undeveloped plot holding the **Bonnet House**, 2 miles ahead and, immediately across Sunrise Boulevard, the **Hugh Taylor Birch State Park**.

Take Sunrise Boulevard east for 4 miles to reach I-95, and travel north for 16 miles to the junction with Route 808 (Palmetto Park Road) leading into **BOCA RATON** ❷. The route passes the **Boca Raton Museum of Art** on the left, and half a mile later, enters **Downtown**

Water taxis

An enjoyable way to get around Fort Lauderdale is with the water taxi, which ferries passengers between the beachside area and Downtown using the New River and the town's canal network. Call to have the taxi collect you from the nearest landing stage (*tel: (954) 467-6677*). Alternatively visit *www.watertaxi.com* for information and schedules.

Accommodation

The Gold Coast is one of Florida's most popular vacation areas and accommodation, while plentiful, varies greatly in price according to season. Between December and May, prices may be three times what they are during the summer, and public holiday periods will find some hotels booked months in advance. During these times, reserve well ahead.

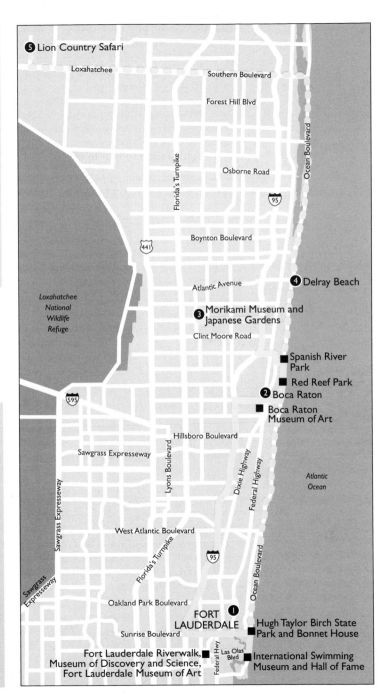

⑤ Lion Country Safari

Loxahatchee

Southern Boulevard

Forest Hill Blvd

Ocean Boulevard

Florida's Turnpike

Osborne Road

95

441

Boynton Boulevard

Loxahatchee National Wildlife Refuge

Atlantic Avenue

④ Delray Beach

③ Morikami Museum and Japanese Gardens

Clint Moore Road

■ Spanish River Park

■ Red Reef Park

② Boca Raton

■ Boca Raton Museum of Art

Hillsboro Boulevard

Sawgrass Expressway

Lyons Boulevard

Dixie Highway

Federal Highway

Atlantic Ocean

595

Sawgrass Expressway

West Atlantic Boulevard

Florida's Turnpike

95

Ocean Boulevard

Sawgrass Expressway

Oakland Park Boulevard

FORT LAUDERDALE ❶

Sunrise Boulevard

■ Hugh Taylor Birch State Park and Bonnet House

Fort Lauderdale Riverwalk, ■ Museum of Discovery and Science, Fort Lauderdale Museum of Art

Federal Hwy

Las Olas Blvd

■ International Swimming Museum and Hall of Fame

Above
Hollywood Beach, North Fort
Lauderdale

⊞ Spanish River Park
$ *3001 N Ocean
Boulevard; tel: (561) 393-
7815. Open daily
0800–sunset.*

Boca Raton. The **Old Town Hall** is to the left on Hwy-1 (Federal Highway), as is the **Mizner Park** shopping mall, site of the **International Museum of Cartoon Art**.

A mile south on Federal Highway, the palm-lined Camino Real is on the left. Take this for the **Boca Raton Resort and Club**, and continue in this direction for Ocean Boulevard, the local section of Hwy-A1A. Turn left, and a mile ahead are **Red Reef Park** and the **Gumbo Limbo Nature Center**. For the next 3 miles, Hwy-A1A skirts the ocean, usually concealed behind rows of Australian pines, before passing **Spanish River Park**.

The north side of the park is bordered by Spanish River Road. Take this for 3 miles west to rejoin I-95. Continue north on I-95, turning west after 4.6 miles on to Linton Boulevard (Route 782). After 3.6 miles, turn south on to Jog Road, following the signs for the **MORIKAMI MUSEUM AND JAPANESE GARDENS ❸**.

Detour: An outlook of sea, sun and sand makes it very tempting to stick to Hwy-A1A as it continues north from Fort Lauderdale. After the vibrant beach strip, however, the outlook becomes a fairly dull residential one with a succession of sedate beachside communities such as **Lauderdale-by-the-Sea** and **Pompano Beach**, which claims to be the 'swordfish capital of the world'.

Peppered with seafood restaurants and small motels, Hwy-A1A continues north crossing the **Hillsboro Inlet** into the community of the same name (on the mainland side and holding some very expensive homes at the end of secluded driveways) and an undeveloped beachside strip dominated by the US Coastguard.

Three miles ahead is **Deerfield Beach**, with a peaceful mile-long beach lined by palms and flanked by a zigzagging boardwalk. Snorkelling and diving are popular local pursuits, thanks to two sections of coral reef lying offshore, as is casting a rod from the grandly titled International Fishing Pier. Three miles north is **South Inlet Park**, another invitingly isolated patch of sand and marking the edge of Boca Raton. Just ahead is the junction with Camino Real, part of the main route.

Detour: Driving 6 miles north on Hwy-A1A from Spanish River Park leads through the barely developed beach areas of **Highland Beach** and **Atlantic Dunes Park** to the very relaxed **DELRAY BEACH ❹**. Enjoy the beach and explore the shops of Atlantic Avenue, before rejoining the main route and continuing to the Morikami Museum and Japanese Gardens. Alternatively, stick to the coast route which continues for 14 very pleasant miles before reaching Route 80. Head 2.5 miles west to reach I-95 or continue west to **LION COUNTRY SAFARI ❺**. Meanwhile, Palm Beach (*see pages 86–93*) is directly ahead.

Detour: Leave I-95 by heading west on Route 80 (Southern Boulevard). Residential areas and commercial estates give way to farmland and areas of scrub and swamp as you continue for 16 miles to the signposted access road to Lion Country Safari. It is an unprepossessing route and a good reminder of how much of south Florida really looks. In comparison, the re-created habitats of the safari park seem luxuriously vegetated.

Below
Rollerblading along Fort Lauderdale's seafront promenade

Palm Beach

Famous throughout the world as a haunt of the rich and famous, Palm Beach lives up to its reputation with sumptuous homes lining immaculately clean streets scented by the tropical shrubbery that blooms year-round in pampered gardens. Yet just a few hours' exploration reveals the town to be a surprisingly small, friendly and accessible place with a palpable sense of community, even if being a member of that community requires a million-dollar-plus annual income and an ability to be socially at ease with the leading politicians, financiers, film stars, sports champions and other celebrities who make it their winter home.

Henry Flagler's Whitehall mansion, the extremely grand Breakers hotel, and the up-market shops of Worth Avenue provide the cornerstones of a visit, but the town is also laden with the nooks and crannies that reveal curious snippets of local history and some of the best of the Mediterranean style architecture that gives Palm Beach its signature appearance.

Sights

ⓘ Palm Beach Chamber of Commerce *45 Cocoanut Row; tel: (561) 655-3282; www.palmbeachchamber.com. Open Mon–Fri 0900–1630; from 1000 in summer.*

The Beach✦
The most unpretentious place in Palm Beach is simply the long and slender beach that runs parallel to the town. Swimming, sunbathing and sandcastle building are all commonly seen here but tanning celebrities are not. Most residents have their own private strand adjacent to their properties.

ⓗ The Breakers *1 S County Road; tel: (561) 655-6611; www.thebreakers.com. Guided tour Wed at 1500.*

The Breakers✦✦✦
Built in 1926, the Breakers hotel casts a commanding presence over Palm Beach. With its palatial size, distinctive twin towers and a golf course which consumes almost the entire width of the island, the Italian Renaissance hotel is Palm Beach's biggest employer and hosts top society occasions.

The current property is the third hotel on the site. The original Breakers was raised in 1896 as oil and transportation magnate Henry Flagler sought to lure the nation's rich and powerful to vacations in

Church of Bethesda-by-the-Sea *141 S County Road; tel: (561) 655-4554; www.bbts.org. Open daily 0800–1700.*

Everglades Club *356 Worth Avenue; tel: (561) 655-7810. Private club, view from street only.*

his newly developed town; both it and a 1903 replacement succumbed to fire. Six million dollars was lavished on the present hotel's construction, using 1200 workers and a brigade of artists and craftsmen brought from Europe.

Word has it that the $2000-a-night suites are only slightly smaller than the lobby, which runs the entire length of the hotel. Step inside and pass beneath the vaulted ceiling and its crystal chandeliers, noting the 1920s brass fittings around the concierge's desk and the fireplaces, the frescoes and the 15th- and 16th-century Flemish tapestries along the walls.

Take a peek inside the mind-numbingly opulent Circle Dining Room, where diners are distracted from their food by the scenes of Italian cities etched on to the ceiling, and turn left into the side room which carries exhibits on the hotel's illustrious past. In the grounds are fountain-bearing courtyards and loggias, a croquet lawn and a path that leads to the hotel's private beach to which guests were once ferried by horse-drawn carriage.

Church of Bethesda-by-the-Sea◆
The mere fact that its Gothic Revival looks are completely at odds with Palm Beach's profusion of Mediterranean architectural styles gives the Episcopalian Church of Bethesda-by-the-Sea a certain appeal. Inside, a gorgeous stained-glass window rises above the high altar. Beside the church, the cloistered **Cluett Memorial Gardens** and their stone benches provide a lovely setting for a snack and a meditation on the transient nature of material things.

Everglades Club◆◆
Self-taught architect Addison Mizner gave Palm Beach its Mediterranean appearance. One of his earliest and best works was the 1918 Everglades Club, complete with fake Moorish bell towers and barrel-tiled roofs. Originally conceived as a convalescent hospital for veterans of World War I, the three-storey building quickly became the base of the most exclusive resort club in the US and remains strictly members only.

Kennedy Compound
Links between Palm Beach and the Kennedy family go back to 1933 when Joseph Kennedy, prominent businessman, ambassador to Britain from 1938, and patriarch of the political dynasty, bought a 2-acre oceanside property at 1095 Ocean Boulevard (private home; no admittance) as a winter retreat. During John Kennedy's presidency, the compound, actually a fairly drab beach house, became grandly known as the Florida White House. In 1993, the Kennedy family sold the compound, allegedly for $4.9 million.

Above
The Breakers Hotel

Mar-a-Lago *1100*
S Ocean Boulevard;
private house, no admission.

Mizner Fountain
S County Road, between
Australian and Chilean
avenues.

Paramount Building
139 N County Road.

Royal Poinciana Chapel
In the grounds of Whitehall;
tel: (561) 655-4212;
www.royalpoincianachapel.org.
Open by appointment only.

Mar-a-Lago**

Not only was breakfast cereal heiress Marjorie Merriweather Post the queen of Palm Beach society for four decades, she also owned what was undoubtedly the island's most extravagant home, Mar-a-Lago. The bright pink building with 118 rooms and sprawling across a 17-acre plot was unveiled to a disbelieving audience in 1927. Some were impressed, some were jealous, others considered the whole thing an $8-million exercise in Mediterranean kitsch.

Even the US government, to whom the house was willed on Post's death in 1973, could not afford its upkeep. In 1985 it was purchased for $15 million by property tycoon Donald Trump with plans to turn it into an exclusive club with $100,000 annual membership fees. A small bronze plaque on Ocean Drive announces the entrance; the overwrought Moorish tower and many other features of the house can be glimpsed over the wall.

Mizner Fountain*

Marking the heart of Palm Beach as Addison Mizner probably envisaged it, the Mizner Fountain, its three basins held by sculptured horses, sits alongside a narrow palm tree-lined pond opposite Palm Beach's modestly sized Town Hall. The surrounding buildings encapsulate the mish-mash of Mediterranean features that Mizner gave the developing town in the early 1920s. Note the imitation wormholes created in stucco walls with hobnailed boots.

Paramount Building*

Although a few of the original features can still be spotted amid a routine collection of shops and offices, the 1927 Paramount Building is one of Palm Beach's celebrated structures. It was designed by Joseph Urban, better known as set designer of the *Ziegfeld Follies*, and was a venue for live performances by stars such as Charlie Chaplin and W C Fields, and movie premières attended by the likes of Douglas Fairbanks and Mary Pickford. Season tickets were charged at $1000 a time.

Royal Poinciana Chapel*

Used by guests staying at Palm Beach's first luxury resort, Henry Flagler's Royal Poinciana Hotel, this clapboard, non-denominational place of worship was raised in 1896 and moved to the grounds of Whitehall (*see page 90*) to make way for the creation of Cocoanut Way. Behind it stands the oldest house in Palm Beach, **Seagull Cottage,** built in 1886 and occupied by Henry Flagler as he awaited the completion of the decidedly grander Whitehall.

St Edwards Church*

This pretty and ornate Catholic church, completed in 1927, has a cast stone baroque entrance that leads into the nave, over which each segment of the 65-ft-high vaulted ceiling is hand painted. Cast from a single piece of Carrara marble, the enormously imposing main altar occupies a 40-ft-high niche. Among many stained-glass windows is one donated by the Kennedys, regulars at Sunday service when in town and whose presence during the presidency of John Kennedy boosted attendances (*see Lake Trail, page 92*).

Society of the Four Arts❖❖

Palm Beach is awash with money and a surprising amount of it floats towards the Society of the Four Arts, founded in 1936 to promote art, literature, music and science. The society's offices, lecture halls and exhibition spaces fill several buildings, most attractive of which is the **Four Arts Library**, a gorgeous Italian-influenced construction in coquina rock with an entrance loggia decorated with classical-style murals depicting the Fine Arts. Across the courtyard, the scrupulously well-maintained **gardens** are a sight to behold.

Whitehall and the Flagler Museum❖❖❖

Oil and transportation magnate Henry Flagler, whose railroad made Florida's east coast accessible, turned Palm Beach into a retreat for the rich from the late 1890s. He built several hotels and lavished $4 million on Whitehall, a home for himself and his third wife for whom it was intended as a wedding present.

Architects Carrère and Hastings, also known for the New York Public Library, created what was eventually labelled 'the Taj Mahal of North America', an extraordinary hotchpotch of ideas and furnishings culled from the aristocratic homes of Europe.

Behind its Doric columns, Whitehall has a marble entrance hall modelled on that of a Roman villa's atrium, a Swiss billiard room, an Italian Renaissance library, an Elizabethan breakfast room, a Louis XIV music room and a 94-ft-long Louis XV ballroom lined by mirrors and illuminated by three vast chandeliers. Upstairs are 14 guest rooms revealing styles ranging from Colonial American to art nouveau and the Flaglers' own rococo suite with Louis XV-style furniture.

Arched loggias lead into the open courtyard at the centre of the house, a refreshing spot to contemplate the architectural excesses and admire the sculptured Venus rising from the fountain overlooked by four satyrs.

Worth Avenue❖❖❖

The only street in Florida where top-dollar stores such as Tiffany & Co, Cartier and Lacoste stand side-by-side, Worth Avenue is Palm Beach's main shopping strip and provides clothing, jewellery and household items for the island's many rich residents, most of whom arrive by Jaguar or Rolls Royce and have their chauffeurs wait as the price of new purchases are added to their accounts.

The mock-Mediterranean style created by Addison Mizner makes Worth Avenue very enjoyable to explore, even for those who can afford to do no more than window shop. Many of the smaller stores are arranged around cobbled courtyards, reached by alleyways (or *vias*), decorated by wall-fountains and hanging flower baskets, with slender spiral staircases accessing upper levels.

Accommodation and food

Despite its well-deserved reputation as a playground of the rich and famous, Palm Beach offers accommodation and food at surprisingly affordable prices, particularly in the summer off-season, for those whose funds render the luxury options off-limits.

Bice $$$ *313 1/2 Worth Avenue; tel: (561) 835-1600; www.biceristorante.com.* Northern Italian cuisines impeccably prepared and presented in a candle-lit setting.

The Breakers $$$ *1 S County Road; tel: (561) 655-6611 or (888) BREAKERS; www.thebreakers.com.* This historic hotel (*see page 86*) has lovely rooms, a private beach and faultless service.

The Chesterfield $$$ *363 Cocoanut Row; tel: (561) 659-5800; www.chesterfieldpb.com.* Offers the unmitigated luxury that is the perfect accompaniment for exploring Palm Beach; includes heated pool, Jacuzzi spa, and the serving of 'English' afternoon tea.

Chuck & Harold's $$–$$$ *207 Royal Poinciana Way; tel: (561) 659-1440; email: chuck@ldry.com; www.muer.com.* Delicious salads, soups and daily specials, best eaten at the sidewalk tables.

Palm Beach Historic Inn $$–$$$ *365 S County Road; tel: (561) 832-4009; www. palmbeachhistoricinn.com.* Small and friendly inn occupying a 1921 building facing the Town Hall.

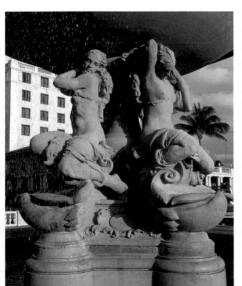

Suggested tour

Length: Main tour, 2 miles; 6 miles with detours.

Duration: 3 hours, 6 hours with detours.

Links: The northern edge of the Gold Coast route (*see pages 74–85*) is 23 miles south of Palm Beach, separated by an attractive stretch of the coastal Hwy-A1A.

Although you should arrive in Palm Beach by car, the main tour can be undertaken mostly on foot. The Lake Trail detour is a good option by bike but can also be covered by walking.

Enter Palm Beach on Royal Palm Bridge, named for its majestic royal palm trees, and the **SOCIETY OF THE FOUR ARTS** ❶ is on the left, adjacent to

🚩 Lake Trail *starts off at Royal Poinciana Way close to Flagler Memorial Bridge.*

🅿 Palm Beach Bicycle Trail Shop *223 Sunrise Avenue; tel: (561) 659-4583.*

the commendable **Philip Hulitar Sculpture Garden ②**. Turn north along Cocoanut Way for **WHITEHALL ③** the former mansion of Henry Flagler, also known as the **Flagler Museum ④**. Within the grounds stands the dainty **ROYAL POINCIANA CHAPEL ⑤**.

Directly ahead across Royal Poinciana Way is the start of the Lake Trail detour. Turning right along busy Royal Poinciana Way leads to N County Road, the twin-towered **BREAKERS ⑥** hotel and its expansive golf course dominating the view to the right. Turn left on N County Road for the **PARAMOUNT BUILDING ⑦** and, just beyond, **ST EDWARDS CHURCH ⑧**. Retrace your steps to explore the elegant interior and ample public spaces of the Breakers.

Continue south along N County Road for the **CHURCH OF BETHESDA-BY-THE-SEA ⑨**, and then turn left along Barton Avenue for a stroll on the sands of Palm Beach's public **BEACH ⑩**. Continuing along Royal Palm Way, turn right into S County Road and look for the entrance on the left into **Phipps Plaza ⑪**, a quiet and rarely visited cul-de-sac with many notable Mediterranean-style buildings.

Walk back along S County Road, crossing Royal Palm Way, reaching the administrative heart of Palm Beach where the **MIZNER FOUNTAIN ⑫** faces the Town Hall. Three blocks south is the junction with **WORTH AVENUE ⑬**. Stroll this high-class shopping street exploring its many courtyards as you go. At the junction with Cocoanut Way, the **EVERGLADES CLUB ⑭**, one of the first buildings in Palm Beach in the Mediterranean style, can be spotted on the south side.

Detour: Palm Beach's almost entirely residential northern reaches are best seen from the 3-mile-long **Lake Trail ⑮** beginning close to the junction of the Flagler Memorial Bridge and Royal Poinciana Way. Ideally undertaken by bicycle, the meandering route passes local landmarks such as **Duck's Nest ⑯** (*561 N Lake Trail*), Palm Beach's oldest continuously occupied home, erected in 1890 from prefabricated material shipped from New York. At that time, boats would bring the faithful to the island's first church, the first **Church of Bethesda-by-the-Sea ⑨**, a shingle-fronted building just beyond Duck's Nest.

The trail expires at the northern tip of the island. Returning along North Ocean Boulevard passes the gatehouses of numerous expansive beachfront estates. These include **La Guerida ⑰** (*No 1095*), bought by Joe Kennedy in 1933, used as a working vacation base in the early 1960s by his son, John F Kennedy, and remaining under Kennedy family ownership until the mid-1990s.

Detour: By car or bike, head south along Ocean Boulevard from the eastern end of Worth Avenue. This route has a lovely strip of beach to the left and stupendous mansions to the right, none more spectacular than the partially concealed **MAR-A-LAGO ⑱**, 2 miles ahead.

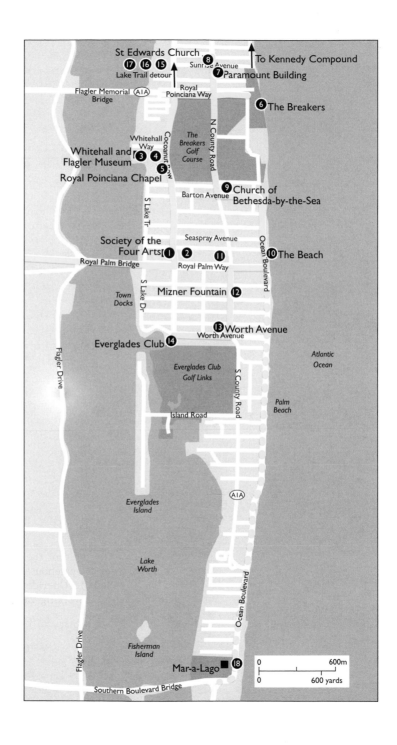

St Edwards Church
⑰ ⑯ ⑮
Lake Trail detour
Sunrise Avenue
⑧
To Kennedy Compound
⑦ Paramount Building
Flagler Memorial (A1A)
Bridge
Royal
Poinciana Way
⑥ The Breakers
Whitehall
Way
The
Breakers
Golf
Course
N County Road
Whitehall and
Flagler Museum ③ ④
⑤
Royal Poinciana Chapel
Coconut Row
⑨ Church of
Bethesda-by-the-Sea
Barton Avenue
S Lake Tr
Society of the
Four Arts ①
②
⑪
Seaspray Avenue
Ocean Boulevard
⑩ The Beach
Royal Palm Bridge
Royal Palm Way
Town
Docks
S Lake Dr
Mizner Fountain ⑫
⑬ Worth Avenue
Worth Avenue
Everglades Club ⑭
Atlantic
Ocean
Everglades Club
Golf Links
S County Road
Palm
Beach
Island Road
Flagler Drive
Everglades
Island
(A1A)
Lake
Worth
Ocean Boulevard
Flagler Drive
Fisherman
Island
Mar-a-Lago ■ ⑱

0		600m
0		600 yards

Southern Boulevard Bridge

Florida Keys

Ratings

Fishing	●●●●●
Nature	●●●●●
Snorkelling and diving	●●●●●
Scenery	●●●●○
Beaches	●●●○○
Children	●●○○○
History	●●○○○
Museums	●●○○○

Few places anywhere in the world have the scenery, history or the romance to match that of the Florida Keys, a chain of islands that spreads from the Florida mainland to Key West. Linked by a single road (Hwy-1, also called the Overseas Highway), each section of the Keys has a personality distinct from its neighbours. One thing they share, however, is a fantastic natural setting: each island like a green speck within a gigantic expanse of sea and sky.

Although the route is packed with visual delights, not least incredible sunsets, many sections are dominated not by nature's handiwork but by the fishing and diving businesses that underpin most local economies. Underwater exploration and numerous types of fishing draw many visitors to the Keys. If these pursuits do not appeal, though, the region's friendly and relaxed mood, epitomised by many of the quiet hotels and unpretentious restaurants, certainly will.

BAHIA HONDA STATE PARK✧✧✧

ⓘ Bahia Honda State Park $ *MM36.8, south of Seven Mile Bridge; tel: (305) 872-2353; www.bahiahondapark.com. Open daily 0800–sunset.*

The best beach in the Keys, a strip of fine white sand that separates the ocean from a tranquil lagoon, flanks the 524-acre Bahia Honda State Park. Also in the park are shady picnic tables, swimming areas and a short foot trail weaving through a tropical hardwood hammock and above mangrove entanglements. White-crowned pigeons, great white herons and roseate spoonbills are among the most regularly sighted examples of the local birdlife.

BIG PINE KEY✧

Several thousand people live on Big Pine Key but the best-known residents are several hundred Key deer, a dwarf species once plentiful throughout the Keys but now found only here. Supplementing the diet of Key West sailors for many years, the deer acquired federal protection in 1954. Though tempting, it is illegal to feed the very tame

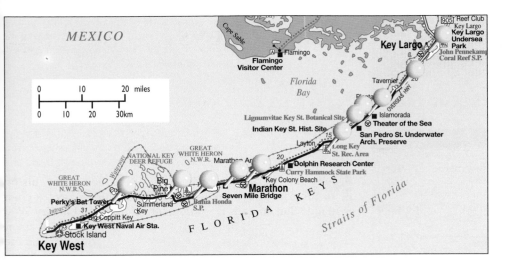

**Lower Keys
Chamber of
Commerce** *MM31, Big
Pine Key; tel: (305) 872-
2411 or (800) 872-3722;
www.lowerkeyschamber.com.
Open Mon–Fri 0900–1700,
Sat–Sun 0900–1500.*

deer which are easily spotted beside Key Deer Boulevard and Watson Boulevard, and are most numerous in the coolness of early morning and evening. Another lure for nature lovers is **Blue Hole**, a former rock quarry now filled with fresh water and home to several alligators and a multitude of other less formidable creatures.

Accommodation and food in Big Pine Key

Addresses in the Keys

Green and white **mile markers** run along Hwy-1 from Key West (MM0) and are used to locate addresses *en route.*

Barnacle Bed & Breakfast *$$ 1557 Long Beach Drive; tel: (305) 872-3298 or (800) 465-9100; email: barnacle@attglobal.net; www.thebarnacle.net.* A Caribbean-style house in a peaceful spot, ideal for exploring this under-visited section of the Keys.

Mangrove Mama's *$$ MM22; tel: (305) 745-3030.* Encapsulates the unpretentious spirit of the Keys, serving top-notch seafood in a rustic and convivial setting.

INDIAN KEY STATE HISTORIC SITE❖❖❖

**Indian Key State
Historic Park** *$
tel: (305) 664-2540;
www.floridastateparks.org/
indiankey. Open
0800–sunset.*

One of the many eccentrics to become footnotes in Keys' history is Jacob Housman who, in 1831, bought 11-acre Indian Key intent on grabbing a share of the Keys' lucrative salvaging business. Housman's initial success made Indian Key an instant town, with shops, wharves, warehouses and even a bowling alley. The unscrupulous Housman was known to deliberately lure vessels to destruction. He lost his salvaging licence and sold the island to botanist James Perrine in 1839. Housman and Perrine were both killed a year later when Indians attacked the island for its stores during the Seminole Wars.

The uninhabited island is overgrown by many of the plant species introduced by Perrine, among them the tea, coffee and sisal that he hoped to exploit commercially. A two-hour guided tour tells the full story of this strange and beguiling island.

ISLAMORADA*

① Islamorada Chamber of Commerce *MM82.5, Islamorada; tel: (305) 664-4503 or (800) 322-5397; www.islamoradachamber.com. Open Mon–Fri 0900–1700, Sat–Sun 0900–1400.*

⊕ Theater of the Sea $$ *MM84.5; tel: (305) 664-2431; www.theaterofthesea.com. Open daily 0930–1600.*

Though popular throughout the Keys, fishing is especially big news at Islamorada, a town spreading for 18 miles across four separate islands and holding the region's densest concentration of charter boats and marinas. Photos of satisfied customers holding their catches aloft – usually man-sized tarpon and marlin – encourage many novices to try their hand on a 'party boat', which carries 20 to 30 enthusiastic beginners out to sea and provides the necessary instruction and equipment for a fruitful day's fishing.

For anyone who prefers to watch marine life rather than land it, the **Theater of the Sea** provides a few pleasant low-key hours with sea lion and dolphin shows, and glass-bottomed boat trips.

Food in Islamorada

Islamorada Fish Company $$ *81532 Overseas Highway; tel: (800) 258-2559; www.islamoradafishco.com.* Packs and exports stone crab and more local marine fare but also serves ultra-fresh squid rings, oysters, and crab cakes along with more substantial seafood main courses. Part of the World Wide Sportsman complex.

Lorelei Restaurant & Cabana $–$$ *MM.82; tel: (305) 664-4656; email: loreleimermaid@bellsouth.net; www.loreleifloridakeys.com.* Seafood and sunsets are on the menu, as are lobster tails and conch chowder, and a host of daily specials.

JOHN PENNEKAMP CORAL REEF STATE PARK❖❖❖

ⓘ John Pennekamp Coral Reef State Park $ *MM 102.6, Key Largo: tel: (305) 451-1202; www.floridastateparks.org/ pennekamp. Open daily 0800–sunset.*

Protecting a large section of the narrow strip of living coral lying 3 miles offshore and continuing for 200 miles to Key West and beyond, John Pennekamp Coral Reef State Park is the gateway to an underwater world of great complexity and beauty. Some 500 fish species, from 4-ft-long barracuda to the dazzlingly coloured parrotfish, plus an amazing mixture of crabs, sea urchins, starfish, snails, lobsters and shrimps, live around the reef. Many can be viewed on the diving, snorkelling and glass-bottomed boat trips available from the park.

Although its most spectacular sections are underwater, the park's 2300-acre land area provides excellent picnic territory. The visitors' centre has displays on the park's natural history and boardwalk trails around its mangrove forests, which can also be navigated by canoe.

KEY LARGO❖

ⓘ Key Largo Chamber of Commerce *MM106, Key Largo; tel: (305) 451-1414 or (800) 822-1088; www.keylargo.org. Open daily 0900–1800.*

ⓘ World Parrot Mission *99150 Overseas Highway; tel: (305) 453-1800; email: info@worldparrotmission.org; www.worldparrotmission.org. Open Tue–Sun 1000–1800, with a 45-minute parrot show at 1130.*

The film of the same name (set around the Keys' 1935 Labor Day hurricane and mostly filmed in Hollywood) has brought Key Largo a fame beyond its due. None the less, further cinematic links are maintained with the **African Queen**, the diminutive vessel that starred in John Houston's 1951 film, now berthed in a local marina. Amid the birdlife spottable on the Florida Keys are the abandoned parrots being cared for by the **World Parrot Mission**, a visit to which will tell you much more than you thought there was to know about the loud and colourful creatures.

Food in Key Largo

Coconuts $$ *MM 101; tel: (305) 453-9794; www.coconutsrestaurant.com.* Large seafood menu and stunning waterfront location.

Ganim's Kountry Kitchen $–$$ *MM 100.5; tel: (305) 451-2895.* Small, friendly spot serving wholesome breakfasts and lunches in generous portions.

Left
Fishing boat and heron

LIGNUMVITAE KEY STATE BOTANICAL SITE❖❖❖

Lignumvitae Key $
Boat from MM77.7,
south of Islamorada; tel:
(305) 664-2540;
www.floridastateparks.org/
lignumvitaekey. Departures
Thur–Mon at 0830 and
1230.

Much of Lignumvitae Key is covered by a shady hammock containing strangler fig, mahogany, gumbo limbo, mastic, poisonwood, pigeon plum and other exotically named tree types, many of them beginning life in the Keys having arrived as wind- or sea-borne seeds. The trees and their curious idiosyncrasies are entertainingly described on a three-hour guided tour.

The conservation of the island is due largely to W J Matheson, a rich industrialist who bought the island in 1919 and raised the coral rock house which still provides its main sign of human habitation.

LONG KEY STATE PARK❖❖

Long Key State
Park $ *Long Key;*
tel: (305) 664-4815;
www.floridastateparks.org/
longkey. Open 0800–sunset.

At the heart of a particularly beautiful segment of the Keys, Long Key State Recreation Area is a mixture of tropical hardwood hammock and mangrove forest interwoven with short nature trails. An observation point brings views of wading birds, especially prevalent here in winter.

MARATHON❖

Marathon
Chamber of
Commerce *MM53.5;*
tel: (305) 743-5417 or
(800) 527-8539;
www.floridakeysmarathon.com.
Open daily 0900–1700.

Crane Point
Hammock
Museum $ *MM50; tel:*
(305) 743-9100;
www.cranepoint.org. Open
Mon–Sat 0900–1700, Sun
1200–1700.

Marathon is said to have acquired its name from workers on the Overseas Railroad who, while camped here in the 1910s, would contemplate the 'marathon' nature of their task to continue the tracks south across the forbidding span now straddled by the Seven Mile Bridge (*see page 101*).

Marathon is the venue of several major fishing tournaments, but a year-round local highlight is **Crane Point Hammock Museum**, providing an excellent introduction to Keys' ecology. The museum has a large children's section separated from the main museum by a 15,000-gallon saltwater lagoon, home to creatures such as bonnethead sharks and barracudas.

A number of foot trails have been devised through the 64 acres of tropical hardwood hammock that the museum occupies. Among them, the **Bahama House Trail** reaches the remains of a 1903 Bahamian settlement and explores the tabby-built (a mixture of shells, coral rock and mud) house that belonged to the colony's founder.

Accommodation in Marathon

Banana Bay Resort $$ *4590 Hwy-1; tel: (305) 743-3500 or (800) BANANA-1; www.bananabay.com.* Large and tastefully decorated rooms, close to the beach. Pool and continental breakfast.

Hawk's Cay Resort & Marina $$$ *MM61 Duck Key; tel: (305) 743-7000 or (888) 443-6393; www.hawkscay.com.* On its own 60-acre island, offering luxury and a staff trained to pamper.

Snorkelling and diving

The keys are prized for their snorkelling and scuba-diving opportunities. **John Pennekamp Coral Reef State Park, Sombrero Reef,** off Marathon, the **San Pedro Underwater Archaeological Park,** off Islamorada, and **Looe Key Marine Sanctuary** are particularly good areas. The necessary equipment, information, guided trips, and the instruction leading to the certificate essential for the use of scuba equipment are provided by scores of dive shops along Hwy-1.

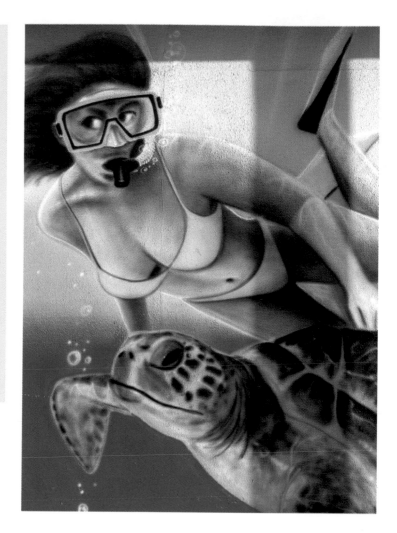

Right
Diver and turtle wall mural

PERKY'S BAT TOWER⬧

 Perky's Bat Tower
off Hwy-1 near MM17.

The rich folklore of the Florida Keys is littered with eccentric schemes but none are more bizarre than that of property speculator Richter C Perky, who devised what he thought was a foolproof plan to tempt settlers to Sugarloaf Key. Aware that mosquitoes deterred many would-be arrivals, Perky raised a 35-ft wooden tower, now remembered as Perky's Bat Tower, and packed it with a mail-order 'bat bait' (thought to have been bat droppings). Perky believed that bats would take up residence in the tower and rid the area of its mosquitoes. He soon went bust, but the tower remains.

Henry Flagler's Overseas Railroad

Hwy-1, the Overseas Highway, follows the route of the Overseas Railroad that was devised by Standard Oil magnate and Florida developer Henry Flagler to link the Keys to the mainland and continue to Key West. Begun in 1904, the line reached Key West eight years later, having claimed the lives of 700 workers and given the Keys a series of multi-arched concrete bridges.

Although the bridges stayed intact, the 200mph winds of the 1935 Labor Day hurricane tore the tracks from the ground. The death toll included 200 people aboard an evacuation train. The loss of the tracks and Americans' growing love affair with the car resulted in the creation of the Overseas Highway, helping the newly accessible Keys become a popular vacation destination. The road crosses many Flagler-era bridges; their environmental impact, not least in changing tidal patterns, is still being assessed.

SEVEN MILE BRIDGE❖❖

The Seven Mile Bridge, completed in 1982 at a cost of $45 million, was a much-needed replacement for the Flagler-era original, easing traffic congestion on Hwy-1 and tall enough to allow ships to pass beneath. The bridge itself is a jaw-dropping sight and the view from it is every bit as spectacular as you might expect.

TAVERNIER❖

Florida Keys Wild Birds Rehabilitation Center
MM93.6; tel: (305) 852-4486; www.fkwbc.org. Open daily 0830–1730. Donation.

First settled by Bahamian farmers and later becoming a pineapple and coconut plantation, Tavernier possess a charming **historic district** and the **Florida Keys Wild Birds Rehabilitation Center**, where sick birds are nursed back to health; many can be seen in various stages of convalescence from a boardwalk trail.

Accommodation in Tavernier

Bay Breeze Motel $$ *160 Sterling Road, MM92.5 Bayside; tel: (305) 852-5248 or (800) 937-5650; www.baybreezemotel.com.* Good rates beside the bay, with spectacular sunsets and a private beach.

Suggested tour

Length: 95 miles.

Duration: Main tour driving time 2.5 hours; detours according to local boat and tour schedules.

Left
Florida Keys highway

Links: It would be criminal to travel the length of the Keys without continuing to Key West (*see pages 104–13*). In the other direction, this route meets the South Miami and the Everglades National Park tour at Florida City (*see pages 64–73*).

As it crosses Florida Bay towards the Keys, the outlook from Hwy-1 is of a vast expanse of ocean dotted with mangrove-fringed islands beneath intensely blue skies. Also known as the Overseas Highway, Hwy-1 runs the length of the Keys (derived from the Spanish word for island, *cayo*) connecting the string of islands between the mainland and Key West.

Two miles after swinging right into **KEY LARGO** ❶, Hwy-1 passes the entrance to **JOHN PENNEKAMP CORAL REEF STATE PARK** ❷, the best place to explore the offshore coral reef. The reef is the reason very few beaches are found along the Keys. From Key Largo, Hwy-1 passes through **TAVERNIER** ❸ and on to the first of the four separate islands that comprise **ISLAMORADA** ❹, the route lined by bait-and-tackle shops, petrol stations, dive centres, small supermarkets and side-roads leading to numerous marinas.

Refreshingly, the next 20 miles or so are among the prettiest sections of Hwy-1. This stretch includes **LONG KEY STATE PARK** ❺ and

Swimming with dolphins

Three places in the Keys let humans swim with dolphins; reservations should be made well in advance and participants must be strong swimmers and used to masks and fins: **Dolphins Plus** (*MM100.5, Key Largo; tel: (305) 451-1993 or (866) 860-7946; www.dolphinsplus.com*); **Dolphin Research Center** (*MM59, Marathon; tel: (305) 289-1121; www.dolphins.org*); and **Theater of the Sea** (*MM84.5, Islamorada; tel: (305) 664-2431*).

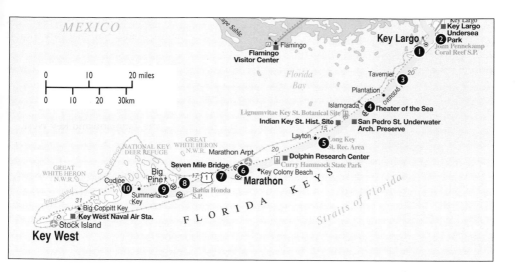

Pigeon Key $ *Tram from visitors' centre, on left of Hwy-1 immediately north of Seven Mile Bridge. Departures on the hour Tue–Sun 0900–1700.*

continues across the 2.3-mile Long Key Bridge into **MARATHON ⑥**. Note the disproportionately large runways of the airport, to the right of Hwy-1, a training strip for B17 bomber pilots during World War II. Immediately south of Marathon is the soaring **SEVEN MILE BRIDGE ⑦** that hits land at **BAHIA HONDA STATE PARK ⑧**, perhaps the most scenic picnic stop in Florida.

Four miles ahead, the route swings right on to **BIG PINE KEY ⑨**. Take a right turn on to Key Deer Boulevard to find the Key Pine deer. Hwy-1 continues on to Sugarloaf Key; turning right just after MM17 leads to **PERKY'S BAT TOWER ⑩**.

Detour: Both Lignumvitae Key and Indian Key are accessible only by boat and are best seen on guided tours. Boat departures, which link with the tours, are from a marked point on **Indian Key Fill**, just south of Islamorada near MM78.

Also worth exploring

Dominated by the enormous Seven Mile Bridge which rises immediately south, **Pigeon Key** provided accommodation for 400 railroad workers from 1908. They were employed in the massive task of erecting the original Seven Mile Bridge, a section of which links Pigeon Key to Hwy-1. Seven wooden cottages on the 5-acre island have been restored and form part of a guided tour starting at the visitors' centre on Knights Key, to the left off Hwy-1 at MM45. No cars are permitted on Pigeon Key, which is reached by tram from the visitors' centre; visitors may also arrive on foot or bicycle.

Left
Dolphin Research Center

Ratings

Ambience	●●●●●
History	●●●●○
Nightlife	●●●●○
Architecture	●●●○○
Children	●●●○○
Museums	●●●○○
Scenery	●●●○○
Beaches	●●○○○

Key West

Key West is the southernmost city in the continental US and one of the most distinctive. Compact and easily walkable, the city's tree-lined streets are studded with pretty 19th-century homes, many of them open to the public. Some once accommodated luminaries such as Ernest Hemingway, one of many writers with local links, while others now function as small museums displaying mementoes of Key West's seafaring past. The settlement originally grew as a centre for salvaging from ships wrecked on the offshore reefs.

Key West's 30,000-strong permanent population, typically relaxed to the point of catatonia, may be swamped by a million annual visitors but the immense tourist influx fails to lessen the charm or dent the sense of individuality in a community that declared itself an independent republic in 1982. At night the open-sided bars, some of them with deep roots in local history, are at the centre of a famously voracious nightlife.

ⓘ Key West Chamber of Commerce 402 Wall Street; tel: (305) 294-2587 or (800) LAST-KEY; www.keywestchamber.org. Open daily 0830–1700.

🏠 Audubon House $ 205 Whitehead Street; tel: (305) 294-2116; www.audubonhouse.com. Open daily 0930–1700.

Sights

Audubon House**

John James Audubon, who visited Key West in 1832 while compiling the wildlife studies that eventually earned him enduring fame as the *Birds of America* series, gives the house its name although links between the artist and the house are tenuous. This attractive, early 19th-century residence was built by a ship's carpenter for a leading Key West citizen, Captain John G Geiger, a salvager and harbour pilot during the days when shipwrecks underpinned the Key West economy.

Re-creating the voices of the Captain and his wife, audio guides (for hire) describe the house and their time in it. An Irish harp, a Chinese tea caddy and Chippendale tables and chairs are among the fixtures and fittings selected to suggest a typical wealthy Key West house of the time. Many Audubon prints line the walls.

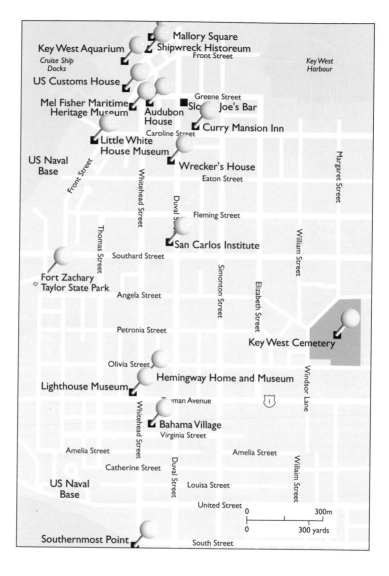

Mallory Square
Shipwreck Historeum
Key West Aquarium
Cruise Ship Docks
Front Street
Key West Harbour
US Customs House
Mel Fisher Maritime Heritage Museum
Greene Street
Sloppy Joe's Bar
Audubon House
Curry Mansion Inn
Caroline Street
Little White House Museum
US Naval Base
Front Street
Wrecker's House
Eaton Street
Whitehead Street
Duval Street
Fleming Street
Margaret Street
San Carlos Institute
Southard Street
Thomas Street
William Street
Fort Zachary Taylor State Park
Angela Street
Simonton Street
Elizabeth Street
Petronia Street
Key West Cemetery
Olivia Street
Hemingway Home and Museum
Windsor Lane
Lighthouse Museum
Whitehead Street
'man Avenue
Bahama Village
Virginia Street
Amelia Street
Amelia Street
Catherine Street
Duval Street
Willaim Street
US Naval Base
Louisa Street
United Street
0   300m
0   300 yards
Southernmost Point
South Street

Bahama Village
bordered by Virginia, Olivia, Fort and Whitehead streets.

Bahama Village*

Many of Key West's 19th-century homes were expensively restored through the 1980s and 1990s. One part of town that retains a rustic appearance, however, is the Bahama Village, originally settled by Bahamians and still occupied by many people of Caribbean descent or origin. The atmosphere is informal and redolent of a Caribbean street with few concessions to tourists amid the scurrying chickens and serious domino games.

🅷 **Curry Mansion Inn**
$ *511 Caroline Street;
tel: (305) 294-5349 or (800)
253-3466;
www.currymansion.com. Open
daily 1000–1700.*

**Fort Zachary Taylor
State Historic Sight $**
*West end of Southard Street,
enter through Truman Annexe
and the grounds of the Little
White House Museum; tel:
(305) 292-6713;
www.floridastateparks.org/
forttaylor. Open daily
0800–dusk.*

Curry Mansion Inn✦✦✦

William Curry, one-time mayor of Key West, made a fortune by supplying salvagers with hardware. In 1855 he began building what grew into the Curry Mansion, greatly expanded by his son in the early 1900s. A plush and rambling affair fronted by an inviting veranda, the mansion's wood-panelled rooms are packed with antiques, including glasswork by Louis Comfort Tiffany, a 1835 piano believed to have belonged to novelist Henry James and Audubon ornithological prints, and is a delight to explore.

Key West folklore suggests that the first Key lime pie (a dessert found throughout the Keys and exciting high passions in devotees) was made here in 1895, when the cook added the newly invented condensed milk to a dish that originated in the Bahamas.

Fort Zachary Taylor State Historic Site✦✦

Fort Zachary Taylor, its red brick buildings unearthed through the 1970s after decades of neglect, was originally intended as part of the US coastal defences and helped Key West become the only city south of the Mason-Dixon line to remain in Union hands through the Civil War. The fort's construction, a process lasting 21 years from 1845, was hindered by outbreaks of yellow fever and hurricanes. The story of the fort, now landlocked but originally 1200 feet from shore and linked to Key West by piers, is outlined in a small museum within one of the vaulted rooms.

Another reason to visit is simply the setting: a tranquil site with fabulous ocean views from the walkways along the top of the fort's 8-ft-thick walls. Nearby, an alluring white-sand beach makes a perfect picnic venue.

Above
Fort Zachary Taylor sculpture

Hemingway Home and Museum $
907 Whitehead Street;
tel: (305) 294-1136;
www.hemingwayhome.com.
Open daily 0900–1700.

Key West Aquarium $
1 Whitehead Street; tel:
(305) 296-2051;
www.keywestaquarium.com.
Open daily 1000–1800.

Key West Cemetery
701 Passover Lane; tel:
(305) 292-8177. Open daily
sunrise–1800; phone for
guided tour details.

Hemingway Home and Museum**

This Spanish Colonial house, built for a wealthy Key West merchant in the 1850s, was in a dilapidated condition when it became Ernest Hemingway's first US home after returning from Europe, where he had established his literary reputation in the 1920s. It stayed under the ownership of the Hemingways (Ernest and his second wife, Pauline) for 30 years, although the writer moved out in 1940 when the marriage ended, leaving many of his possessions here but storing his manuscripts in the backroom of a local bar.

Key West was an unlikely setting for a man fast becoming a giant of American literature but Hemingway coveted the deep-sea fishing, the many bars and the easy-going nature of the locals, once describing the town as 'the St Tropez of the poor'. Hemingway wrote about Key West in *To Have And Have Not*, one of two novels (the other was *For Whom The Bell Tolls*) written here in a hunting trophy-lined study accessed from the main house by rope bridge.

Simple furnishings and the writer's knick-knacks are revealed on the guided tours, as is the $20,000 swimming pool, the first in Key West. The tour also recounts a few of the many stories about Hemingway in Key West. Among other achievements, Hemingway's custom helped make Sloppy Joe's bar a legend and his appearance inspired what is now the annual Hemingway lookalike contest, held each July, part of the **Hemingway Days** festival that commemorates the writer and his Key West links.

Key West Aquarium*

It may not be state-of-the-art but the Key West Aquarium is an enjoyable place to pass an hour, with sharks, stingrays, turtles, spiny lobsters, angel fish, sea cucumbers, guitar fish and other oddities of the deep in tanks arranged around wooden walkways.

The 50,000-gallon Atlantic Shores exhibit re-creates conditions around a coral reef of the kind found off the Keys, highlighting the delicate and complex reef ecology and showing some of its community including barracuda, tarpon, starfish and the very peculiar reef squid.

The aquarium has shark-feeding sessions (times are posted) and free guided tours throughout the day. It also has a place in local history; opening in 1934 it was one of the first open-air aquariums in the US and part of Key West's attempts to boost tourism and stimulate its economy after the Depression.

Key West Cemetery*

A bronze statue commemorating the 266 sailors who perished in the explosion of the USS *Maine* in Havana harbour in 1898, triggering the Spanish-American War, stands at the heart of the 21-acre Key West Cemetery. Many of the tombs, however, are much less solemn and reflect the famously easy-going attitude of the town with dozens of humorous epitaphs, such as 'I told you I was sick' and 'Call me for dinner'. Guided

Lighthouse Museum $ 938 Whitehead Street; tel: (305) 294-0012; www.kwahs.com. Open daily 0930–1630.

Little White House Museum $ 111 Front Street; tel: (305) 294-9911; www.trumanlittlewhitehouse.com. Open daily 0900–1700.

Below
Mallory Square Sunset Festival

tours tell the amusing story of the cemetery, which replaced an earlier one destroyed by a hurricane, and includes a pets section.

Lighthouse Museum*

Dating from 1847, the Key West Lighthouse was among the first in Florida, a fact underlining the immense importance of Key West as a salvaging centre. The former lighthouse keeper's cottage, a dainty structure clad in termite-resistant Dade County pine, houses entertaining relics of Key West's maritime past and displays on the trials and tribulations of lighthouse keeping. Climbing 88 steps leads to the balcony just beneath the light itself and an impressive view across the town.

Little White House Museum**

President Harry S Truman first visited Key West in 1946 and found the climate and the informality much to his liking. He subsequently enjoyed frequent working vacations in this 1890 house, originally built for the commandant of Key West's US naval base and once housing inventor Thomas Edison, employed by the navy during World War I to develop depth charges.

The house is evocatively maintained in the style of Truman's time and packed with small but intriguing mementoes of his stay. They include the modestly sized desk from which the country was sometimes governed during a period that included the Korean War and the rise of McCarthyism. In Key West, however, Truman is best remembered for playing poker into the small hours and his fondness for the coconut cake made by a local woman.

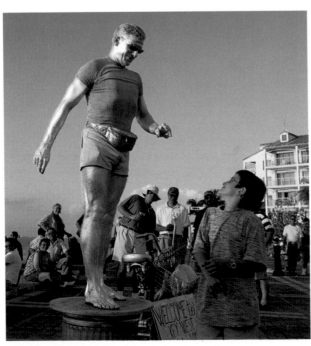

Mallory Square***

Clowns, jugglers, unicyclists and busking musicians are all likely to be found at Mallory Square for the nightly **Sunset Festival**. What began in Key West's pre-tourist days as a hippie ritual has now evolved into a major celebration that attracts every tourist in town, as well as a large number of locals who never tire of the spectacle. Crowds aside, the festival is fun and the sunset is genuinely spectacular.

Mel Fisher Maritime Heritage Museum $$ 200 Greene Street; tel: (305) 294-2633; www.melfisher.org. Open daily 0930–1700.

San Carlos Institute 516 Duval Street; tel: (305) 294-3887. Open Tue–Sun 1100–1800.

Shipwreck Historeum $$ 1 Whitehead Street; tel: (305) 292-8990; email: shipwreck@historictours.com; www.shipwreckhistoreum.com. Open daily 0945–1645.

Mel Fisher Maritime Heritage Museum**

Among the many vessels to come to grief on the treacherous reef system lying off the coast of Florida were those plying the route between Spain and the Spanish colonies in the Caribbean and Americas. The wrecks and the valuable cargo they carried provide a cue for modern-day treasure seekers to study old maps and make use of the latest technology in the hope of locating a major find. Mel Fisher, former California surf shop owner, was more successful than most in this field. In 1985, after years of searching, he located the *Nuestra Señora de Atocha*, a Spanish galleon sunk in 1622. The cargo retrieved from the ship was valued at $400 million.

The museum displays relics from the galleon, an impressive if small stash (much has been sold) of gold and silver jewellery, coins and religious items, and documents the search that lasted 16 years and took the life of Fisher's son. Remnants from the *Henrietta Marie*, the only working slave shipwreck to have been excavated are also displayed. The second floor has temporary exhibitions, focusing on underwater archaeology and other aspects of seafaring.

San Carlos Institute***

Founded in 1871 by Cuban exiles as a campaigning base for Cuban independence, the San Carlos Institute provided a school and social centre for the Cuban community in Key West (the backbone of a cigar industry flourishing in the late 1800s) and later moved into this pretty, baroque structure completed in 1924. Designed by Francisco Centurión, a leading Cuban architect, the interior of the new building had Cuban-tiled floors, mosaics reflecting Cuba's six regions, and elegant marble staircases. Upkeep was financed by the Cuban government who used its as a consulate until 1961.

The building, restored during the late 1980s, now justifiably claims to have Key West's most beautiful interior. Exhibits on Cuban themes fill three floors, one of them devoted to the life and work of the revered poet and independence fighter José Martí. Other sections illustrate the many links between Cuba, Florida and Key West.

Conch Train $ tel: (305) 294-5161; www.historictours.com/keywest. Daily 0930–1600. This 90-minute guided shunt around Key West orientates and informs. Board at *Mallory Square* or *3850 N Roosevelt Boulevard*. Similar tours are run by **Old Town Trolley** (tel: (305) 292-8906), which can be joined from 14 marked stops around Key West.

Shipwreck Historeum*

Using actors, lasers, and booty from the *Isaac Allerton*, a ship that sank in 1856 and was excavated in the 1980s, the Historeum re-creates the daily life of Key West in the mid-19th century, a period when it was among the richest cities per capita in the US through the proceeds of salvaging.

Competition to be first to a wreck was intense. Before the advent of radar and radio, salvagers would be alerted of a wreck by the shouts of lookouts posted in elevated points around the shoreline (though in some cases they simply put to sea and hoped for the worst). One such was **Tift Wrecker's Lookout**, re-created on the Historeum's second floor. From it, shipwrecks are unlikely to be spotted but there is a fine view over Key West and beyond.

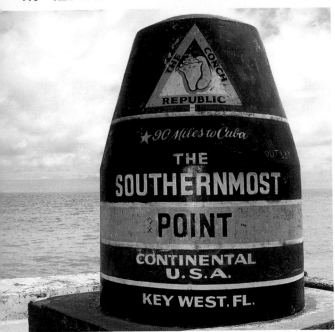

Southernmost Point⁺

At the foot of Whitehead Street, a large red, yellow and black buoy marks the southernmost point in the continental US, just 90 miles from Cuba. Among the most-photographed features of Key West, the buoy weighs several tons to prevent tourists taking it home as a souvenir. Come early to avoid the crowds and enjoy a stroll across the tiny palm-tree-lined **South Beach**.

US Customs House⁺

The divinely proportioned US Customs House, raised in 1891 and costing $108,000, has a suitably imposing presence in this town of clapboard homes. Besides its customs role, the redbrick Romanesque Revival structure has served as a federal court, post office, coastguard headquarters and US Navy office. The fact that the interior is as grand as the exterior will be proven when, after years of closure, the building becomes the home of the **Key West Museum of Art and History**.

Wrecker's House
$ 322 Duval Street; tel: (305) 294-9502; www.keysdirectory.com/oldesthouse. Open daily 1000–1600.

US Custom/Key West Museum of Art and History $ corner of Greene and Front streets; tel: (305) 295-6616; www.kwahs.com/customhouse.htm. Open daily 0900–1700.

Wrecker's House⁺⁺

Built around 1829, the clapboard Wrecker's House is believed to be the oldest house in Key West. Its first occupant was Captain Francis Watlington, whose salvaging success accounts for the plethora of 19th-century furnishings filling this compact but comfortable dwelling. Many of the architectural features were typical of Key West at the time: the widow's walk, the ship's hatch in the ceiling that provided ventilation, the cistern that collected rainwater from the gutters, and an outdoor kitchen to reduce risk of fire.

Accommodation and food

Key West Restaurants News and information on many of Key West's restaurants can be found at www.keywestmenu.com

Camille's $–$$ 1202 Simonton Street; tel: (305) 296-4811; email: camilleskeywest@aol.com; www.camilleskeywest.com. Open for breakfast, lunch and dinner with a constantly changing menu including cashew waffles and stone crab claws.

Curry Mansion Inn $$$ 511 Caroline Street; tel: (305) 294-5349 or (800) 253-3466; www.currymansion.com. Historic mansion (see page 106). Several rooms with four-poster beds.

Above
The southernmost point in the USA

El Patio Motel $–$$ *800 Washington Street; tel: (305) 296-6531 or (866) 533-5189; www.elpatiomotel.com.* Small, reliable and in a good location.

Pier House Resort $$$ *1 Duval Street; tel: (305) 296-4600 or (800) 327-8340; www.pierhouse.com.* A setting on the Gulf of Mexico ensures sunsets as splendid as the service in this luxury resort, a short walk from the main points of interest.

South Beach Seafood & Raw Bar $$ *1405 Duval Street; tel: (305) 294-2830.* Offers breakfast, lunch and dinner but most popular for its large portions of fresh seafood served with ocean views.

Southernmost Hotel $$ *1319 Duval Street; tel: (305) 296-6577 or (800) 354-4455; www.oldtownresorts.com.* Comfortable rooms, two poolside bars and a rooftop sundeck.

Square One $$$ *1075 Duval Street; tel: (305) 296-4300; www.squareonerestaurant.com.* Scallops on a bed of poached spinach is just one of the chef's special creations; a pianist adds to the ambience.

Turtle Kraals $–$$ *Lands End Village, 231 Margaret Street; tel: (305) 294-2640; email: info@turtlekraals.com; www.turtlekraals.com.* The ramshackle exterior of what was once a turtle cannery conceals some of the best seafood in Key West.

Right
Captain Tony's Saloon

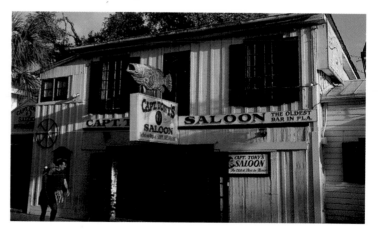

Key West's bars

Whether to follow in the footsteps of Ernest Hemingway or simply succumb to the relaxed mood, Key West is noted for the open-sided bars where locals and tourists mingle to while away the balmy evenings.

Captain Tony's Saloon *428 Greene Street; tel: (305) 294-1838; www.capttonyssaloon.com.* The site of Sloppy Joe's during the Hemingway era and very much part of local folklore.

Green Parrot *601 Whitehead Street; tel: (305) 294-6133; www.greenparrot.com.* Live music at weekends and always a jukebox with a tremendous stash of blues, zydecko, rockabilly and reggae.

Margaritaville Café *500 Duval Street; tel: (305) 292-1435; www.margaritaville.com.* Owned by singer-songwriter and long-time Key West resident Jimmy Buffett and named after one of his biggest hits. Good live music and frozen margaritas.

Sloppy Joe's *201 Duval Street; tel: (305) 294-5717; www.sloppyjoes.com.* Always crowded, Sloppy Joe's dates from 1933 and has become very touristy, partly through its exaggerated Hemingway connection.

Boat tours

Many Key West companies offer deep-sea fishing, snorkelling and diving trips, glass-bottomed boat trips to coral reefs, nature tours and champagne-fuelled sunset celebration cruises. Among them are:

Discovery Undersea Tours *251 Margaret Street; tel: (305) 293-0099 or (800) 262-0099; www.discoveryunderseatours.com*

Schooner Liberty *245 Front Street; tel: (305) 292-0332; email: info@libertyfleet.com; www.libertyfleet.com* Put out on the 80-foot schooner *Liberty* for morning, afternoon or sunset cruises beneath the sails.

Lucky Fleet Inc *Land's End Marina; tel: (800) 292-3096 or (800) 294-7988; www.luckyfleet.com*

Mosquito Coast Wildlife Tours *310 Duval Street; tel: (305) 294-7178; www.mosquitocoast.net*

Suggested tour

Length: Main tour 1.5 miles, 3 miles with detours.

Duration: Main tour 2 hours, 4 hours with detours.

Links: The Florida Keys (*see pages 94–103*).

The main route is an easy walk around the historic heart of Key West, beginning on **MALLORY SQUARE ❶**. From here, the **KEY WEST AQUARIUM ❷**, the **SHIPWRECK HISTOREUM ❸**, the **US CUSTOMS HOUSE ❹** and the **MEL FISHER MARITIME HERITAGE MUSEUM ❺** are all within a few strides. Also close by, at the corner of Greene and Whitehead streets, is **AUDUBON HOUSE ❻**.

Two blocks east, Duval Street forms Key West's main commercial artery and is lined by clapboard buildings housing art galleries, boutiques and souvenir shops. Facing you is the legendary **Sloppy Joe's** bar. Walk a block south along Duval Street and turn east on to Caroline Street for the **CURRY MANSION INN ❼**. Go west on Caroline Street for the **LITTLE WHITE HOUSE ❽**.

Return to Duval Street for the **WRECKER'S HOUSE ❾**, between Caroline and Eaton streets. Directly south, on the junction with Eaton Street, Stands **St Paul's Episcopal Church**, its vaulted wooden ceiling resembling an inverted ship's hull.

A block south on Duval Street is the **SAN CARLOS INSTITUTE ❿**. Continue south for three blocks to Olivia Street, then turn right for the **HEMINGWAY HOME AND MUSEUM ⓫** and the neighbouring **LIGHTHOUSE MUSEUM ⓬**. Adjacent are the streets of the **BAHAMA VILLAGE ⓭**. Continue south along Whitehead Street for the **SOUTHERNMOST POINT ⓮**.

Detour: From the Little White House Museum, walk along Front Street into narrow Emma Street, which meets Southard Street. Turn right here and follow the signs for the **FORT ZACHARY TAYLOR STATE PARK 15**.

Detour: To reach **KEY WEST CEMETERY 16** from Duval Street, walk three blocks east on Eaton Street, passing the **Donkey Milk House** (*No 613*), a restored Greek Revival home open for tours, and the **Bahama House** (*No 408*), built in the Bahamas and brought here by its owner in 1846, before turning right along William Street and continuing south.

Coast to coast across the Everglades

Ratings

Nature	●●●●●
History	●●●●○
Outdoor activities	●●●●○
Boating	●●●○○
Scenery	●●●○○
Children	●●○○○
Beaches	●○○○○
Museums	●○○○○

The busy and dull I-75 is the main link between south Florida's east and west coasts but the first road to cross the Everglades, gouging a path through swamp and sawgrass prairie stimulating a boom in south Florida's fortunes, was Hwy-41 (the Tamiami Trail), opened in 1928. Today, the two-lane Hwy-41 is a journey through Florida's frontier history, passing thinly populated settlements where fugitives, smugglers and moonshiners once flourished, and where the lack of development brings frontier folklore to life.

Despite being decimated by logging, drainage and human demands for drinking water, the Everglades are very much alive. This route includes everything from steamy swamps to strands of stately royal palm trees, although the view from the road is usually a mind-bogglingly huge expanse of sawgrass. Shark Valley is one highlight; a boat trip from Chokoloskee another. Both will enjoyably initiate newcomers into the complexities of the Everglades.

BIG CYPRESS NATIONAL PRESERVE✧✧

ⓘ Gulf Coast Ranger Station *Route 29, Chokoloskee; tel: (239) 695-3311. Open daily 0830–1700.*

Part of the 2400-square-mile Big Cypress Swamp, the preserve, is noted for the slender belts of dwarf and big cypress trees growing along the sides of freshwater channels (or sloughs). Despite the devastation caused by the lumber industry, a few giant cypresses still remain, distinguished by their flared bases. The trees provide a rich and sheltered habitat for many varieties of bird life, including bald eagles and wood storks, an incentive for the birdwatchers who keenly gather with binoculars and cameras on the short boardwalk trail.

Among other creatures regularly spotted are alligators, turkeys and deer; the very rare Florida panther (secretive big cats that face an uncertain future, although now they are subject to protection and intensive research) and mink are occasionally seen. At the visitors' centre, a short film documents the complex Everglades' ecosystem of which the swamp forms a vital part, and highlights the damage limitation exercise that brought federal protection to this portion of it in 1974. *www.nps.gov/bicy*

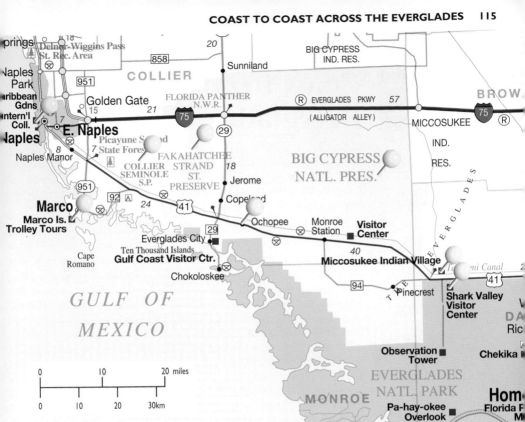

COLLIER-SEMINOLE STATE PARK❖❖

❶ Collier-Seminole State Park $ *20200 S Tamiami Trail; tel: (239) 394-3397; www.floridastateparks.org/ collier-seminole. Open daily 0800–sunset; boat trips 0900–1600.*

Cypress swamps, hardwood hammocks, pinelands, mangrove forests and other features typical of the Everglades landscape make up the 6000-acre Collier-Seminole State Park. The most eye-catching elements, however, are the rows of Florida royal palms, a species of palm that rises with great elegance and sometimes reaches 120ft high.

Pontoon boat trips on the aptly named Blackwater River which runs through the park are an enjoyable way to experience the varied terrain and, with the guide's commentary, gain insights into local nature (canoes are available for rent). Also in the park, a short foot trail leads to a raised viewing platform from which wood storks, bald eagles, woodpeckers, alligators, mangrove foxes and squirrels might be spotted.

Near the entrance to the park, look out for the weighty slab of metal known as the walking dredge, used to clear a route through the jungle-like foliage for the building of Hwy-41 in the 1920s. The slow progress it made earned it its nickname.

FAKAHATCHEE STRAND STATE PRESERVE✦

ⓘ Fakahatchee Strand State Preserve *Off Hwy-41, 7 miles west of junction with Route 29; tel: (239) 695-4593; www.floridastateparks.org/ fakahatcheestrand. Open dawn–dusk.*

Particularly if you missed them at Collier-Seminole State Park, the Florida royal palms that grace Fakahatchee Strand are well worth making the effort to see, as are the enormous number and variety of epiphytic plants, including a wonderful array of orchids that bloom throughout the year. A mile-long boardwalk trail leads to a strand of virgin cypress and into Big Cypress Swamp, one of the few sections of old-growth cypress left intact by the lumber industry. The primordial scene is completed by the steamy atmosphere and a complement of watchful alligators.

MARCO ISLAND✦✦

ⓘ Marco Island Chamber of Commerce *1102 N Collier Boulevard; tel: (239) 394-7549; www.marcoislandchamber.org. Open Mon–Fri 0900–1700.*

ⓣ Marco Island trolley tours $ *tel: (941) 394-1600. Open daily 1000–1645.*

The most northerly link in the Ten Thousand Island chain, Marco Island is studded with up-market resort hotels and expensive homes, and also boasts one of the country's largest bald eagle colonies nesting in its tall pine trees. Remains dating back to the Calusa people of 3500 years ago have been found on the islands and shell mounds, the debris of many generations of prehistoric clam and oyster harvesting, can still be seen.

The island's past and present is outlined on the stress-free **trolley tours**, which last 90-minutes but permit visitors to hop on and off as the mood takes them. One place you might be tempted to do so is **Tigertail Beach Park**. On any sunny weekend, the park is filled with locals flying kites, jogging, or just sunbathing and wildlife-watching: pelicans and ospreys proliferate and dolphins are known to swim close to the shore.

MICCOSUKEE INDIAN VILLAGE✦

ⓣ Miccosukee Indian Village $ *On Hwy-41, half-a-mile west of Shark Valley entrance; tel: (305) 223-8380; www.miccosukeeresort.com/ mivillage.html. Open daily 0900–1700.*

ⓣ Miccosukee Restaurant $ *Miccosukee Indian Village, Hwy-41; tel: (305) 223-8380. A mixture of standard American diner fare and old-time Florida favourites such as alligator, frogs' legs and catfish, given a Miccosukee treatment.*

Like the Seminoles, with whom they share many cultural traits and history, the Miccosukee are descended from the Creek people of the American Southeast and were driven into the Everglades following the Seminole wars. Speaking a unique language, many Miccosukee now inhabit the 76-square-mile reservation in the Everglades on which the Miccosukee Indian Village stands.

Anyone interested in finding out about Miccosukee lifestyles and beliefs will regard the commercially orientated village as a disappointment. There are demonstrations of alligator wrestling, and handicrafts such as baskets and beadwork are made and offered for sale. Only the small museum provides a slightly more substantial commentary on the tribe.

Miccosukee-operated airboat rides press deeper into the Everglades, reaching a gathering of traditional open-sided 'chickee' structures surrounded by sawgrass. These are suggestive of everyday Miccosukee life but leave visitors with nothing to do once there other than buy souvenirs.

NAPLES✧✧

ⓘ Naples Area Chamber of Commerce *3620 N Hwy-41; tel: (239) 262 6376; www.napleschamber.org. Open Mon–Fri 0830–1700.*

Designer boutiques, high-class restaurants, million-dollar homes and more golf courses per head of population than any other place in Florida help make Naples a byword for wealth and exclusivity. Unlike its glamorous east-coast counterpart, Palm Beach, Naples' residents typically keep a low profile and view celebrity status as rather vulgar.

The half-hour guided tour of the 1887 **Palm Cottage**, its construction financed by Walter S Haldeman, the newspaper proprietor who tried unsuccessfully to develop the area, provides background on Naples' humble origins: it stayed a quiet fishing settlement until the arrival of the railway and the completion of the Tamiami Trail.

Below
Fifth Avenue South, Naples

Above
Third Street South, Naples

An easy walk from the cottage leads to **Naples Pier**, erected in the 1880s and re-built in 1961 following its third demolition by a hurricane. A haunt of pelicans and fishermen, the pier gives stupendous views across the town's palm-fringed beaches and to the excellent **Lowdermilk Park**, 2 miles north. Stroll from the pier to **Fifth Avenue** and window-shop amid Naples' showpiece stores and art galleries, many of them housed in the former boatyards that serviced the fishing fleet based on Naples Bay, now a departure point for sightseeing cruises.

Accommodation and food in Naples

The Lemon Tree Inn $$ *250 9th Street South; tel: (239) 262-1414 or (888) 800-LEMO; email: ltreeinn@aol.com; www.lemontreeeinn.com.* Bed-and-breakfast option in the oldest part of Naples, an easy walk to everywhere and offering all the free lemonade you can drink.

The Registry Resort $$$ *475 Seagate Drive; tel: (239) 597-3232; www.registryresort.com.* Despite having 475 fully-equipped rooms and several golf courses, this first-class hotel enjoys a low-key charm. Guests reach the beach via a boardwalk through a mangrove forest.

Residence Inn $–$$ *4075 Tamiami Trail; tel: (239) 659-1300 or (800) 331-3131; www.naplesresidenceinn.com.* Clean and dependable, one of the Marriott Hotel Group's less expensive chains.

The Riverwalk Fish & Ale House $$ *Tin City, 1200 5th Avenue; tel: (239) 263-2734; www.riverwalktincity.com.* Seafood, salad and sandwiches served with a view of Naples Bay, plus a long list of beers and exotic cocktails.

Zoe's $$–$$$ *720 5th Avenue South; tel: (239) 261-1221.* Stylish up-market place to dine on European-influenced American fare; doubles as a no less stylish nightspot.

OCHOPEE✦

The tiny white-painted wooden structure that stands in the minuscule settlement of Ochopee, created as a lumber camp in the 1920s, is not a misplaced garden shed but the smallest and most-photographed post office in the US.

SHARK VALLEY✦✦✦

Shark Valley $ *Off Hwy-41, 25 miles west of Miami; tel: (305) 221 8776; www.nps.gov/ever/visit/activ-sv.htm. Entrance open daily 0830–1800; Visitor Center open daily 0830–1715.*

At first glance, the Shark Valley section of Everglades National Park seems devoid of life but the two-hour **tram tour**, led and narrated by a park ranger, along a 15-mile paved loop road, reveals a great deal about the unique ecology and wildlife of the area and stops regularly for close-up looks at the multitude of creatures that inhabit this curious terrain. In summer, heavy rains can put much of Shark Valley, including all the trails and roads, under water.

During September and October, a mother alligator tending her young is a common sight, particularly around the artificial lakes known as 'borrow pits' that also attract wading birds and anhingas (snake birds). Midway along the loop road, a 65-ft-high **observation tower** offers views reaching into the distance and downwards to a large pond usually teeming with turtles, otters and alligators.

The tram tour provides a welcome initiation into the wonders of Shark Valley, while a bicycle trip along the same road allows further appreciation of the setting and its wildlife. In addition to the usual protection against mosquitoes and the sun, cyclists must carry ample drinking water and heed the safety precautions issued when hiring a bike from the park's rental outlet. Be particularly wary of close encounters with snakes and alligators when moving to the side of the road to allow the tram to pass.

While the loop trail is the main feature of Shark Valley, make time for two short trails close to the visitors' centre: the **Bobcat Boardwalk** and the **Otter Cave Hammock Trail**, both of which penetrate hardwood hammocks.

Suggested tour

Length: Main route, 300 miles; 350 miles with detours.

Duration: 6 hours; allow 3–4 extra hours for both detours. With limited time, concentrate on Shark Valley, plus Marco Island and Naples for their beaches and dining, or Collier-Seminole State Park and Big Cypress National Preserve for nature.

Links: The eastern part of this route can easily be joined from Miami. Hwy-41 is a continuation of SW 8th Street, the main commercial strip of Miami's Little Havana (*see pages 52–63*). On the west coast, continuing for 36 miles on Hwy-41 north from Naples you reach Fort Myers (*see pages 126–29*).

From Miami, Hwy-41 begins its Everglades crossing west of the Florida Turnpike. The outlook remains similar for much of the route: sawgrass as far as the eye can see; billboards advertising airboat rides; and minuscule settlements that originated as lumber camps and now have a shop and petrol station. **Cooperstown**, which claims a population of just eight, and the evocatively named **Frog City**, are two of the first.

Thirty-six miles from Miami, the entrance for the **SHARK VALLEY ❶** section of Everglades National Park is to the left; a mile further lies the **MICCOSUKEE INDIAN VILLAGE ❷** , occupying an area of the Everglades designated as a Miccosukee reservation. Three miles on, Hwy-41 deviates from a straight route for the first time at the aptly-named **Fortymile Bend**, also the junction for the **Route 94** detour (*see overleaf*).

Fiftymile Bend is 10 miles ahead on Hwy-41 and 7 miles further is the entrance to **BIG CYPRESS NATIONAL PRESERVE ❸** . A further 3 miles on Hwy-41 is **Monroe Station**, a modest settlement that grew in the 1920s as a lumber camp. An annual wild hog barbecue remains the major event here, where the proprietor of the local store will perform 'swamp weddings'.

Right
Everglades resident

Twelve miles further west, little **OCHOPEE** ❹ is sometimes overwhelmed by tour buses as passengers pause just long enough to photograph its tiny post office. Equally good as souvenir snaps are the Panther Crossing signs which appear for the next few miles, albeit optimistically as the Florida panther is close to extinction. The junction with Route 29 is 4 miles west of Ochopee; turn to the left for Everglades City and Chokoloskee (*see opposite*) or right for **FAKAHATCHEE STRAND STATE PRESERVE** ❺.

From a junction 17 miles further west on Hwy-41, Route 951 covers the 9 miles to **MARCO ISLAND** ❻. On the way, the outlook shifts from sawgrass to mangrove as the distinctions between land and sea become blurred. To reach **NAPLES** ❼, return to Hwy-41 and head west for 7 miles.

Detour: A pot-holed road liable to flooding but none the less accessible to two-wheeled vehicles, **Route 94** leaves Hwy-41 at Fortymile Bend and charts a 26-mile single-lane course through a cypress hammock and may bring views through the car windows (if you do step out, be alert for snakes) of deer and alligator, and other creatures that gather around the roadside channels which are the only source of water through the dry winter. On the way is an **Interpretative Center** and the **Tree Snail Hammock Nature Trail**, named for the colourful tree snails that can usually be seen.

Captain Doug House's Original Jet Air Boat Adventure $ *State Road 29; tel: (800) 282-9194; www.florida-everglades.com/airboat/home.htm.* Of the many airboat across the waterways of the Everglades this is among the least environmentally harmful. Daily, departures every 30 mins.

Museum of the Everglades $ *105 W Broadway, Everglades City; tel: (239) 695-0008; www.florida-everglades.com/evercty/museum.htm. Open Tue–Sat 1100–1600.*

Smallwood Store Museum *Chokoloskee; tel: (239) 695-2989. Open Dec–May, daily 1000–1700; Jun–Nov, Fri–Tue 1000–1600.*

Rod and Gun Lodge $$ *200 S Riverside Drive, Everglades City; tel: (239) 695-2101.* Hearty portions of seafood, so fresh it was swimming only hours ago.

Detour: Five miles south of Hwy-41 on Route 29, **Everglades City** has a population of just 300 and grew as a base for the building of the Tamiami Trail. Its founder, W S Allen, hoped he would be remembered as the originator of south Florida's biggest city but the lasting landmark of his time is the white-framed building that holds the **Rod and Gun Lodge**, one of the US's most exclusive sports clubs in the days when the Everglades were synonymous with hunting and fishing rather than appreciation of nature. The club's members included presidents and other national notables. Now open to all, it offers accommodation and food, a lobby filled with stuffed fish and the club crest: an American eagle with fishing rod and rifle. Close by, a 1920s laundry dating from the construction of Hwy-41 now, as the **Museum of the Everglades**, documents the history of the region's human habitation.

Continue south on Route 29 to **Chokoloskee**, even smaller than Everglades City but with a history to call its own documented in the **Smallwood Store**, a trading post established in 1906.

Chokoloskee is a departure point for **boat tours**, some independent, others licensed by the National Parks Service who also operate the **Gulf Coast Ranger Station**, the main source of local information. The boat tour commentary reveals a few of the mysteries of the mangrove, a vital component of the ecosystem, as the boat weaves steadily around the labyrinthine waterways.

Creatures such as mangrove racoons, and bird life such as bald eagles, ospreys and great white herons all find the area to their liking and can often be spotted. Passing the shell mounds left by early Native Americans and recounting tales of the larger-than-life characters who were the area's first white settlers, the tour paints a colourful picture of human settlement in this extreme terrain.

Fort Myers and the Lee County Islands

Ratings

Beaches	●●●●●
Nature	●●●●○
Scenery	●●●●○
Beachcombing	●●●○○
Children	●●●○○
History	●●●○○
Sunsets	●●●○○
Museums	●●○○○

The historic city of Fort Myers and the unspoilt islands that flank the mouth of the broad Caloosahatchee River that runs beside it are among the most appealing yet relatively undiscovered sections of Florida's west coast. Inventor Thomas Edison was one of the first to find the slow pace and the idyllic subtropical scenery to his liking; his winter home is an essential stop. The palm trees Edison planted in the town still grace the route between Fort Myers and the islands.

The islands range from the developed Estero Island, holding vibrant Fort Myers Beach, to Captiva and Sanibel islands, where large tracts provide wildlife refuges and pocket-sized beaches drawing thousands of avid shell collectors. In one of the state's happiest marriages between humans and nature, there are plentiful opportunities to spot dolphins and other marine life surprisingly close to the shore, and on the boat trips that make other even less developed islands accessible.

CABBAGE KEY*

Cabbage Key Inn
tel: (239) 283-2278;
fax: (239) 283-1384;
www.cabbage-key.com

An estimated $25,000 worth of dollar bills line the walls of the rustic restaurant on Cabbage Key (accessible only by boat), each signed by the person who left it and part of a tradition established in the 1940s when a customer, worried that he may not have sufficient funds to buy a drink on his return from a fishing trip, left a dollar behind with his name on it. The restaurant occupies the Cabbage Key Inn, which was originally built in 1938 by Mary Roberts Rhinehart, author of mystery stories, as a winter home for her son.

CAPTIVA ISLAND***

Chapel-by-the-Sea
End of Wiles Drive, off
Sanibel-Captiva Road.

Inhabited only by a few hundred privacy-loving souls and largely undeveloped, save for the luxury South Seas Plantation resort (departure point for boat trips to Cabbage Key) that occupies its northern tip, Captiva Island is a must-see even though there is just

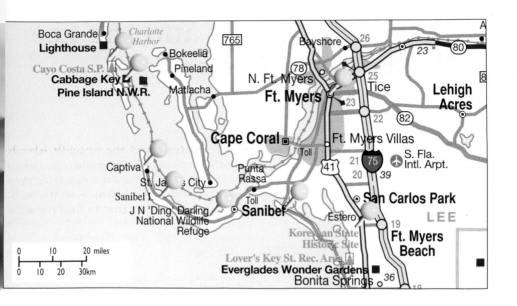

one place specifically meriting a visit. This is the weather-beaten, white clapboard **Chapel-by-the-Sea**, built in 1901 as the local school and converted to religious use by Methodists before becoming interdenominational.

Now mostly used for weddings, the church has a palm-shaded **cemetery** that provides a resting place for early islanders, including William Howard Binder, whose headstone remembers him as 'First Homesteader Captiva Island, 1888'.

Accommodation on Captiva Island

The Bubble Room $$ *15001 Captiva Road; tel: (239) 472-5558; www.bubbleroomrestaurant.com.* An effervescent atmosphere and 1940s style décor tend to overshadow the hearty portions of seafood and steak.

South Seas Plantation $$$ *PO Box 194; tel: (239) 472-5111 or (800) 965-7772; www.southseaplantation.com.* Full-service resort with all imaginable facilities spread across the northern tip of Captiva Island.

CAYO COSTA STATE PARK❖❖

Cayo Costa State Park $ *tel: (941) 964-0375; www.floridastateparks.org/cayocosta. Open daily 0800–sunset. Accessible only by boat; see page 132.*

The only human occupant of Cayo Costa Island, a park ranger, shares the island with abundant bird life and has first pick of the shells that wash ashore on the 9 glorious miles of white-sanded beach lining the western side. The eastern side is composed of mangrove swamps, oak palm hammocks and pinelands. The secluded island can be reached only by boat and can be explored on 5 miles of foot trails. Besides the many shells, look on the beach for the footprints of loggerhead turtles, who come ashore at night to lay their eggs in the sand.

FORT MYERS❖

ℹ️ **Lee County Visitor and Convention Bureau**, 2180 W 1st Street; tel: (941) 338-3500 or (800) 237-6444; www.leeislandcoast.com

🏠 **Burroughs Home $** 2505 1st Street; tel: (941) 332-6125. Open Tue–Fri 1100–1500. Currently closed for renovations.

South West Florida Museum of History $ 2300 Peck Street; tel: (239) 332-5955; www.cityftmyers.com. Open Tue–Sat 1000–1700, Sun 1200–1600.

Edison Winter Home $$ (includes Ford Winter Home) 2350 McGregor Boulevard; tel: (239) 334-7419; www.edison-ford-estate.com. Open Mon–Sat 0900–1600, Sun 1200–1600.

Set beside the broad Caloosahatchee River, Fort Myers has a relaxed air and is enhanced by the many stately royal palms that line its main artery, McGregor Boulevard. Modern Fort Myers sprawls well beyond the sway of the river but this commercially vibrant city keeps much from its first period of growth intact in the small Downtown district centred on 1st Street.

Once the largest and most luxurious house in Fort Myers, the handsome Georgian Revival **Burroughs Home** was built in 1901 for $15,000 and purchased by Midwestern banker and cattle baron Nelson T Burroughs in 1919. A mahogany fireplace, a spiral staircase and detailed reconstruction of the house as it was in the early 1900s add to the appeal, as do tours conducted by costumed guides taking the roles of the Burroughs' daughters, who inherited the house on their father's death in 1932. In character, the guides recount the story of the house and its occupants, and the social life of the time when the Edisons, Fords and tyre-mogul Harvey Firestone were regular visitors.

The **South West Florida Museum of History**, housed in a restored former railway depot, arranges local history into neat segments, from the prehistory of the Calusa people – a major native grouping settled throughout southwest Florida with marine skills believed to have taken them as far as Cuba – and relics from Spanish shipwrecks, to notable individuals such as Doctor Franklin Miles, inventor of *Alka Seltzer*. In the grounds, the 84-ft-long *Esperanza*, a private Pullman carriage, gives a taste of the luxury available to well-heeled rail travellers in the 1930s.

Thomas Edison, inventor of the incandescent light bulb, the phonograph, the cine projector and the generating system that brought power to cities, wintered at the 14-acre riverside site now known as the **Edison Winter Home** from 1886 until his death in 1931. Advised to move to Florida from New Jersey for health reasons, Edison relished the local climate for the opportunity to grow tropical plants and trees, utilising their raw material in his experiments (bamboo had provided the filament in Edison's early light bulbs).

The caringly tended and frangipani-scented **gardens** are a highlight of a visit. They include such exotic trees as the African sausage, fried egg and giant tulip, amid a variety of palms, a profusion of wild orchids and many other plants. Also here is the 14-ft-high golden rod tree cultivated for its sap, instrumental in Edison's attempts to develop new forms of natural rubber during the 1920s.

Above
Exotic foliage, Edison Winter
Home

With its shady porches, Edison's two-storey **house** was designed for the Florida climate but constructed in Maine prior to being shipped south: one of the first pre-fabricated dwellings in the US. Still illuminated by the carbon filament bulbs of Edison's time, the house reveals the elegant yet simple style enjoyed by the inventor and his second wife.

Edison's **laboratory** is evocatively maintained as he left it with rows of test tubes, glass beakers and tripods. Note the small cot to one side of the lab: it was here that Edison would take catnaps during experiments. The colossal impact of Edison's work on the modern world is put in context by the adjoining **museum**, stocking many of his creations and allowing a chronological assessment of his achievements, made all the more remarkable by the fact that his life included just three months of formal education.

Leading car manufacturer and pioneer of the assembly line production system, Henry Ford also enjoyed a long-lasting friendship with Thomas Edison (who had encouraged Ford with his first automobile ideas) and in 1916 bought the winter home next door to the great inventor. For a man who died in 1947 leaving a fortune conservatively estimated at $500 million, the **Ford Winter Home** is a surprisingly unelaborate affair equipped with the 1920s fixtures and fittings of the kind that surrounded the Fords (Henry and his wife) during their occupancy.

Above
White ibis, Sanibel Island

The Fords' time in Fort Myers, particularly their close links with the Edisons, is outlined on the guided tours as they pass through the house and across the very pleasant 3-acre gardens of palms, citrus trees and tropical plants.

FORT MYERS BEACH AND SAN CARLOS ISLAND❖❖

Fort Myers Beach occupies the long and narrow Estero Island and is lined by a fine 7-mile strip of white sand. A homely mood prevails despite the high concentration of motels, seafood restaurants and boat charter services. To the north, **Bodwitch Regional Park** wraps 7 acres of greenery around an attractive beach, with a boardwalk linking it to picnic areas.

To the south are the less developed **San Carlos Island** and **Carl Johnson Park**, where a boardwalk trail to the beach passes rows of Australian pines and crosses a forest of mangrove. The gorgeous **Lover's Key**, also accessible on a small passenger-carrying 'tractor', is at the end of the trail and boasts one of the area's quietest and prettiest beaches.

Accommodation in Fort Myers Beach

Edgewater Inn $$ *781 Estero Boulevard; tel: (239) 765-5959; www.edgewaterfmb.com.* Small, but the pick of the area's many accommodations with a good position on the northern end of Estero Island and choice of one- and two-bedded rooms.

J N 'DING' DARLING NATIONAL WILDLIFE REFUGE✦✦✦

J N 'Ding' Darling National Wildlife Refuge $
1 Wildlife Drive, Sanibel Island; tel: (941) 472-1100; www.dingdarlingsociety.com. Wildlife Drive open Sat–Thur 1 hour after sunrise–30 mins before sunset. Closed Sun. Education Center: daily 0900–1700.

Named for the political cartoonist who signed his creations 'Ding' and was also a leading conservationist, this refuge protects a 6000-acre tract on the northern side of Sanibel Island. During springtime, roseate spoonbills can often be sighted at sunset; in summer, night herons, mottled ducks and blue herons may appear and year-round ospreys, racoons, brown pelicans and a very large colony of alligators are frequently seen. The 5-mile Wildlife Drive can be navigated by car but renting a bike from the visitor centre improves the chances of spotting the well-camouflaged creatures.

KORESHAN STATE HISTORIC SITE✦✦

Koreshan State Historic Site $ *off Corkscrew Road, Estero; tel: (239) 992-0311; www.floridastateparks.org/koreshan. Open daily 0800–1700.*

The most successful of several utopian-minded communities which sought to establish themselves in Florida over the turn of the 20th century, the Koreshan Unity sect were led by Cyrus Teed (aka 'Koresh'), who claimed that an angelic visitation had convinced him that the world was not a globe but concave, set around the inner edge of a giant sphere.

Some 250 Koreshans lived here during the early 1900s, vowed to celibacy outside marriage, equality between the sexes and shared property ownership as they prepared the 305-acre site for ten million anticipated settlers in the 'New Jerusalem'. Although the last Koreshan lived until 1982, Teed's death in 1908 signalled the sect's decline and its land was donated to the state in 1961. The restored Koreshan homes and communal buildings can be toured and aspects of their curious and intriguing philosophy discovered.

SANIBEL ISLAND✦✦✦

Sanibel-Captiva Visitors Center
1159 Causeway Road; tel: (239) 472-1080; www.sanibel-captiva.org. Open Mon–Sat 0900–2000, Sun 1000–1800.

A slender, curving island, a third of which is taken up by a wildlife refuge, Sanibel Island attracts shell collectors from near and far, over-eager gatherers sometimes acquiring the bent-back condition known as the 'Sanibel stoop'. The island was linked to the mainland by bridge only as recently as 1963, and retains a distinct and very individual identity, many of its long-time residents tracing their lineage

Above
Sanibel Island beachcombers

back to the hardy farmers and fishermen who settled here in the 1890s. The 98-ft-high **Sanibel Lighthouse** was raised in 1884 after many years of campaigning by islanders. The still-operating lighthouse and two adjoining keepers' cottages, raised on stilts to avoid high tides, are the island's oldest buildings. Adjacent to the lighthouse, the south-facing **Sanibel Beach** misses the strong tides that deposit shells on the island's other beaches but is popular with sunbathers and swimmers, and those who come to watch out in the hope of seeing the dolphins that are regularly sighted at sea.

Sanibel Historical Village and Museum $ *950 Dunlop Road; tel: (239) 472-4648; www.bestofsanibelcaptiva.com. Open Dec–Easter, Wed–Sat 1000–1600, Sun 1200–1600; rest of year, closed Sun.*

Bailey-Matthews Shell Museum $ *3075 Sanibel-Captiva Road; tel: (239) 395-2233 or (888) 679-6450; www.shellmuseum.org. Open daily 1000–1600.*

Sanibel Captiva Conservation Foundation $ *3333 Sanibel-Captiva Road; tel: (239) 472-2329; www.sccf.org. Open late-Nov–Easter, Mon–Sat 0830–1600; rest of year Mon–Sat 0830–1500.*

Sanibel's history may be insignificant in world terms but is very highly regarded and zealously maintained by islanders, and is on display in the **Sanibel Historical Village and Museum**. Inside a 1913 'cracker' cottage (the term applied to the simple woodframed dwelling that provided typical living quarters for Florida settlers of the time), are rooms lined with historical artefacts, such as Calusa relics, Spanish shipwreck items, and the paraphernalia of early-1900s island life. The former Sanibel Post Office and Bailey's General Store and Gas Station, dating from the 1920s, are restored in period style and form part of the village complex.

The importance of shells to Sanibel Island should not be underestimated. The east–west orientation of the island and its position at the junction of several currents brings a rich harvest of shells at every low tide. The intriguing **Bailey-Matthews Shell Museum**, which claims to display a third of the 10,000 shell types found in the world, gives some clues as to why people hit the local beaches in the first rays of dawn with hopes of spotting a brown speckled junonia.

Reached by a foot bridge passing through pinelands and over mangrove swamps, **Bowman's Beach** is the most popular strand on Sanibel Island, with showers, a shady picnic area and dramatic sunsets.

Accommodation and food on Sanibel Island

The Lighthouse Café $ *Seahorse Shopping Center, 362 Periwinkle Way; tel: (239) 472-0303; www.lighthousecafe.com.* Serving breakfasts and lunches for over 25 years; early risers might tackle the shrimp, crabmeat and scallop that sits on a croissant and forms part of the 'seafood benedict' breakfast special.

West Wind Inn $$ *3345 West Gulf Drive; tel: (239) 472-1541 or (800) 824-0476 from US and Canada; (00 800) 897-44321 from UK; www.westwindinn.com.* Nicely located for exploring the island, with large comfortable rooms and the beach just steps away.

Suggested tour

Length: Main route, 50 miles; 73 miles with beach detour; 103 miles with the Koreshan State Historic Site detour.

Duration: Main route driving time 2 hours; 3 hours with beach detour; 4–5 hours with Koreshan State Historic Site detour. Allow additional time, and preferably an extra day, for the boat trip to Cayo Costa State Park.

The suggested tour assumes a start in Sanibel and Captiva islands and takes around 5 hours, focusing on Sanibel and Captiva islands and the main sights of Fort Myers, covering a distance of some 50 miles.

Above
Basking alligator

The Fort Myers Beach detour will add an extra 2 hours or so. The Koreshan State Historic Site and Cayo Costa State Park are much lengthier detours, best undertaken on a separate day.

Links: Coast to coast across the Everglades (*see pages 114–23*) and The Culture Coast (*see pages 162–71*). Although the tour can easily be joined from any point on its route, the description begins with Captiva and Sanibel islands, on the assumption that you spend the previous night there.

The Sanibel-Captiva Road passes attractive **Turner Beach** before leaving Sanibel and reaching the ruggedly vegetated **CAPTIVA ISLAND** ❶. Becoming Captiva Drive, the road continues for 3 barely inhabited miles passing Wiles Drive, leading to the **Chapel-by-the Sea**. The main route expires 2 miles further at the South Seas Plantation, where boats continue to **CABBAGE KEY** ❷.

Returning to Sanibel, Bowman's Beach Road branches to the right off the Sanibel-Captiva Road to the excellent **Bowman's Beach**. The main route continues alongside the **J N 'DING' DARLING NATIONAL WILDLIFE REFUGE** ❸, its main entrance 3.5 miles ahead.

Continuing, the route joins Periwinkle Way, which cuts through the residential and commercial heart of **SANIBEL ISLAND** ❹. On the right, the **Sanibel Captiva Conservation Foundation** is a worthwhile stop for its boardwalk trails over mangrove swamps. Also on the right a short distance ahead is the two-storey stucco-fronted building holding the **Bailey-Matthews Shell Museum**.

A further few minutes' drive reaches Dunlop Road on the left, leading to the **Sanibel Historical Village and Museum**. Return to Periwinkle Way and head east for 3.5 miles to the spindly **Sanibel Lighthouse**, adjacent to the welcoming **Sanibel Beach**.

Boat trips

To Cabbage Key $$
daily from South Seas Plantation, operated by Captiva Cruises; tel: (239) 472-5300; www.captivacruises.com; phone for times.

To Cayo Costa State Park $$ *from Pineland Marina, 13921 Waterfront Drive, Pineland, operated by* **Tropic Star**; *tel: (239) 283-0015; www.tropicstarcruises.com*

Retrace the route along Periwinkle Way for 1 mile to Causeway Boulevard, which leads to the 3.25-mile **toll bridge** to the mainland. The bridge brings spectacular views of San Carlos Bay and the densely concentrated mangrove forming the Matlacha Pass Wildlife Refuge. As it touches ground, Causeway Boulevard becomes MacGregor Boulevard which continues for 15 miles into the heart of **FORT MYERS** ❺ and is the site of the neighbouring **Edison** and **Ford Winter Homes**.

Detour: To reach **FORT MYERS BEACH** ❻ from the bridge, take Route 869 for 2.2 miles, turning south along San Carlos Boulevard; Estero Island is 3.5 miles ahead. The route continues for 6 miles through the commercialised beach strip before reaching the more peaceful **SAN CARLOS ISLAND** ❼.

Detour: Avoid the residential sprawl to the south of Fort Myers by driving 3.5 miles east from the Downtown area on Anderson Avenue (Route 82) to reach I-75, then head south for 14 miles, exiting westbound at the junction with Corkscrew Swamp Road. The **KORESHAN STATE HISTORIC SITE ❽** is 2.4 miles ahead, near the junction with Hwy-41.

Detour by boat: Without a vessel of your own, the only way to reach the divinely secluded **CAYO COSTA STATE PARK ❾** is by boat from Pineland, near the northern tip of Pine Island (*see below*).

Also worth exploring

An escape from both the urban development of Fort Myers and the trappings of mainstream tourism around the area's sandy beaches, **Pine Island** is sited between the mainland and the main barrier islands. Reach it from Fort Myers by crossing the Caloosahatchee River on Cleveland Avenue, after 2 miles turning left on Route 78. This continues for 15 miles and crosses the 'fishingest bridge in the USA' on to the island.

Almost entirely fringed by mangrove, the Pine Island economy revolves around fishing. Redfish, spotted seatrout and other species are regularly hooked from the many piers; tarpon and marlin are the main rewards for trips out to sea. Route 767 runs the length of Pine Island. Take it north to reach **Bokeelia**, departure point for boats to Cayo Costa State Park and also the site of a small museum recording local nature and history.

Tampa

Ratings

Children	●●●●
Museums	●●●●
Architecture	●●●
Crafts	●●●
Food	●●●
History	●●●
Nature	●●●
Theme parks	●●●

Tampa is the major city of Florida's west coast, and at first sight is large and uninteresting. Yet concealed within its urban sprawl, it has several neighbourhoods of great distinction that repay exploration by foot. Downtown Tampa showcases a fine mixture of old and new architecture and noteworthy attractions from the past, such as the 1890s luxury hotel built by Henry Plant whose railroad put Tampa on the map, and from the present with the splendid Florida Aquarium and an impressive art museum.

A few miles away, Ybor City was for decades a largely Spanish-speaking centre for cigar manufacture; its atmospheric streets are now revitalised with craft shops filling historic redbrick buildings. Further afield, Busch Gardens is a long-running and extremely popular theme park, where state-of-the-art roller-coaster rides vie for attention with elephants and lions. With the Museum of Science and Industry, Tampa has one of Florida's most technologically innovative and child-friendly institutions.

Sights

ⓘ Tampa Bay Visitor Information Center
Channelside, 1000 Channelside Drive; tel: (813) 223-2752; www.visittampabay.com. Open Mon–Sat 0930–1730, Sun 1100–1700.

Ybor City Information Center *1600 E 8th Avenue, Ybor City; tel: (813) 248-3712; www.ybor.org. Open Mon–Sat 1000–1800, Sun 1200–1800.*

Busch Gardens**

What began as a bird sanctuary in the grounds of the Anheuser-Busch brewery in the 1950s grew swiftly into the wildlife showcase of Busch Gardens, still among the biggest tourist attractions in Florida. Spread across 300 acres, the park divides into sections that replicate an African country or region with a combination of animals, thrills-and-spills rides and theatrical shows.

Major animal habitats include the 80-acre **Serengeti Plain**, where antelope, rhinos, giraffes, hippos and more can be spotted; **Myombe Reserve**, with gorillas and chimpanzees in a re-created tropical rain-forest complete with mist; **Claw Island**, inhabited by white and yellow Bengal tigers; and the **Elephant Habitat**, where Asian elephants dwell beside a water hole watched by humans from a raised viewing level.

Busch Gardens' reputation among roller-coaster devotees is well deserved. **Kumba** is one of the scariest such rides yet devised, reaching

Busch Gardens
& Museum of Science and Industry

E 13th Avenue

YBOR
CITY

Palm Avenue

E 8th Avenue

Ybor Square

José Martí Park

Seventh Avenue

Ybor City
Museum

Columbia
Restaurant

Tampa Street

Florida Avenue

N 18th Street

N 22nd Street

N 17th Street

Nick Nuccio Parkway

Crosstown Expresseway

Twiggs Street

N Marion St

Twiggs Street

Tampa Theatre

E Kennedy Boulevard

Jackson Street

S Meridian Street

N 12th Street

Ybor Channel

Ashley Ave

Hillsborough R

Tampa Museum of Art

Henry B
Plant Museum

W Kennedy Boulevard

TAMPA

Franklin Street Mall

Whiting Street

North Boulevard

Borein Street

De Park Avenue

Channelside Drive

Florida Aquarium

Tampa Bay
History Center

Crosstown Expressway

W Platt Street

Hyde Park

South Boulevard

Bayshore Boulevard

Davis Boulevard

Seddon Channel

Harbour Island

S Beneficial Drive

Sparkman Channel

Hillsborough
Bay

0   600m
0   600 yards

Busch Gardens $$$
*3000 E Busch Boulevard;
tel: (813) 987-5082 or (888)
800-5447;
www.buschgardens.com.
Open daily 0900–1800,
extended hours on holidays.*

**Columbia
Restaurant $$** *Corner
of 7th Avenue and 21st Street,
Ybor City; tel: (813) 248-4961;
www.columbiarestaurant.com*

City Hall *Corner of
Franklin Street and
Kennedy Boulevard.*

Sacred Heart Church
*Corner of Florida Avenue and
Twiggs Street; tel: (813) 229-
1595; www.sacredheartfla.org*

speeds of 60mph and heights of 140ft. Slightly less terrifying are the double-spiralled **Python** and the **Scorpion**, which includes a 60-ft drop. Similarly exciting are water rides such as **Congo River Rapids** and **Tanganyika Tidal Wave**, a jungle adventure culminating in a 55-ft drop over a waterfall. Calmer, infant-geared amusements fill the **Land of the Dragons** area.

Columbia Restaurant◆
Originating as a street corner café for Ybor City cigar-makers in 1905, the Colombia Restaurant grew into one of Tampa's most celebrated dining places (as well as the largest, filling an entire block). Note the exterior's exquisite tilework and peek inside for the displays recounting the Columbia's illustrious history. The Spanish cuisine, served by bow-tied waiters, is enlivened by flamenco dancing each evening.

Downtown Tampa◆
Dominated by modern high-rise offices and the people who work in them, Downtown Tampa occupies a compact area beside the Hillsborough River. The attractively pedestrianised Franklin Street, the Channelside complex, and prolific public art reflect the successful efforts to enhance the area, while abundant historical markers provide an easily followed guide to Tampa's past. Take a look at the pleasingly *beaux-arts* **City Hall**, dating from 1915 and the powerful Romanesque form of the 1905 **Sacred Heart Church**.

Below
Henry B Plant Museum

⓭ Florida Aquarium
$ *701 Channelside Drive; tel: (813) 273-4000; www.flaquarium.org. Open daily 0900–1700.*

Harbour Island *777 S Harbour Island Boulevard; tel: (813) 229-5324, events hotline tel: (813) 229-5000 or (800) 822-4200; www.wyndham.com*

Henry B Plant Museum
$ *401 W Kennedy Boulevard; tel: (831) 254-1891; www.plantmuseum.com. Open Tue–Sat 1000–1600, Sun 1200–1600.*

Hyde Park *Centred on Swann Avenue, between Bayshore Boulevard and Platt Street.*

Old Hyde Park Village, *Swann and Dakota Avenues; tel: (813) 251-3500; www.oldhydepark.com*

Florida Aquarium**

Inside a blue-green glass dome that makes the building resemble a gigantic shell, the $84 million Florida Aquarium showcases the natural wonders of the state's aquatic habitats and ecosystems. From freshwater springs and sawgrass marshes to cypress swamps and beaches, visitors tour the galleries symbolically following the progress of a single drop of water. On the way they encounter some of the 4000 species found in Florida, from tiny molluscs to ever-busy river otters.

The Florida Coral Reefs Gallery includes a simulated 60-ft dive to a piece of living coral, bringing close-up views of darting eels, prowling barracudas and colourful reef denizens such as the rainbow parrot fish. The extraordinary story of the coral's creation is cogently explained and a few of its weird and wonderful shapes displayed.

Harbour Island*

One of the many improvements to Downtown Tampa in the 1990s was the transformation of Harbour Island from disused cargo dock to site of luxury condominiums, a smart hotel and a shopping mall. Gift shops and boutiques make for amiable browsing in the mall, which also holds several restaurants and a food court; weekends and holidays bring free waterfront entertainment.

Henry B Plant Museum***

The Henry B Plant Museum, built by transport magnate Plant whose railroad reached Tampa in the 1880s and triggered the city's growth, occupies part of the former Tampa Bay Hotel, its distinctive Moorish minarets rising beside the Hillsborough River.

Opened in 1891, the 500-room hotel was the first building in Tampa with electricity and carried its guests through the grounds and along the quarter-mile-long lobby by rickshaw. In operation for just ten years, the hotel became neglected after Plant's death in 1899 and has been occupied by the University of Tampa since 1933.

One wing houses the museum where a remarkable stash of Wedgwood china, Florentine and Venetian mirrors, and all manner of antiques and statuary – gathered by Plant and his wife on a $500,000 shopping trip to Europe and Asia – indicate the opulence that hotel guests once enjoyed.

Hyde Park**

Hyde Park provides a welcome contrast to modern Tampa with several blocks of wood-framed and brick-built homes dating from the late 1800s to the 1920s. In styles ranging from Gothic and neo-classical to Mediterranean and Colonial, the homes were mostly built for the well-to-do settlers who arrived in Tampa as the city boomed following the arrival of Henry Plant's railroad and the opening of the Tampa Bay Hotel (*see Henry B Plant Museum, above*). A focal-point are the shops of **Old Hyde Park Village**.

José Martí Park
*Corner of 8th Avenue
and 13th Street, Ybor City.*

**Museum of Science and
Industry $$** *4801 E Fowler
Avenue; tel: (813) 987-
6300; www.mosi.org. Open
daily 0900–closing hours
vary.*

**Tampa Bay History
Center $** *225 S Franklin
Street; tel: (813) 228-0097;
www.tampabayhistorycenter.
org. Open Tue–Sat
1000–1700, closed
Sun–Mon.*

**Tampa Museum of Art
$** *600 N Ashley Drive;
tel: (813) 274-8130;
www. tampagov.net/
dept_museum. Open
Tue–Sat 1100–1700.*

Tampa Theatre
*711 Franklin Street;
tel: (831) 274-8286;
www.tampatheatre.org.
Guided tours ($) usually
twice monthly.*

On tree-lined streets with little traffic, the old homes, now among the most sought-after in the city, make for an enjoyable driving tour. The shops and restaurants of **Old Hyde Park Village** provide a weekend rendezvous for locals with free entertainment outside pricey shops and restaurants. As you leave, drive along **Bayshore Boulevard** which scenically skirts Tampa Bay.

José Martí Park✦
Revered Cuban poet and independence fighter José Martí frequently visited Cubans in the US to raise money for the struggle against Cuba's Spanish rulers. In Ybor City he addressed cigar workers from the steps of what is now Ybor Square. Many donated part of their earnings to buy the arms and ammunition that helped bring about Cuban independence in 1898. This small park bears a statue of Martí, hand outstretched in mid-oration.

Museum of Science and Industry✦✦
It may prove hard to tear young and inquisitive minds away from the innovative interactive and multimedia exhibits of this tremendous museum. Be it the workings of the human body, the life cycle of a butterfly, a simulated hurricane or the three-dimensional walk-through Florida postcard, the exhibits never fail to entertain and inform. Adjoining are a planetarium and an IMAX cinema where highly realistic films are projected on to a 10,500-sq-ft screen.

Tampa Bay History Center✦
A non-profit educational institution currently operating a history and heritage museum in Downtown Tampa. The museum takes you on a journey through Florida and US history, archaeology, folk life, artefacts and memorabilia.

Tampa Museum of Art✦✦
Dividing its energies and half its gallery space to temporary exhibitions, this highly regarded museum often attracts prestigious travelling shows. Space limits the amount that can be displayed from the permanent stock, which spans classical antiquities – including some treasured painted Greek vases – sculpture, photography, and modern painting from artists such as Jim Dine, Robert Rauschenberg and Frank Stella.

Tampa Theatre✦✦
The Tampa Theatre, completed in 1926, was heralded as 'the South's most beautiful theatre' when fashion dictated that cinema interiors should be as lavish and as fantastical as the films they screened. Inspired by the opera houses of Europe and intending the interior to resemble an outdoor auditorium, architect John Emberson hoped the audience would be enchanted by 'colonnades of graceful arches,

romantic balconies, the towers of ancient castles, and the mystical beauty of an old Spanish cathedral window'. Specially designed lighting and smoke machines create the illusion of stars and clouds passing across a night-time sky. The wonderfully restored interior can be admired at a film screening or on twice-monthly guided tours.

Right
Ybor City wall mural depicting the area in the 1920s

Ybor City◆◆◆

Ybor City (which covers just a few blocks despite its name) is a lively and historic corner of Tampa, filled with craft shops and studios. Its main streets are lined by brick buildings with decorative tilework and illuminated by five-globe street lamps.

The city takes its name from Don Vicente Martinez Ybor who in 1886 arrived in what was then a palmetto-covered scrubland and opened what would become the world's largest cigar factory, employing 4000 people. Most of the cigar workers were Cubans, a major component in what soon became a multiethnic community of 20,000 including Spanish, Italian, German and Jewish settlers. Ybor City gave birth to the country's first tri-lingual newspaper, *La Gaceta*, which continues to be published in Spanish, Italian and English.

The decline in the cigar industry led to the splintering of the local community and Ybor City became badly rundown. A revitalisation programme launched in the late 1980s bore great dividends, putting many of the historic buildings to fresh use and encouraging the plethora of new restaurants, bars and clubs that make Ybor City one of Tampa's busiest nightlife areas.

Ybor City Museum**

This small collection charts the rise of Ybor City and occupies the former Ferlita Bakery, opened here in 1923 when its original premises burnt down. Enormous bread ovens recall the bakery, while expanded photos depict the massed cigar workers in what is now Ybor Square (*see below*) and record the fundraising visits of José Martí (*see page 138*).

Other exhibits highlight the local community's ethnic mix and the decline in hand-rolled cigar consumption that signalled the demise of Ybor City. The tiny **Cigar Worker's Cottage** (the Casita) dates from 1895 and reveals much about the simple domestic arrangements experienced by Ybor City residents of the time.

ⓘ Ybor City Museum $ *1818 9th Avenue, Ybor City; tel: (813) 247-6323; www.ybormuseum.org. Open daily 0900–1700.*

◐ Ybor Square *1911 N 13th Street, Ybor City; tel: (813) 247-4497. Open Mon–Fri 1000–1800, Sat 1200–1730.*

Ybor Square*

The cigar factory that provided the focal point of life for 40 years to the 1930s is now Ybor Square, occupied by a variety of shops and eateries. Although the building is steeped in history, the only place where the aroma of tobacco lingers is at the small Tampa Rico Cigar Company on the first floor. Here, amid a wealth of smoking accessories and souvenirs, hand-rolled cigars are still made and sold.

Accommodation and food

Apart from a plethora of chain motels close to Busch Gardens and business-oriented chain hotels in Downtown, Tampa offers little attractively priced or well-located accommodation. It makes sense to visit the city as a day-trip from the St Petersburg area, to which there are good road links (avoid rush hours) and where there are many more overnight options.

Bernini $$–$$$ *1702 E 7th Avenue; tel: (813) 248 0099.* Pasta, pizza and more Italian fare in an elegant setting.

Blackhawk Coffee Cafe $–$$ *Old Hyde Park Village, 1628 W Snow Circle, Hyde Park; tel: (813) 258-1600; www.blackhawkcoffeecafe.com.* Makes much of serving coffee in real ceramic cups, as well as offering a range of other drinks and nibbles, and a wide selection of reading materials.

Columbia Restaurant $$ *2117 E 7th Avenue; tel: (813) 248-4961; www.columbiarestaurant.com.* Originating as a street corner café for Ybor cigar-makers, now one of Tampa's most celebrated dining places.

Don Vincente de Ybor Historic Inn $$ *1915 Republica de Cuba; tel: (813) 241-4545; www.donvicenteinn.com.* Occupying the 1895 building erected by the founder of Ybor City and offering plush one-bedroomed suites in a perfect location.

Gram's Place $–$$ *3109 Ola Avenue North; tel: (813) 221-0956; www.grams-inn-tampa.com.* A plain neighbourhood conceals this friendly

Above
Ybor Square cigar factory

bed-and-breakfast spot housed in two adjoining cottages and devoted to the memory and music of country-rock legend Gram Parsons.

Hilton Garden Inn $$–$$$ *1700 E 9th Avenue; Ybor City; tel: (813) 769-9267; www.hiltongardeninn.com.* Comfortable if slightly generic accommodations with high speed internet access included.

Old Hyde Park Village Farmers Market *Main Fountain Area, Hyde Park.* Every Saturday (0900–1400) these stalls are stacked with fresh fruit, vegetables, cheeses, breads and other local produce.

Wyndham Lodge Harbour Island Hotel $$$ *725 S Harbour Island Boulevard; tel: (813) 229-5000 or (800) 631-4200; www.wyndham.com.* Up-market option, complete with marina for boat-owning guests, adjacent to Harbour Island and within walking distance of Downtown Tampa.

Suggested tour

Length: Main route, 8 miles; Florida Aquarium detour 1.5 miles; Museum of Science and Industry 10 miles (from Downtown Tampa); Busch Gardens 10 miles (from Downtown Tampa).

Duration: Main route, 45 minutes driving time; Florida Aquarium detour 10 minutes driving time; Museum of Science and Industry and Busch Gardens each 20 minutes driving time from Downtown Tampa.

Links: Easily accessed by I-4 and I-275 and with the Tampa Crosstown Expressway connecting the city to I-75, Tampa links easily with St Petersburg and its beaches (*see pages 144–53*), Between Tampa and Orlando (*see pages 172–79*) and The Culture Coast (*see pages 162–71*).

Downtown Tampa and Ybor City, each best explored by foot but requiring a car to travel between them, and Hyde Park, form the main route. The Florida Aquarium is an easy detour from the Downtown route and a good location for kids. An extra day is required to do justice to the Museum of Science and Industry and Busch Gardens.

From the Fort Brooke Parking Garage, the People Mover monorail provides easy access to **HARBOUR ISLAND ❶**. In the other direction, walk along Franklin Street, taking in **TAMPA BAY HISTORY CENTER ❷**, into the heart of **DOWNTOWN TAMPA ❸**. Crossing Kennedy Boulevard reveals the elegant **City Hall ❹** on the right, architecturally holding its own amid glass and steel high-rises. Two blocks ahead, the forceful **Sacred Heart Church ❺** is to the right on Twiggs Street.

Continue on Franklin Street, crossing Zack Street for the **TAMPA THEATRE ❻** on the right. Return to Zack Street, turn right and walk two blocks to the Hillsborough River, passing the gleaming **Curtis Hixon Convention Center ❼** to reach the **TAMPA MUSEUM OF ART ❽**. Looming across the river is the unmistakable Moorish profile of the former Tampa Bay Hotel, now holding the **HENRY B PLANT MUSEUM ❾**; reach it by crossing the Kennedy Boulevard bridge.

Southwest of the museum lies **HYDE PARK ⑩**. This can be reached on foot, but if you are planning to continue to Ybor City, retrieve your car and use it to cruise the historic homes of Hyde Park. To reach **YBOR CITY ⑪**, take Cass Street which becomes Nuccio Boulevard. After 3 miles, turn right on to 8th Avenue and use the car park facing **YBOR SQUARE ⑫**. From elsewhere, reach the same destination by taking the Ybor City exit off I-4 on to 21st Street, turning right on Palm Avenue, and after four blocks, left on to 13th Street.

Facing Ybor Square across 8th Avenue is the small **JOSE MARTI PARK ⑬**. Walk east along 8th Avenue, passing numerous one-off shops, many of them outlets for locally based artisans (more line 7th Avenue). Go left on to 18th Street and, passing **Centennial Park ⑭**, right on to 9th Avenue for **YBOR CITY MUSEUM ⑮**. From the museum, walk two blocks south on 19th Street, turning left on to 7th Avenue where the **COLUMBIA RESTAURANT ⑯** fills the block between 21st and 22nd streets, greatly expanded since it opened in 1905 as a cigar workers' café.

Detour: On the western edge of Downtown Tampa, the **FLORIDA AQUARIUM ⑰** is a just over half-a-mile from the heart of Downtown Tampa; reach it along Channelside Drive from the southern end of Franklin Street. The route passes the new and expanding **Cruise Ship Terminal ⑱**.

Detour: Deep within the characterless urban sprawl that fills much of northern Tampa, **BUSCH GARDENS ⑲** are easily accessed from Downtown Tampa or Ybor City from I-275. Leave at Exit 33, heading east on to Busch Boulevard. The gardens are signposted 2 miles ahead.

Detour: A mile northeast of Busch Gardens, the **MUSEUM OF SCIENCE AND INDUSTRY ⑳** is accessed from Exit 34 off I-275, then heading east for 3 miles on Fowler Boulevard.

Also worth exploring

⊖ Hillsborough River State Park $ 20 miles northeast of Downtown Tampa, from I-4 take Exit 6 on to Hwy-301; the park entrance is on the left after 14 miles; tel: (813) 986-1020. Open daily 0800–sunset.

If the network of freeway interchanges engulfing Tampa makes the city seem too much of a metropolis, find a bucolic escape within the 3000-acre **Hillsborough River State Park**. The river from which the park takes its name forms dashing rapids as it passes over limestone outcrops; elsewhere in the park it becomes placid enough for boating. Nature trails pick through the park's swamplands and penetrate its hammocks of magnolia, bald cypress, live oak and sabal palm to reach shady picnic areas.

The park occupies the site of Fort Foster, built in 1837 as a base for US soldiers during the Second Seminole War. At weekends there are guided tours of the fort's reconstructed wooden buildings. A major battle between the soldiers and the Seminoles they came to subdue is enthusiastically re-enacted during March.

275

41

Busch Gardens ⑲
& Museum of Science and Industry ⑳

Florida Avenue

Tampa Street

E 13th Avenue

N 19th Street

4

E Palm Avenue

YBOR CITY ⑪

N 18th Street

N 22nd Street

Ybor Square ⑫

E 8th Avenue

⑮

Ybor City ⑭
Museum

José Martí Park ⑬

Seventh Avenue

⑯

Columbia
Restaurant

275

N 17th Street

Nick Nuccio Parkway

Crosstown Expressway

41

N Marion Street

Twiggs Street

Ybor Channel

Ashley Drive

⑥ Tampa Theatre

Twiggs Street

Hillsborough River

⑦

E Kennedy Boulevard

S Meridian Street

N 12th Street

⑧

⑤

Tampa Museum of Art

④

Jackson Street

Henry B
Plant Museum

⑨

Franklin Street Mall

Whiting Street

W Kennedy Boulevard

③

TAMPA

Borein Street

Channelside Drive

⑰ Florida Aquarium

S Hyde Park Avenue

② Tampa Bay
History Center

⑱

sstown Expressway

W Platt Street

South Boulevard

⑩

Hyde Park

① Harbour Island

S Beneficial Drive

Sparkman Channel

Bayshore Boulevard

Davis Boulevard

Seddon Channel

Hillsborough
Bay

0   600m

0   600 yards

St Petersburg and its beaches

Ratings

Beaches	●●●●●
Scenery	●●●●○
Arts and crafts	●●●○○
Boat trips	●●●○○
Children	●●●○○
History	●●●○○
Nature	●●●○○
Museums	●●○○○

Along the western edge of the Pinellas Peninsula, which divides Tampa Bay from the Gulf of Mexico, nature has sculptured a 25-mile string of barrier islands with idyllic beaches, soul-stirring sunsets and some of Florida's most benevolent weather with barely a cloud seen all year. Predictably the area is a major hit with international travellers and much is an unbroken line of hotels, motels, beachside bars and seafood restaurants.

Amid the commercialism, however, this route reveals sights to savour, ranging from a wild bird sanctuary to a luxury pink hotel of the 1920s. And with the seductively pristine Caladesi Island comes a glimpse of the area as it looked before the advent of package tourism. Across the peninsula from the beaches, St Petersburg is a town in the throes of upward mobility, evolving as a major centre for arts and culture as well as sheltering oddities in its midsts such as an ex-Soviet submarine.

CALADESI ISLAND STATE PARK✦✦✦

Caladesi Island State Park $
tel: (727) 469-5918;
www.floridastateparks.org/
caladesiisland. Open daily
0800–sunset; accessible by
boat only $ from Honeymoon
Island – operated by Caladesi
Connection; tel: (727) 734-
5263.

Beautifully unspoilt Caladesi Island, accessible only by boat, is a welcome reminder of how all of Florida's barrier islands looked before the dawn of mass tourism. From the mangrove-enshrouded landing stage, where a snack bar is a rare sign of human habitation, a short boardwalk trail runs to a usually deserted 2-mile-long white-sand beach. If shell collecting, sunbathing and swimming are not sufficient to pass the time, take the 2.5-mile nature trail cutting through the pine flatlands and oak hammocks amid the tall grasses of the island's interior.

CLEARWATER BEACH✦✦

Anchoring the northern end of an 18-mile string of holiday islands, Clearwater Beach has a friendly atmosphere, enjoyable restaurants and a cluster of nightspots. Small motels fill the side-streets while more expensive accommodation boasts enviable locations overlooking

ⓘ Clearwater Beach Information Center *1 Causeway Boulevard; tel: (727) 446-2424; www.clearwaterflorida.org. Open daily 1000–1800 or later.*

ⓗ Clearwater Marine Aquarium *$ 249 Windward Passage; tel: (727) 441-1790; www.cmaquarium.org. Open Mon–Fri 0900–1700, Sat 0900–1600, Sun 1100–1600.*

Captain Memo's Pirate Cruise *$$ from Clearwater Beach Marina; tel: (727) 446-2587; www.captmemo.com. Board a mock pirate vessel for swashbuckling treasure hunts and dolphin discovery trips.*

the Gulf. Although the main attraction is a very broad white-sand beach, Clearwater Beach is also a major departure point for short boat trips, such as sunset cruises and 'pirate' ships.

The commendable **Clear-water Marine Aquarium** rescues and rehabilitates injured marine mammals, sea turtles and river otters; it also has exhibits on Florida's coastal ecology, and tanks of stingrays and sharks.

Accommodation and food in Clearwater Beach

Clearwater Beach Hotel *$$–$$$ 500 Mandalay Avenue; tel: (727) 441-2425 or (800) 292-2295; www.clearwaterbeachhotel.com.* On the beach and a short walk from the heart of the town, one of the area's nicest and oldest, though fully modernised, places to stay.

EbbTide Suites *$$ 621 Bay Esplanade; tel: (727) 441-4121 or (800) 635-0620; email: ebbtide@gate.net; www.clearwaterbeachresorts.com.* Smallish suites equipped with kitchens.

Frenchy's Saltwater Café *$ 419 Poinsettia Avenue; tel: (727) 461-6295; www.frenchysonline.com.* Deservedly popular for its great-value seafood such as conch chowder and grilled grouper sandwiches. Success has spawned several local branches.

Tropical Breeze Motel *$–$$ 333 Hamden Drive; tel: (727) 442-6865 or (888) 530-1088; www.tropicalbreezeresort.com.* Clean and simple rooms in a good location. The motel also has its own fishing dock and a barbecue and picnic area.

Caladesi Island State Park

Clearwater Beach

Sand Key Park

Suncoast Bird Sanctuary

Ulmerton Road

John's Pass Village

Gulf of Mexico

Florida Holocaust Museum

The Pier

Museu of Fir Ar

Salvador Dali Museum

Don Cesar Resort

Pass-a-Grille

Fort de Soto Park

Fort Harrison Avenue

Gulf Boulevard

Eisenhower Boulevard

Old Tampa Bay

Tyrone Boulevard

66th Street N

Pinellas Bayway

DON CESAR RESORT✣✣

Don Cesar Resort
3400 Gulf Boulevard, St Pete Beach; tel: (727) 360-1881 or (866) 728-2206; www.doncesar.com

The unmistakable Don Cesar Resort, a large and intensely pink creation in concrete and stucco, looms beside Gulf Boulevard and occupies 7 beachfront acres. Raised in the 1920s for $1.5 million, this luxury hotel (known simply as 'the Don') attracted high-calibre guests such as Franklin Roosevelt and F Scott Fitzgerald in its short-lived heyday. The Depression heralded decades of neglect until the property was restored and re-opened in the 1970s.

Despite the marble fountains, Italian crystal chandeliers, French candelabra and Cuban tiles, the interior does not quite match the pizzazz of the Moorish-Mediterranean exterior. None the less, take a look inside this piece of local history and, if possible, join the illuminating guided tour for the full story on this remarkable edifice and Thomas Rawle, the Boston-born man who built it.

FORT DE SOTO PARK✣✣

Fort de Soto Park
Mullet Key; tel: (727) 582-2267; www.fortdesoto.com. Open daily dawn–dusk. Free.

In 1849, Robert E Lee, then an army engineer but later to find lasting fame as leader of the Confederate Army in the Civil War, recommended that Mullet Key, one of five small islands south of St Pete Beach, be fortified as part of Florida's coastal defences. Not until 50 years later during the Spanish-American War did Fort de Soto come into being. Used as a training base in the two world wars, the curious if rather paltry remains of the fort can be explored on a history trail, described in a free leaflet.

Today, the park is better known for its fabulous stretch of beach and plentiful palm-shaded picnic tables. The view across the mouth of Tampa Bay is a stunning one with passing freighters and the shimmering profile of the soaring Sunshine Skyway Bridge (*see The Culture Coast, pages 162–71*).

JOHN'S PASS VILLAGE✣

John's Pass Village
Madeira Beach; www.johnspass.com

John's Pass Village is a group of art galleries, clothing, jewellery and souvenir shops in intentionally ramshackle structures, loosely based on the fishing village established here from the 1870s. The unusual merchandise of many of the stores makes for amiable browsing. A fleet of pleasure boats and fishing charter vessels, and numerous restaurants, add to the appeal. One of the area's major events is the seafood festival held here each November.

Right
Great blue heron

PASS-A-GRILLE*

Gulf Beaches Historical Museum
115 10th Avenue; tel: (727) 552-1610. Open mid-May–mid-Sept Fri–Sat 1000–1600, Sun 1300–1600; rest of year Thur–Sat 1000–1600, Sun 1300–1600. Free.

Hurricane Seafood Restaurant $$ 807 Gulf Way, Pass-a-Grille; tel: (727) 360-9558; www.thehurricane.com. Delectable fish sandwiches are among the most ordered dishes in this enjoyable eatery.

At the southern tip of the barrier island chain, Pass-a-Grille is the only local beach community not dominated by tourists, motels and high-rise condominiums. The village began as a fishing settlement in the 1910s and still holds some of the dainty cottages of that time, along with the seafood eateries and bars that have been serving locals for years. The **Gulf Beaches Historical Museum** captures the homely mood with a modest but engaging run-down on local history. The quiet beach is a fine place to enjoy the sunset.

ST PETERSBURG**

St Petersburg Chamber of Commerce 100 2nd Avenue N; tel: (727) 821-4069; www.stpete.com. Open Mon–Fri 0830–1700.

Tampa Bay Beaches Chamber of Commerce 6990 Gulf Boulevard, St Pete Beach; tel: (727) 360-6957; www.tampabaybeaches.com. Open Mon–Fri 0900–1700.

Florida International Museum $$ 100 2nd Street; tel: (727) 822-3693; www.floridamuseum.org. Open Mon–Sat 1000–1700, Sun 1200–1700.

St Petersburg was once best known as one of the US's sunniest retirement communities, but during the last few years has beome an increasingly respected centre for the arts and has gained a younger population. Several new museums have joined the already established and well regarded Fine Arts and Salvador Dali museums.

Many new arrivals, employed in the area's expanding financial and service sector industries, are attracted to St Petersburg for its successful blend of old and new architecture, and the several miles of landscaped parks beside Tampa Bay.

Also overlooking the bay is the **Renaissance Vinoy Resort**, originally the Vinoy Park Hotel; for two decades following its 1925 opening it encouraged the rich and famous to winter in St Petersburg. President Calvin Cooleridge and baseball superstar Babe Ruth were just two early guests. Given a $93 million facelift after years of neglect, the hotel re-opened in 1992.

Almost two million people attended the first four exhibitions staged at the **Florida International Museum**, which opened in 1995 to show large-scale exhibitions from around the globe across 20,000ft of

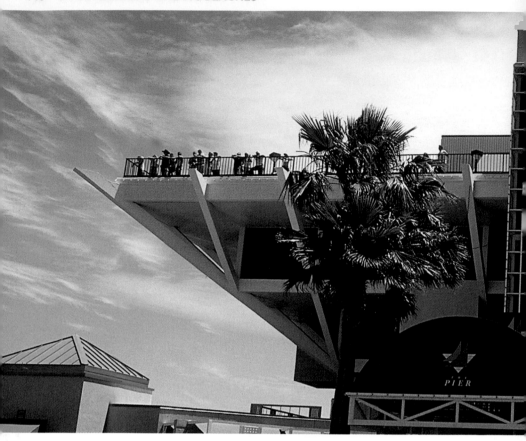

🛈 **The Pier** *Eastern foot
of 2nd Avenue; tel:*
(727) 821-6443;
*www.stpete-pier.com. Open
Mon–Thur 1000–2100,
Fri–Sat 1000–2200, Sun
1100–1900.*

**St Petersburg Museum
of History $**
*335 2nd Avenue NE; tel:
(727) 894-1052; www.
stpetemuseumofhistory.org.
Open Mon–Sat 1000–1700,
Sun 1300–1700.*

display space in a former department store. The first exhibition
displayed Romanov treasures borrowed from Moscow's Kremlin
museums; later ones have focused on the *Titanic*, Ancient Egypt,
Alexander the Great and the lost civilisations of Peru. To prevent
overcrowding, visitors must usually make a reservation ahead of arrival.

Resembling an upside-down pyramid, the **Pier**, actually the name
given to the building on the end of the half-mile-long pier itself, is the
most eye-catching object on the St Petersburg waterfront. The five-
storey-high structure is popular for its restaurants and small aquarium
and each evening makes a pleasant base to enjoy free entertainment
and the cool breezes crossing the bay.

Lined by jet-ski and boat rental stands, the approach to the Pier also
passes the **St Petersburg Museum of History** with its entertaining
accounts of local history from Native American finds to the story of
the world's first commercial airline flight, which took place here in
1914 when the mayor was flown to Tampa by airboat.

With its collections arranged in small galleries spread through the
ground floor of a Palladian-style villa, the **Museum of Fine Arts**

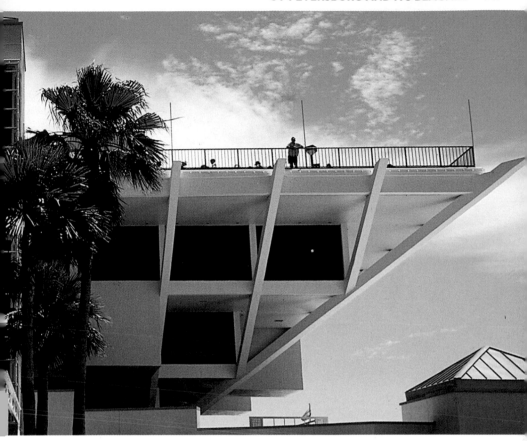

Above
The Pier, St Petersburg

Museum of Fine Art
255 Beach Drive NE;
tel: (727) 896-2667;
www.fine-arts.org. Open
Tue–Sat 1000–1700,
Sun 1300–1700.

**Florida Holocaust
Museum** 55 5th Street S;
tel: (727) 820-0100 or (800)
960-7448;
www.flholocaustmuseum.org.
Open Mon–Fri 1000–1700,
Sat–Sun 1200–1700.

creates an air of intimacy ideally suited for viewing the displayed art. The permanent collections include pre-Columbian, Native American and Asian artefacts but the museum wins most acclaim for its 19th- and 20th-century French and American paintings. The French art includes striking canvases by Cézanne, Gauguin, Daumier, Renoir, and Monet, whose *Houses of Parliament*, a shimmering depiction of a fogbound London, is the gem. The American art ranges from Whistler to Lichtenstein and includes several of Georgia O'Keeffe's close-up flower paintings, notably the powerful and vibrant *Poppy*.

In contrast to the happy-go-lucky holiday atmosphere that pervades St Petersburg, the **Florida Holocaust Museum** details the Nazi genocide against the Jews with an inevitably saddening collection of exhibits. These include a 15-ton boxcar used for transportation to concentration camps, inmates' art, and much more, including a much broader picture of anti-Semitism and intolerance through the ages.

The last thing most people expect to find in Florida is one of the world's most complete chronicles of the career of Spanish surrealist Salvador Dali, but with more than a thousand of the artist's works

Salvador Dali Museum $ *1000 3rd Street; tel: (727) 823-3767; www.salvadordalimuseum.org. Open Mon–Sat 0930–1730, Sun 1200–1730.*

from 1914 to 1980, the **Salvador Dali Museum** justifies such a description and opened in 1982 to house the collection amassed by a Cleveland industrialist who befriended Dali. The rotating permanent collection includes works such as *Daddy Longlegs of the Evening… Hope!* and *Slave Market with the Disappearing Bust of Voltaire*, featuring Dali's strange imagery and vividly coloured dream-like landscapes, rich in Freudian symbolism, that helped define surrealism from the 1940s for a mass audience (while purists dismissed Dali for his commercialism).

Intriguingly, the museum also shows some of Dali's early canvases, revealing his orthodox artistic skills while mimicking Impressionist and Cubist styles. By contrast, the culmination of Dali's career might be the monumental canvases, mostly created during the 1950s and 1960s and each at least a year in the making, such as *The Hallucinogenic Toreador* and *The Discovery of America by Christopher Columbus*, in which he grapples with major themes of history and religion, and lets his penchant for double images run wild.

Accommodation and food in St Petersburg

Although the bulk of the area's accommodation is concentrated at the beaches, St Petersburg has a growing number of viable options, usually less busy than its Gulf-side counterparts.

Dolphin Beach Resort $$ *4900 Gulf Boulevard, St Pete Beach; tel: (727) 360-7011 or (800) 237-8916; www.dolphinbeach.com.* A giant among the many small motels in the vicinity with 174 rooms and nightly entertainment in the cocktail lounge.

Mansion House $$ *105 5th Avenue NE, St Petersburg; tel: (727) 821-9391 or (800) 274-7520; www.mansionbandb.com.* Believed to have been the home of St Petersburg's first mayor, this offers six guest rooms – one with beamed ceiling and four-poster bed – and a full English breakfast.

Woody's Waterfront Café & Beach Bar $–$$ *738 Sunset Way, St Pete Beach; tel: (727) 360-9165.* Begun as a bait hut serving hot dogs to local fisherman and now offering seafood, burgers and steaks in an informal atmosphere. Live music most evenings.

Sand Key Park❖❖

Sand Key Park *1060 Gulf Boulevard; tel: (727) 595-7611. Open daily 0700–sunset. Donation.*

Among the scores of beachfront parks intended to prettify the Florida coast, few come bigger or better than Sand Key Park, 65 acres of dazzlingly white-sand beach fringed by greenery. Ranked among the best in the US, the beach stretches for 12 miles, its popular northernmost section evocatively flanked by tall palm trees.

SUNCOAST SEABIRD SANCTUARY✤

Suncoast Seabird Sanctuary *18328 Gulf Boulevard, Indian Shores; tel: (727) 391-6211; www.seabirdsanctuary.org. Open daily 0900–2100; guided tours Wed and 2nd, 3rd and 4th Sun of the month at 1400.*

The Suncoast Seabird Sanctuary began when a local zoologist found a broken-winged cormorant on Gulf Boulevard in 1971, and has grown into the US's largest wild-bird hospital. In various stages of recuperation, some 600 birds commonly injured by fishing lines or environmental pollution can be seen. Many are large brown pelicans, ubiquitous along the Gulf beaches, although herons and egrets are also plentiful. More exotic patients have included Arctic loons and peregrine falcons.

Right
Renaissance Vinoy Hotel,
St Petersburg

Suggested tour

The Lobster Pot
$$$ 17814 Gulf
Boulevard, Redington Shores;
tel: (727) 391-8592;
www.lobsterpotrestaurant.com.
Although serving many
varieties of seafood,
lobster cooked in a
multitude of styles draws
the crowds.

Length: Main tour, 20 miles. Add 8 miles to reach Downtown St Petersburg and 23 miles to tour Pass-a-Grille and Fort de Soto and return.

Duration: Main tour driving time, 1 hour. Allow a day to cover the main route and one detour; another half-day is necessary to cover all the detours. The Caladesi ferry runs twice-daily, allowing a maximum of 4 hours on the island.

Links: Tampa (*see pages 134–43*), The Nature Coast and rural Florida (*see pages 154–61*), The Culture Coast (*see pages 162–71*).

The main tour is a simple drive through the adjoining barrier island beach communities following the single road that links them. The remainder of the day should be spent on one or more of the coastal detours, venturing inland to St Petersburg, and exploring this bayside town on foot, or enjoying the seclusion of Caladesi Island.

Take any route to **CLEARWATER BEACH ①**. With its beckoning beach and abundance of hotels and motels, this provides a good introduction to the beach communities. Head south along Coronado Drive, which sweeps eastwards to cross the bridge on to the palm-lined **SAND KEY PARK ②**. Becoming Gulf Boulevard, the road continues for 3 miles, passing the tall condominiums of **Belleair Shores** and, 5 miles further, reaching **Indian Shores** where the **SUNCOAST SEABIRD SANCTUARY ③** is on the right, shortly after the junction with Park Boulevard.

For the next 5 miles the outlook is one of hotels, restaurants and slender pathways providing beach access as the route moves through undistinguished **Redington Beach** and into **Madeira Beach**, at the southern end of which is **JOHN'S PASS VILLAGE ④**. From Madeira Beach, a large concrete bridge carries Gulf Boulevard on to **Treasure Island**, boasting one of the area's nicest strands.

Ten miles on, the route passes through the highly developed centre of **St Pete Beach** (formerly called St Petersburg Beach, the name some signs continue to use) before encountering the **DON CESAR RESORT ⑤**, rising mirage-like beside the beach.

Boat trips

Dolphin Landings $$
4737 Gulf Boulevard,
St Pete Beach;
tel: (727) 360-7411;
www.dolphinlandings.com.
Sunset cruises and
dolphin-watching
excursions.

Detour: City Beach Marina, on the south side of Route 60 on the bay side of Clearwater Beach, is the local departure point for the ferry to **CALADESI ISLAND STATE PARK ⑥**. Take a picnic lunch and spend several blissful hours at this pristine spot.

Detour: From the Don Cesar Resort, Pass-a-Grille Road continues south into the largely residential **PASS-A-GRILLE ⑦**, a contrast to the more touristed beach areas. The **Gulf Beaches Historical Museum** is found by turning right along 10th Avenue. From the museum, return to the Don

Great Explorations $$ *1925 4th Street; tel: (727) 821-8992; www.greatexplorations.org. Open Mon–Sat 1000–1630, Sun 1200–1630.*

Cesar Resort and turn right on to Pinellas Bay South (toll), continuing for 1.5 miles before swinging right across a series of slender islands and, after 6.6 miles, reaching the junction with Anderson Boulevard. Turn right here and continue for 1.5 miles to **FORT DE SOTO PARK ❽** and a winning outlook across Tampa Bay.

Detour: The most direct route to St Petersburg from the beaches is Route 150, which leaves Gulf Boulevard at Treasure Island, becoming Central Avenue as it crosses the Pinellas Peninsula and, after 8 miles, reaching Downtown St Petersburg.

The Downtown area is best seen on foot. At the end of an extended causeway running from 2nd Avenue is **The Pier**. At the pier's foot is the **St Petersburg Museum of History**. A few steps north is the **Museum of Fine Arts**, a few blocks west, the **Florida Holocaust Museum**, while the extravagant **Renaissance Vinoy Resort** can be spotted on the north side of the yacht marina.

Walking inland along 2nd Avenue for three blocks you reach the **Florida International Museum**. A mile south along Fourth Street N is **Great Explorations**, an enjoyable museum of hands-on exhibits aimed at kids. A block east is the outstanding **Salvador Dali Museum**.

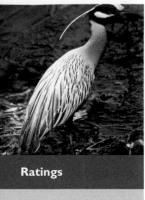

The Nature Coast and rural Florida

Ratings

Nature	●●●●●
Arts and crafts	●●●○○
Boat trips	●●●○○
Geology	●●●○○
History	●●●○○
Museums	●●●○○
Scenery	●●●○○
Children	●●○○○

Freshwater springs, sinkholes, nature refuges and thoroughbred horse farms all feature in the Nature Coast, where sandy beaches and hi-tech theme parks are conspicuous by their absence. Instead, the land meets the sea in a vast expanse of mangrove and marshlands, and quiet coastal roads terminate at pocket-sized communities that seldom see a visitor. The region also holds two of Florida's oldest tourist attractions: the dancing mermaids of Weeki Wachee and the glass-bottomed boat trips at Silver Springs.

Linking the larger coastal towns, the tour takes in Tarpon Springs, evolved from a community of Greek sponge divers, Crystal River, renowned for its frequently seen manatees, and Cedar Key, a secluded island settlement and one of Florida's most attractive off-the-beaten-track communities. Inland, the route explores rural central Florida, including the university town of Gainesville, and Ocala, set amid the pastoral surrounds that have raised some of the nation's champion racehorses.

CEDAR KEY✧✧✧

ⓘ Cedar Key Historical Society Museum $ *609 2nd Street; tel: (352) 543-5549; www.floridastateparks.org/ cedarkeymuseum. Open Mon–Sat 1100–1600, Sun 1400–1600.*

Cedar Key State Museum $ *12231 SW166 Court; tel: (352) 543-5350. Open Thur–Mon 0900–1700.*

ⓧ The Captain's Table $–$$ *Dock Street; tel: (352) 543-5441. On stilts this spot is ideal for sampling local favourites.*

With timber-framed, tin-roofed buildings and sidewalks overhung by wooden balconies, Cedar Key is a picture of a bygone Florida. A century ago it was a thriving port with an important railway line and regular boat connections to New Orleans, Key West and Cuba. By contrast, the local pace today is slow and relaxed. Among a population of several hundred attracted to live here by the easy-going atmosphere and laid-back pace are numerous artists whose work is displayed in local craft shops and art galleries. Others here earn a living from the sea, harvesting crabs and oysters or running boat trips to the **Cedar Key Wildlife Refuge**, a group of tiny islands providing nesting grounds for ospreys, pelicans and other species.

To emphasise its past importance, Cedar Key has two historical collections: the **Cedar Key Historical Society Museum** and the smaller **Cedar Key State Museum**, both tracing the 19th-century heyday of the town. The latter boasts an immense shell collection, illustrating the huge variety of exotic shells to be found in the region.

DIXIE

High Springs Station Mus.
340 Bell 7 78 ALACHUA Keystone Hts.
Alachua 15 441 Waldo Florahome
232 17 Fairbanks 225 14 24
129 47 22 San Felasco Hammock St. Pres. 441 26 Orange Hts. Putnam Hall
351 Wannee Newberry 222 76 Gainesville Reg. Arpt. 16 PUTNAM
Shamrock 26 26 26
Cross City Old Town Trenton 337 Univ. of Florida Arredondo 75 6 Gainesville 21 30 20 Interlachen Ravine St. Garde
Fann Spri. ALT 27 Rochelle 16 Hawthorne 21 Kenwood
357 Manatee Springs S.P. 320 15 Chiefland 27 41 Paynes Prairie St. Pres. 301 Lochloosa
347 339 Archer 8 R 74 Micanopy 18 Island Grove 315 Oklawaha Lake
Shired Island 347 Bronson Raleigh 17 McIntosh 73 Citra
349 13 Williston 318 72 Orange Lake M. K. Rawlings S.H.S.
Suwannee 336 12 316 Reddick 32 Fort McCoy OCALA
345 Ellzey 337 121 Montbrook Spar. 316 NATIONAL
LOWER SUWANNEE NATIONAL WILDLIFE REFUGE 326 Otter Cr. 41 MARION 11 75 Anthony Silver Sprs. FOREST
Cedar Key Scrub St. Res. Gulf Hammock 326 Morriston 71 Kendrick Silver Springs & Wild Waters Lynne
Cedar Key St. Museum 24 326 LEVY 14 GOETHE ST. FOR. Romeo 25 27 Martel 70 Ocala 35
Cedar Keys Waccasassa Bay 337 328 69 68 Santos Belleview Ocklawaha 27 441
CEDAR KEYS N.W.R. Lebanon 41 40 Westwood Acres 5 Eastlake Weir
19 98 336 Dunnellon Springs S.P. 484 200 R Lady Lake
Inglis 40 488 26 Marion Oaks 67 Pedro 42 Summerfield 31 Weirsdale L. Griffin S.R.A.
Yankeetown 495 Citrus Sprs. 41 Holder 21 Dallas Oxford 301
Beverly Hills Hernando 19 475 66 Wildwood S 8 Leesburg
Crystal River St. Arch. Site Crystal River N.W.R. 44 CITRUS 470 309 304 Coleman 14
Crystal River Lecanto 44 Inverness Port Cooper Sumterville SUMTER 48
Homosassa Springs 490 491 18 C.R. Lake Panasoffkee 64 Center Hill 48
Homosassa Springs St. Wildlife Park WITHLACOOCHEE ST. FOR. Floral City 41 26 Bushnell 33 6
Homosassa McKethan Lake Rec. Area Pineola 63 St. Catherine Minneola
Yulee Sugar Mill Ruins S.H.S. 98 Istachatta 48 476 Dade Battlefield S.H.S.
Chassahowitzka 15 HERNANDO Nobleton R 62 Webster
CHASSAHOWITZKA N.W.R. Brooksville 21 Ridge Manor 50 21 WITHLACOOCHEE
Weeki Wachee Gardens 10 Spring Lake 61 5 Trilby ST. FOR.
Bayport 50 Weeki Wachee 98 575 Lacoochee 471
Weeki Wachee Springs and Buccaneer Bay 574 19 Masaryktown 541 575
Hernando Beach Spring Hill 581 15 60 Blanton
Aripeka 17 41 San Antonio 75 Pioneer Florida Mus.
Hudson 19 Gowers Corner PASCO 59 9 San
Bayonet Point 52 11 Pasco St. Dade City
Jasmine Estates 12 583 Leo Coll. 301 Richland
Port Richey Trinity Coll. of Florida 12 58 Wesley Chapel Zimberton 54 98
New Port Richey 10 Elfers Land O Lakes 27 Betmar Acres Zephyrhills
Anclote Key St. Preserve 54 Denham Crystal Sprs. 33
Tarpon Sprs. Holiday Odessa R R 13 Providence Gibsonia
Palm Harbor Lutz 57 Kathleen 22
GULF OF MEXICO 597 12 Thonotosassa 39 16 Auburndale
Oldsmar 589 275 Plant City Lakeland
Dunedin 19 Safety Harbor Tampa 4 12 13 10 16 Winston Eaton Park Highland City
Clearwater PINELLAS Dover 14 Medulla 18 37
Belleair Beach Larg 92 Brandon

GULF OF MEXICO

0 10 20 miles
0 10 20km

CRYSTAL RIVER NATIONAL WILDLIFE REFUGE❖

Ⓜ Crystal River National Wildlife Refuge tel: (352) 563-2088; www.crystalriver.fws.gov. Open Mon–Fri 0730–1600. Free.

Almost transparent warm spring water makes this offshore refuge a good place to see manatees, which congregate here during the winter. The bulbous, 10-ft-long creatures, one of Florida's most loved but endangered creatures, can be admired from a boat, though it is permitted to swim, snorkel and scuba dive. Boat trips and guided dives are readily available in the area.

CRYSTAL RIVER STATE ARCHAEOLOGICAL SITE❖❖

ⓘ Citrus County Chamber of Commerce 28 NW Highway 19, Crystal River; tel: (352) 795-3149; www.citruscountychamber.com. Open Mon–Thur 0830–1700, Fri 0830–1600.

Ⓜ Crystal River State Archaeological Site $ 3400 N Museum Point Road; tel: (352) 795-3817; www.floridastateparks. org/crystalriver. Open daily 0900–1700.

Native Americans are believed to have occupied islands in the Crystal River area from 200 BC and to have buried their dead at this 14-acre site where burial mounds, temple mounds and midden mounds (built from the discarded shells of the seafood that underpinned the native diet) remain.

The story of the mounds, the largest 235ft long, and finds such as arrowheads and tools, are documented at the visitors' centre. Curiously, much less is known about the site's two ceremonial stones believed to have been used in solar rituals. Their similarity to stones found in Central America has prompted speculation on local links with the ancient people of Mexico's Yucatan Peninsula and on native skills in long-distance boat travel.

GAINESVILLE❖

ⓘ Alachua County Visitors & Convention Bureau 30 E University Avenue; tel: (352) 374-5231 or (866) 778-5002; www.visitgainesville.net. Open Mon–Fri 0830–1700.

The University of Florida and its 40,000 students bring a youthful and energetic air to the rural town of Gainesville. The university is the oldest in the state, dating from 1853, and its 2000-acre campus holds several museums including the **Florida Museum of Natural History** (University of Florida; tel: (352) 392-1721. Open Mon–Sat 1000–1700, Sun 1300–1700) with a plethora of fossils, mounted butterflies and insects, and displays on Florida ecosystems. Gainesville itself has many streets lined by graceful live oaks and a well-tended **historic area** with elegant homes from the late 1800s.

MANATEE SPRINGS STATE PARK❖

Ⓜ Manatee Springs State Park $ near Chiefland; tel: (352) 493-6072; www.floridastateparks.org/ manateesprings. Open daily 0800–sunset.

The first-magnitude natural spring that gives this park its name is among the most powerful of Florida's 320 springs, daily issuing 117 millions gallons of crystal-clear water. The result is a fascinating ecosystem, which can be studied at close hand as a boardwalk weaves through the park's cypress and maple tree-lined swamps bringing occasional views of wading birds, alligators and bald eagles.

OCALA✧

ⓘ Ocala-Marion Chamber of Commerce *110 E Silver Springs Boulevard; tel: (352) 629-8051; www.ocalacc.com. Open Mon–Fri 0830–1700.*

ⓜ Appleton Museum of Art $ *4333 NE Silver Springs Boulevard; tel: (352) 236-7100; www.appletonmuseum.org. Open Tue–Sun 1000–1800.*

Don Garlits Museum of Drag Racing $ *13700 SW 16th Avenue; tel: (352) 245-8661; www.garlits.com. Open daily 0900–1700.*

ⓒ Seven Sisters Inn $$–$$$ *820 SE King Street; tel: (352) 867-1170 or (800) 250-3469; email: sevensistersinn@msn.com; www.7sistersinn.com.* Handsome bed-and-breakfast inn with beautifully furnished rooms in an 1888 house.

Ⓗ Horse Farm Tours: Florida Thoroughbred Breeders and Owners Association *4727 NW 80th Avenue; tel: (352) 629-2160; www.ftboa.com.* Many of the horse farms in the Ocala area open their doors for free tours at a particular time each week. Details can be checked with the above, as well as with the local Chamber of Commerce.

Ocala's thoroughbred horse industry became established in the 1950s following the success of the locally bred Needles in the Kentucky Derby and Belmont Stakes. The undulating pastures on the northwestern outskirts of Ocala hold 600 breeding and training farms employing 25,000 people on plots from 10 to 5000 acres; many of them welcome visitors.

Ocala itself is a place of quiet streets and quieter lifestyles. In this unlikely setting is the $8.5 million **Appleton Museum of Art**, a repository of cultural treasures that would not be misplaced in a major city. The marble-clad museum's stash spans classical antiquities, pre-Columbian art, Asian arts and crafts, and has a floor devoted to 18th- and 19th-century European art.

By contrast, Ocala's other major historical collection is the **Don Garlits Museum of Drag Racing**, where trophies, posters, press cuttings and the ultra-sleek drag cars themselves chart the rise of drag racing from humble origins in 1930s California to one of the US's most popular forms of motor sport.

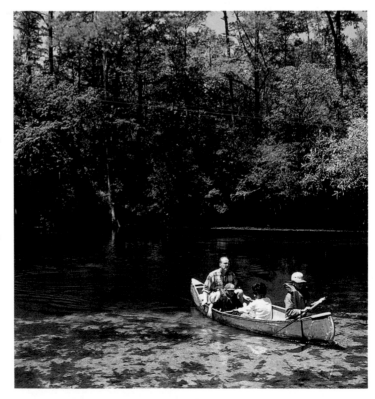

PAYNES PRAIRIE STATE PRESERVE✤✤

ⓘ Paynes Prairie State Preserve $
Near Micanopy; tel: (352) 466-3397; www.floridastateparks.org/ paynesprairie. Open daily 0800–sunset.

Anyone who thinks the Everglades are Florida's wildest place should reserve judgement until they have seen Paynes Prairie State Preserve, a 20,000-acre expanse of swamp, hammocks, pinelands, ponds, sinkholes and prairie that is simultaneously forbidding and compelling. Sandhill cranes, eagles and hawks, wading birds, alligators and otters are among the creatures that thrive in these varied habitats. Follow a short trail to an observation tower for the best viewing point.

SILVER SPRINGS✤✤

ⓘ Silver Springs $$
5656 E Silver Springs Road; Ocala; tel: (352) 236-2121; www.silversprings.com

Silver Springs was one of Florida's earliest tourist attractions, drawing northerners in the late 1800s to view the natural springs, palms and live oaks hung with Spanish moss. Much of the town looks just as good today, even though the original park has expanded to a themed complex with animal shows and various jeep and boat 'safaris', and 'jungle cruises' venturing into the 350-acre site to view an imported population of zebra, deer, emu, ostrich, giraffe and gibbon, as well as many native alligators. There are excellent narrated glass-bottomed boat trips to several of the springs.

TARPON SPRINGS✤✤✤

ⓘ Tarpon Springs Cultural Center,
101 S Pinellas Avenue; tel: (727) 942-3540. Open Mon–Fri 0800–1700, Sat 1000–1700. Free.

St Nicolas Greek Orthodox Cathedral
36 N Pinellas Avenue; tel: (727) 937-3540; www.epiphanycity.org. Open daily 0800–1600.

Settled by Greek sponge divers in the early 1900s, Tarpon Springs became and remains a predominantly Greek community even though the sponge-diving trade was effectively ended by increased production of synthetic sponges. Greek food, music and souvenirs are sold at the tourist-orienated shops lining Dodecanese Boulevard, adjacent to the **sponge docks** where boats carry visitors to re-created sponge dives. The techniques and history of the local sponge trade are documented in the **Tarpon Springs Cultural Center**.

The rest of Tarpon Springs is much less crowded and boasts the resplendent Byzantine Revival **St Nicolas Greek Orthodox Cathedral,** starting point of the US's biggest Epiphany procession and holding an allegedly weeping icon of St Nicolas.

WEEKI WACHEE SPRINGS✤

ⓘ Weeki Wachee Springs $$ *Hwy-19; tel: (352) 596-206; www.weekiwachee.com. Open daily 0930–1730. Shorter hours in winter.*

At Weeki Wachee Springs, built around a freshwater spring, mermaids perform choreographed underwater dances. The Wilderness River Cruise passes through a typically Floridian landscape populated by otters, racoons and wood storks, to a pelican reserve where injured seabirds are brought back to health.

YULEE SUGAR MILL RUINS STATE HISTORIC PARK❖

Yulee Sugar Mill Ruins State Historic Park $ *Route 490, near Homosassa; tel: (352) 795-3817; www.floridastateparks.org/ yuleesugarmill. Open daily 0800–sunset.*

Ruined limestone buildings are all that remain of the 5100-acre sugar plantation that thrived here in the 1850s. Worked by a thousand slaves, the plantation belonged to David Yulee, Florida's first member of Congress and a founder of the trans-Florida railway which carried goods between the Atlantic and Gulf coasts.

Suggested tour

Buccaneer Bay $$ *Hwy-19 near Weeki Wachee; tel: (352) 596-2062. Open late-Mar–Labor Day, daily 1000–1700 or later.*

Length: 168 miles, 258 miles with detours.

Duration: The main tour can be covered in 6–8 hours, but allow two days to take in the detours and spend time in deserving small towns.

Links: Tarpon Springs is 16 miles north of Clearwater Beach, making for a simple connection via Alt Hwy-19 with St Petersburg and its beaches (*see pages 144–53*).

Alt Hwy-19 provides a main route through **TARPON SPRINGS** ❶; the sponge docks are a short distance west on Dodecanese Boulevard. Continuing north, Alt Hwy-19 joins Hwy-19 3.6 miles from Tarpon Springs and passes several condominium communities before the high-rises give way to the forests that dominate the view on both sides of a very straight road.

Manatees

One of the delights of natural Florida is the West Indian manatee (also known as the sea cow on account of its fondness for aquatic grasses and plants), found in the state's warm and shallow coastal waters, rivers and springs. Despite resembling a bloated seal, the manatee, which can reach 14ft in length and typically weighs around 1000lb, has a gentle manner and moves gracefully through the water. Florida manatees, though protected since colonial times, are facing extinction largely due to human impact on the environment.

Twenty-six miles from Tarpon Springs, the junction with Route 50 finds the neighbouring attractions of **WEEKI WACHEE SPRINGS** ❷ and **Buccaneer Bay**, a water park built around one of the area's freshwater springs.

Continuing north on Hwy-19 for 24 miles, Route 490 branches to the left. This route reaches the entry point for **Homosassa Springs State Wildlife Park** and passes the **YULEE SUGAR MILL RUINS STATE HISTORIC PARK** ❸ before continuing into the small town of **Homosassa**. Sugar mill owner David Yulee brought short-lived prosperity to the tiny but attractive Homosassa in the 1800s, extending his cross-Florida railway here from Cedar Key.

Returning to Hwy-19, **Crystal River** is 9 miles north. Turn left along Route 44 and wind around Kings Bay, departure point for trips to **CRYSTAL RIVER NATIONAL WILDLIFE REFUGE** ❹. Returning to Hwy-19, the signposted turning for **CRYSTAL RIVER STATE ARCHAEOLOGICAL SITE** ❺ is 4 miles north, the site enjoying a tranquil setting on the north bank of the Crystal River.

Hwy-19 continues for 8.5 miles before crossing the **Florida Barge Canal**, a relic of an ill-fated attempt to provide a coast-to-coast transport route, and bends to the right at **Inglis**, marking the junction with Route 40.

**ⓘ Devil's Millhopper
State Geological
Site** $ *4732 NW 53rd
Avenue, Gainesville; tel:
(352) 336-2008;
www.floridastateparks.org/
devilsmillhopper. Open daily
0800–sunset.*

**☾ Magnolia
Plantation Bed and
Breakfast Inn** $$
*309 SE 7th Street;
tel: (352) 375-6653;
www.magnoliabnb.com.
Every room is named for a
tree in this quiet, antique-
filled house dating from
1885.*

The Grady House $$
*420 NW 1st Avenue, High
Springs; tel: (904) 454-
2206; www.gradyhouse.com.
It's well worth continuing
20 miles north from
Gainesville for this
excellent bed-and-
breakfast inn, where the
rooms are cosy and the
owners are a great source
of local knowledge.*

ⓘ The Sovereign $$$
*12 SE 2nd Avenue;
tel: (352) 378-6307;
www.sovereign-
restaurant.com. Eclectic
but always outstanding
American cuisine made
more enjoyable by the
setting, a converted barn.*

Venture along Route 40 on any weekend and the marinas around the small town of **Yankeetown** will be lined by the pick-up trucks of local fisherman.

Twenty-one miles north of Inglis, Hwy-19 meets Route 24. Turn right and head east for 36 miles to reach **GAINESVILLE ❻**. A few miles west of Gainesville, I-75 provides a speedy link to **OCALA ❼**, 30 miles south. Eight miles east of Ocala on Silver Springs Boulevard is **SILVER SPRINGS ❽**.

Detour: Turning left off Hwy-19 on to Route 24 leads for 21 miles through the marshlands of **Waccasassa State Preserve** before reaching the coast and crossing on to the island holding **CEDAR KEY ❾**. The only route out of Cedar Key is the one you arrived on, but after 9 miles turn left on to Route 345 to **Chiefland**, 19.5 miles ahead. Briefly re-join Hwy-19 before taking Route 320 west for 7 miles to **MANATEE SPRINGS STATE PARK ❿**.

Detour: With time in hand, travel south from Gainesville toward Ocala on the slower but more scenic Hwy-441. This passes through the moody landscapes of **PAYNES PRAIRIE STATE PRESERVE ⓫**, its main entrance on the left, 7.5 miles from Gainesville. About 4.5 miles ahead, Route 25A leads to **MICANOPY ⓬**. Like **McIntosh**, 5 miles further south on Hwy-441, Micanopy is a small town with several 19th-century buildings now holding antique shops. Continuing south for 17 miles, the route passes through the calcium-enriched pastures of the thoroughbred horse farms north of Ocala.

Detour: This detour from a detour can be joined from Hwy-441, close to Micanopy. Travel 10 miles east on Route 346 and turn right at the junction with Route 325, reaching **Cross Creek** after 3.5 miles. The home of Marjorie Kinnan Rawlings is signposted. Leave Cross Creek heading south on Route 325, after 4.8 miles turning right on to Hwy-301 and re-joining Hwy-441 9.2 miles further.

Also worth exploring

Jumping into one of the many natural springs is one way to cool off in this part of Florida, another is by descending into the **Devil's Millhopper**, a 120-ft-deep sinkhole 7 miles north of Gainesville. Caused by rainwater eroding underground limestone deposits, forming a cavern and eventually causing the roof to fall in, sinkholes are common in Florida – around 400 new ones appear annually – but this is among the largest, its story detailed by a short video shown at the visitors' centre. A wooden walkway and staircase provides access to the sinkhole's depths, where the temperatures are markedly lower than at the surface and the vegetation resembles that commonly seen in cooler, northerly regions.

ALACHUA

High Springs
Station Mus.
340
Bell GILCHRIST
Alachua
441
Fairbanks
225 24
Waldo
Keystone
Hts.
Florahome

DIXIE
232
Wannee
129
47
San Felasco
Hammock St. Pres.
222
26
16
Gainesville
Reg. Arpt.
Putnam
Hall
PUTNAM

351
Shamrock
Old
Town
Newberry
26
26
Univ. of Florida
Arredondo
Gainesville
21 30
20
Campville
Interlachen
Ravine St. C

Cross
City
Trenton
337
75
Gainesville
Rochelle 16
Hawthorne
301
21
Kenwood

Fanning
Springs
339
27
41
R
74
Paynes Prairie
St. Pres.
Lochloosa

ALT
27
15
Archer
121
Micanopy
18
Island
Grove
315

357
10
320
Chiefland
24
8
McIntosh
Citra
Oklawaha
lake

Shired
Island
347
Bronson
Raleigh
Williston
318
Orange Lake
M. K.
Rawlings
S.H.S.
316
Fort
McCoy
OCA

349
336
12
12
41
Reddick
Sparr
MARION

Suwannee
347
Ellzey
Otter Cr.
337
121
Montbrook
32
75
Anthony
Silver
Sprs.
NATIO
FORE

LOWER
NATIONAL
WILDLIFE
REFUGE
345
Rosewood
326
Cedar Key
Scrub St. Res.
326
Morriston
326
25
27
Kendrick
200A
8
35
Lynne

326
24
21
Gulf
Hammock
14
Romeo
328
Martel
70
71
7
Silver
Springs
& Wild
Waters

Cedar Key
St. Museum
Cedar Keys
9
Waccasassa St. Pres.
Lebanon
337
69
68
Ocala
Santos
475

CEDAR KEYS
N.W.R.
Cedar
Key
Waccasassa
Bay
GOETHE
ST. FOR.
40
Westwood
Acres
200
R
Belleview

Inglis
40
336
Dunnellon
41
Springs S.P.
484
R
27
441
Ocklawaha

GULF
Yankeetown
488
Citrus
Sprs.
26
Marion
Oaks
67
Pedro
475
301
Eastlake Wei

495
41
Holder
21
Dallas
42
Summerfield
Weirsdale

OF
21
5
Beverly Hills
Hernando
19
475
301
Wildwood
Lady Lake
L. Griffi
S.R.A

Crystal River St. Arch. Site
Crystal River N.W.R.
4
44
CITRUS
44
Inverness
Lake
470
309
66
S
Leesburg

MEXICO
Crystal River
Lecanto
18
491
Panasoffkee
Coleman
S
14

Homosassa Springs
490
Ft Cooper
41
Sumterville
471
48
33

Homosassa Springs St. Wildlife Park
Homosassa
3
WITHLACOOCHEE
ST. FOR.
Floral City
McKethan
Lake
Rec. Area
Pineola
48
63
SUMTER
Bushnell
Center
Hill
Minneola

Yulee Sugar Mill Ruins S.H.S.
Chassahowitzka
98
Istachatta
476
Dade Battlefield
S.H.S.
Webster
6

CHASSAHOWITZKA
N.W.R.
HERNANDO
15
Nobleton
R
St. Catherine
21

Weeki Wachee Gardens
Bayport
2
Brooksville
10
98
Ridge
Manor
50
21

Weeki Wachee Springs and Buccaneer Bay
13
50
Weeki Wachee
Spring
Lake
61
Trilby
575
Lacoochee
471
WITHLACOOCHEE
ST. FOR.

Hernando Beach
Spring Hill
574
19
541
Masaryktown
575
10

Aripeka
19
41
581
75
Blanton
Pioneer Florida Mus.

Hudson
Gowers
Corner
60
San
Antonio
Dade City

Bayonet Point
52
11
583
Pasco
St.
Leo Coll.
301
Richland
Lumberton
54
98
33

Jasmine Estates
Port Richey
Trinity
Coll. of
Florida
9
Wesley
Chapel
Zephyrhills
Crystal Sprs.
Providence

New Port Richey
Elfers
Land O'
Lakes
27
Betmar
Acres
Kathleen
22
Gibsonia

Anclote Key St. Preserve
54
Denham
R
R
13
Auburndale

Tarpon Sprs.
1
Holiday
Odessa
Lutz
57
Crystal Sprs.
10 16

Harbor
16
597
275
Thonotosassa
39
10 16
471

0 10 20 miles
0 10 20km
Oldsmar
15
589
4
Winston
Lakeland
Eaton Park
Highland
City

Dunedin
Clearwater
19
Safety
Harbor
Tampa
60
Dover
Plant
City
Medulla
16

PINELLAS

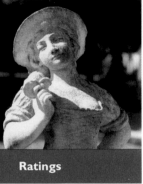

The Culture Coast

Ratings

Beaches	●●●●●
Nature	●●●●●
Art	●●●○○
Children	●●●○○
History	●●●○○
Scenery	●●●○○
Museums	●●○○○
Shopping	●●●●●

A wealthy circus owner with a passion for European art gave this section of Florida's west coast a reputation as a cultural hotspot from the 1920s. The legacy is most strongly felt in Sarasota where galleries, performing arts venues and a major collection of baroque art contribute to the appeal of one of the state's most enjoyable small cities. Sarasota is the only mainland area featured as part of this route, which otherwise sticks to the coast.

Long and slender barrier islands form a 35-mile frame to the Culture Coast, linked for the most part by a continuous road lined on one side by Australian pines and on the other by some of the state's finest white-sand beaches. The islands hold insular, affluent communities each concerned to protect the environment – ospreys and egrets are still more common visitors to parts of this region than tourists – from the rampant development seen elsewhere along the coast.

ANNA MARIA ISLAND❖❖

ℹ️ **Anna Maria Island Chamber of Commerce** *5313 Gulf Drive N; tel: (941) 778-1541; www.annamariaislandchamber. org. Open Mon–Fri 0900– 1700.*

Anna Maria Island stretches for 7.5 miles and is the northernmost of the barrier islands that separate the Gulf of Mexico from the Intracoastal Waterway. The pick of its many white-sand beaches are **Coquina Beach** and **Bayfront Park**. To discover more about the island and its three towns, browse the entertaining **Anna Maria Historical Society Museum**.

DE SOTO NATIONAL MEMORIAL❖❖

🏛️ **De Soto National Memorial** *North end of 75th Street NE, Bradenton; tel: (941) 792-0458; www.nps.gov/deso. Open daily 0900–1700.*

Spaniard Hernando de Soto and a force of 600 soldiers are believed to have landed hereabouts in 1539, the start of a four-year, 4000-mile trek that would bring the first European sighting of the Mississippi River. Failing to find the gold believed to be buried in Florida or establish the colonies that De Soto had promised the Spanish king, the expedition also claimed the lives of De Soto and half his men.

Tierra
Verde
PINELLAS
N.W.R.
679
19
SUNSHINE
679
A
SKYWAY
275
Fort
DeSoto
Park
Fort
DeSoto
Southwest Channel
Intracoastal Waterway

TAMIAMI
Sun City
41
Gillette
683
Rubonia
44   45
ERIE   RD
Tierra Ceia
Madiera Bickel
Mound St. Arch. Site
19
683
301
Portovant
Indian Mound
Memphis
Palmetto
DeSoto
Natl. Mem.
South Florida
Mus. & Bishop
Planetarium
Gamble
Plantation S.H.S.
Ellenton
Anna
Maria   789
Holmes
Beach
Anna
Maria Key
789
Palma
Sola
Bradenton
Columbia Blake
Med. Ctr.
Ct.
Hse.
Manatee
64
Manatee Village
Hist. Park
Samoset
64   42
75
Cortez
684
44TH AV W.
26TH ST
DeSoto Sq.
Mall
70
Bradenton Beach
GULF DR
Sarasota Bay
Oneco
ONECO - MYAKKA CITY RD
41
Longboat Key
Longboat
Key
789
Bayshore
Gardens
Whitfield
Estates
301
683A
Braden
GULF   OF
Sarasota-
Bradenton
Intl. Airport
Tallevast
UNIVERSITY PKWY   40
MEXICO
J. RINGLING
John & Mable
Ringling House
and Museums
Sarasota
Jungle
Gard
41
Sarasota Kennel
Club
Ed
Smith
Stad.
Sarasota
Kensington
Park
780
Mote Marine Aquarium
Ct. Hse.
Fruitville
Marie Selby
Botanical Gardens
39
South Lido Park
Sarasota Mem. Hosp.
Lido
Key
758
773
BEE RIDGE RD
38
Siesta
Key
Bee Ridge
CLARK   RD
72
Coral Cove
Sarasota
Square
37
Crescent
Beach
Siesta
Key

0   10   20 miles
0   10   20   30km

An explanatory video at the visitors' centre describes the expedition and its small museum displays a few related artefacts. Outside, a boardwalk trail through the mangrove swamps suggests the type of terrain through which De Soto and his band of men would have hacked their first steps.

GAMBLE PLANTATION STATE HISTORIC SITE✥✥

Gamble Plantation
$ 3708 Patten Avenue, Ellenton; tel: (941) 723-4536;
www.floridastateparks.org/gambleplantation/default.asp.
Open daily 0800–1630;
guided tours, Mon & Thur–Sun 0930, 1030, 1300, 1400, 1500, 1600.

This excellently maintained ten-room antebellum mansion was built in the mid-1800s for Major Robert Gamble who oversaw a 3500-acre sugar plantation from it. A small museum documents Gamble's life and decline as falling sugar prices forced him to sell the house and grounds. Other exhibits record the arrival here in 1865 of Judah P Benjamin, Secretary of State in the Confederate government, fleeing Union troops. An accomplished lawyer, Benjamin escaped by boat to England where he became a leading member of the British Bar.

MARIE SELBY BOTANICAL GARDENS✥✥

These fragrant and colourful 11 acres, which evolved from the garden of Marie Selby who moved with her oil magnate husband to a bayfront home here in the 1920s, should delight even the least horticulturally minded visitor. The gardens also enjoy a magnificent setting overlooking Sarasota Bay (*811 S Palm Avenue, Sarasota; tel: (941) 366-5730; www.selby.org. Open daily 1000–1700*).

Walkways wind between the individually planted sections revealing cacti, cycads, native Florida plants, herbs and the Tropical Food Garden with oddities such as the giant-leaf edible hibiscus and the liquorice-flavoured black sapote among pineapple, papaya and banana trees. The path continues through groves of banyan and pine and a remarkable forest of bamboo.

MOTE MARINE AQUARIUM*

Mote Marine Aquarium $ 1600 Ken Thompson Parkway, Lido Key; tel: (941) 388-4441; www.mote.org. Open daily 1000–1700.

Primarily a research facility specialising in the study of sharks and environmental pollution, this aquarium blends science and entertainment to good effect. The displays and exhibitions highlight the many problems faced by Florida's marine life while allowing close-up views of creatures as diverse as sea horses and sharks. Another large tank holds two male manatees: try to see them when they chomp through some of the lettuce, cabbage and carrots that forms part of their vegetarian diet.

RINGLING HOUSE AND MUSEUMS***

Ringling House and Museums $$ 5401 Bayshore Drive, Sarasota; tel: (941) 359-5700; www.ringling.org. Open daily 1000–1730.

The Ringling House, known as Ca'd'Zan ('House of John' in Venetian dialect) is among the most beautiful homes in Florida. It was built as a winter residence for circus owner John Ringling and his wife Mable. Set beside Sarasota Bay and completed in 1926, the house is modelled on a Venetian Gothic palace but incorporates many other Mediterranean features.

Ringling's intention was for guests to arrive by gondola and cross a 200-ft-wide terrace, decorated with exquisite tilework, before entering the house. Present-day visitors pass a palm-lined driveway to reach the house and continue into the marble-floored court, the main living area and venue for large dinner parties. The $50,000 Aeolian organ that Mable sometimes played stands on one side, while columns of Mexican onyx rise toward a 30-ft-high ceiling.

Other ground-floor rooms include the Ballroom, with ceiling panels by the *Ziegfeld Follies'* set designer; the Taproom, with its stained-glass panels; and the French Renaissance-style Dining Room. Upstairs, John Ringling's bedroom holds an eight-piece French Empire-style suite; the adjoining bathroom has a Siena marble bathtub. Mable, meanwhile, slept amid a nine-piece suite in Louis XV-style on pillows of Venetian, Belgian and Irish lace.

Restored to its 1920s appearance, the house gives a warm impression of the Ringlings. Unfortunately, their enjoyment of the house did not last long. Mable died in 1929 and the Depression eroded much of the $200 million Ringling fortune; John himself died in 1936.

John Ringling began buying art while touring Europe looking for new talent for his circus. He took a particular shine to baroque art, then financially and critically undervalued, and amassed what is now one of the finest private collections in the world.

Surrounded by replica Greek and Roman statuary, the **Ringling Art Museum** has some 10,000 pieces, none more impressive than the four large-scale canvases by Rubens, painted around 1625 and commissioned by a Hapsburg archduchess as tapestry cartoons. Other excellent baroque works, such as Piero di Cosimo's absorbing *Building*

Opposite
Marie Selby Botanical Gardens

of a Palace, feature among the selections from the permanent collections, expanded considerably since Ringling's time. Temporary shows often focus on contemporary art.

Opened after John Ringling's death, the **Circus Gallery** sits rather oddly amid the estate's art and architectural treasures but records the great years of the Ringing Brothers circus, at its peak through the 1920s and 1930s before transport costs and changing tastes led to its demise. A fine collection of circus posters and interesting accounts of dwarf acts, such as Tom Thumb and Emmet Lee Kelly, are among the exhibits.

Also in the grounds is the 18th-century **Asolo Theater**, a 300-seat horseshoe-shaped auditorium built in Italy and transported here

Below
Ringling Museum complex

brick by brick in 1950, now used for educational programmes and other events.

SARASOTA✦✦✦

ℹ **Sarasota Convention & Visitors Bureau** 665 N Hwy-41; tel: (941) 957-1877 or (800) 522-9799; www.sarasotafl.org. Open Mon–Sat 0900–1700.

Sarasota, one of the few places in Florida where locals might be more familiar with Italian opera than Mickey Mouse, is a small and cultured city in a splendid setting. Given a taste for the fine arts by circus-owner John Ringling (*see opposite*) in the 1920s and set beside a gorgeous bay, Downtown Sarasota occupies an easily walked area. Intimate cafés and restaurants are grouped on and around Main Street, as are a number of antiques shops, art galleries and book stores ideal for browsing.

Food in Sarasota

The Bijou Café $$–$$$ *1287 First Street; tel: (941) 366-8111; www.bijoucafe.net.* More of a self-consciously chic restaurant than a café but a prime spot for a gastronomically-cultured lunch or dinner.

Phillippi Creek Village Restaurant and Oyster Bar $$ *5353 Tamiami Trail; tel: (941) 925-4444; www.creekseafood.com.* Experience casual waterfront dining at this family-run restaurant. Locals say it is the best seafood for miles.

Sugar & Spice $–$$ *4000 Cattlemen Road; tel: (941) 342-1649.* Traditional Amish cooking which includes turkey dinners, large sandwiches and delicious cakes and tarts.

SIESTA KEY✦

ℹ **Siesta Key Chamber of Commerce** 5100 Ocean Boulevard; tel: (941) 349-3800 or (888) 837-3969; www.siestakeychamber.com. Open Mon–Fri 0900–1700.

Siesta Key is prized for the powdery texture of its white-sand beaches, composed of almost pure quartz with little shell or other debris to get trapped between the toes of sunbathers and swimmers. The appeal of its beaches is slightly lessened by the soulless high-rise condos that loom beside them but both crowds and condos thin towards the southern end of the island.

Accommodation in Siesta Key

Crescent View Beach Club $$–$$$ *6512 Midnight Pass Road; tel: (941) 349-2000 or (800) 344-7171; www.crescentviewbeachclub.com.* One- and two-bedroom apartments, and a heated pool, a shell's throw from the beach.

Turtles $$ *8875 Midnight Pass Road; tel: (941) 346-2207.* Waterfront dining; the daily seafood specials are unbeatable.

SOUTH LIDO PARK✿✿

South Lido Beach Park *Open daily 0900–sunset. Free.*

On weekdays, comparatively few people take advantage of this excellent 100-acre beach park fringed by tall rows of Australian pine. The peaceful landscapes range from the Gulf-side beaches to the north side's mangrove-lined bay, which can be explored on a boardwalk trail and by rented canoe. Directly south are views across Big Pass to Siesta Key; east across Sarasota Bay is the Downtown Sarasota skyline.

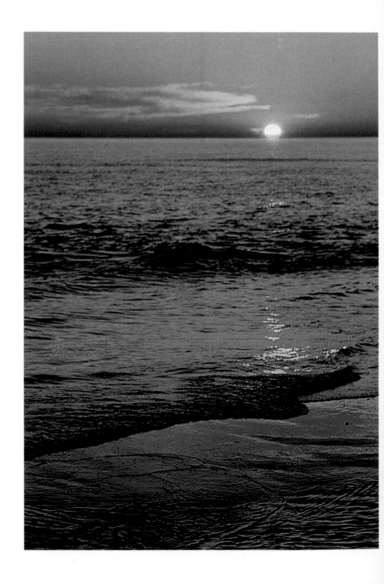

Right
South Lido Park sunset

SUNSHINE SKYWAY BRIDGE❖❖

ⓘ Longboat Key Chamber of Commerce *6854 Gulf of Mexico Drive, Longboat Key; tel: (941) 383-2466; www.longboatkeychamber.com. Open Mon–Fri 0900–1700.*

ⓑ Pelican Man's Bird Sanctuary *$ 1708 Ken Thompson Parkway, Lido Key; tel: (941) 388-4444; www.pelicanman.org. Open daily 1000–1700.*

ⓒ Starfish Motel *$–$$ 2929 Gulf of Mexico Drive, Longboat Key; tel: (941) 383-3117; email: starfish2@comcast.net; www.starfishmotel.com. Good-priced rooms with kitchens and Gulf views; picnic and barbecue areas for guests' use.*

Casa Del Mar *$$ 4621 Gulf of Mexico Drive, Longboat Key; tel: (941) 383 5549; email: info@casadelmar.net; www.casadelmar.net. Red-roofed rooms set beside the private white-sanded beach.*

ⓓ Café on the Bay *$$–$$$ 2630 Harbourside Drive; Longboat Key; tel: (941) 383-0440; www.cafeonthebay.com. Varied Florida cuisine sometimes with a Caribbean twist, such as the coconut shrimp; complete with sunset views.*

This vital traffic link and accomplished piece of engineering carries I-275 for 15 miles across the mouth of Tampa Bay, reaching 250ft at its highest point. It cost $215 million and replaced an earlier bridge, struck by a tanker during a storm in 1980. The collision caused the deaths of 35 people as vehicles fell from the collapsed central span. The southern section of the old bridge now serves as an over-long fishing pier; the submerged span has become an artificial reef.

Suggested tour

Length: Main tour 48 miles, 70 miles with detours.

Duration: Driving time 2 hours, 3 hours with detours.

Links: To the north, the Sunshine Skyway Bridge links this tour with St Petersburg and its beaches (*see pages 144–53*). Heading south, Hwy-41 or I-75 provide access to Fort Myers and the Lee County Islands (*see pages 124–33*).

After crossing Tampa Bay with the **SUNSHINE SKYWAY BRIDGE ❶**, I-275 continues over the mangrove-skirted **Tierra Ceia Island**, dotted by prehistoric shell mounds. Join Route 55 which, after 2.5 miles, connects with Hwy-41 to head south through **Palmetto** on the north bank of the broad Manatee River. Hwy-41 continues across the river into **Bradenton**, more given to commerce and industry than its Culture Coast neighbours.

Half-a-mile after the river crossing, turn right on to Route 64 (Manatee Avenue). This charts an uninspiring course with numerous traffic lights but is the main route to the rewarding barrier island beach communities. The first of these is **Holmes Beach**, 9 miles ahead and one of three separately-governed communities of **ANNA MARIA ISLAND ❷**.

Turn left on to E Bay Drive which quickly joins Gulf Boulevard, the main artery linking the barrier island chain. After 1.75 miles, the route passes **Bradenton Beach**, an unpretentious community where most visitor interest focuses on the excellent **Coquina Beach** occupying Anna Maria Island's southern tip.

Crossing from Anna Maria Island on to **Longboat Key**, the route becomes Gulf of Mexico Drive and for the next 11 miles passes condominiums, beachfront resorts, golf courses and a few small motels. A fine, unbroken strip of sand lines the Gulf. Just before reaching Lido Key, a left turn on to Ken Thompson Parkway leads to the **MOTE MARINE AQUARIUM ❸**. Adjacent to the aquaruim is **Pelican Man's Bird Sanctuary**, a volunteer-run organisation that cares for several thousand injured birds annually; pelicans, owls and cormorants can be viewed from a boardwalk.

Anna Maria Historical Society Museum *402 Pine Avenue; tel: (941) 778-0492; Open May–Sept, Tue–Thur and Sat 1000–1200; Oct–Apr, Tue–Thur and Sat 1000–1500. Free.*

Harrington House *$$$ 5625 Gulf Drive, Holmes Beach, Anna Maria Island; tel: (941) 778-5444 or (888) 828 5566; www.harringtonhouse.com.* Extremely charming beachside bed-and-breakfast inn with 13 antique-filled rooms.

Accommodation and food

Beachside hotels and resorts are found all along the coast, while scores of inexpensive motels line the approach roads into mainland cities, particularly on Hwy-41 as it approaches Sarasota. Food is no less readily available, whether you want to grab a wholesome snack while sightseeing or indulge in a leisurely seafood dinner while watching the sunset.

Reaching Lido Key, the route becomes John Ringling Parkway, named after the circus owner who made these barrier islands accessible from the mainland and who bought much of the replica neo-classical statuary that decorates **St Armands Circle**, directly ahead and ringed by boutiques and speciality shops.

Running east from St Armands Circle, John Ringling Boulevard passes the Sarasota Yacht Club and the small island of Bird Key as it crosses Sarasota Bay, reaching **SARASOTA** 2.25 miles ahead. Follow signs for Main Street to explore Downtown Sarasota, directly ahead. Turn left along Hwy-41 for the **RINGLING HOUSE AND MUSEUMS** ❹, 3.75 miles north. Turn right along Bayfront Drive to pass the pleasantly landscaped Bayfront Park and reach the **MARIE SELBY BOTANICAL GARDENS** ❺.

Stay on Bayfront Drive (the local section of Hwy-41) as it swings left and ascends a hill to reach the junction with Hwy-319 (Washington Boulevard). Turn right and continue south. After 1.8 miles, turn right on to Siesta Drive and the most populated section of **SIESTA KEY** ❻ is a mile ahead. On Siesta Key, Siesta Drive becomes Higel Avenue. After 0.75 miles, Midnight Pass Road forks to the left. Take this for 1.8 miles to reach the junction with Beach Drive where **Siesta Public Beach** occupies 2400ft of shoreline.

Continuing south on Midnight Pass Road penetrates the less developed portions of Siesta Key, reaching the rarely crowded **Crescent Beach** and **Turtle Beach**. After 5 miles, the road expires facing Midnight Pass.

Detour: From Palmetto, turn left on to Hwy-331 towards Ellenton. After 2.7 miles of this busy route, watch for the signposted turning for **GAMBLE PLANTATION STATE HISTORIC SITE** ❼, located on the north side of the route off Ellenton Gillete Road.

Detour: Between Bradenton and Anna Maria Island, 4.6 miles from the junction with Hwy-41, turn right along 75th Street NE. Although little on this tree-lined residential street suggests it, 2.4 miles ahead is the **DE SOTO NATIONAL MEMORIAL** ❽, remembering a 16th-century Spanish landing.

Detour: To see more of **Anna Maria Island** continue on Manatee Avenue from Holmes Beach and turn right on to Gulf Boulevard. After 3 miles, turn right on Pine Avenue for the **Anna Maria Historical Society Museum**. Directly ahead is the engagingly ramshackle **Anna Maria Pier**. To the left is **Bayfront Park**, the heart of this relaxed coastal community.

Detour: From St Armands Circle, take Benjamin Franklin Drive, which for half-a-mile swings along the edge of **Lido Beach**, a favourite spot for sunset strolls on the sand. The edge of the beach marks the start of a tree-lined hotel strip running for less than a mile until the route reaches the entrance to **SOUTH LIDO PARK** ❾.

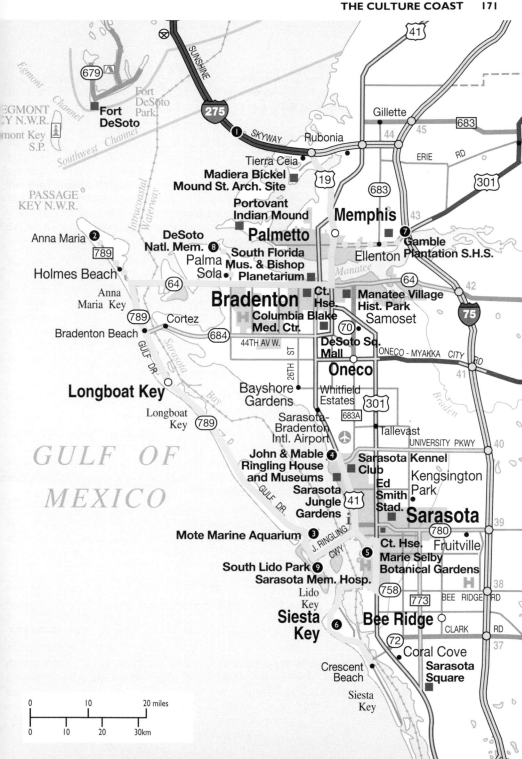

679

275 SUNSHINE SKYWAY

Fort DeSoto
Fort DeSoto Park

EGMONT
KEY N.W.R.
gmont Key
S.P.

Egmont Channel

Southwest Channel

Intracoastal Waterway

PASSAGE
KEY N.W.R.

Anna Maria ❷

789

Holmes Beach

Anna Maria Key

789

Bradenton Beach

Cortez

684

GULF DR.

Sarasota Bay

Longboat Key

Longboat Key

789

GULF OF

MEXICO

Rubonia

Tierra Ceia

Madiera Bickel
Mound St. Arch. Site

19

Portovant
Indian Mound

DeSoto
Natl. Mem. ❽

Palma Sola

Palmetto

South Florida
Mus. & Bishop
Planetarium

64

Bradenton

Columbia Blake
Med. Ctr.

44TH AV W.

26TH ST

Ct.
Hse.

70

DeSoto Sq.
Mall

Manatee River

Manatee Village
Hist. Park

Samoset

Oneco

ONECO - MYAKKA CITY RD

Bayshore
Gardens

Whitfield
Estates

301

683A

Tallevast

UNIVERSITY PKWY

Sarasota-
Bradenton
Intl. Airport

John & Mable ❹
Ringling House
and Museums

Sarasota
Jungle
Gardens

41

Sarasota Kennel
Club

Ed
Smith
Stad.

Kengsington
Park

Sarasota

780

Mote Marine Aquarium

❸ J. RINGLING CWY

Ct. Hse.

Fruitville

South Lido Park ❾
Sarasota Mem. Hosp.

Lido
Key

❺

Marie Selby
Botanical Gardens

758

773

BEE RIDGE RD

**Siesta
Key**

❻

Bee Ridge

CLARK RD

72

Coral Cove

Crescent
Beach

Sarasota
Square

Siesta
Key

41

Gillette

44

45

683

ERIE RD

683

301

Memphis

43

❼ Gamble
Plantation S.H.S.

Ellenton

64

42

75

Braden River

41

39

40

37

38

0   10   20 miles

0   10   20   30km

Between Tampa and Orlando

Ratings

Gardens	●●●●●
Architecture	●●●●○
Lakes	●●●●○
Nature	●●●●○
Scenery	●●●●○
History	●●●○○
Children	●●○○○
Museums	●●○○○

Theme parks and tourism may be the mainstays of central Florida's economy today but once it was citrus that underpinned the region's prosperity, as it kept the rest of the nation supplied with orange juice through winter snows. Small towns set amid the world's largest concentration of citrus groves form the core of this tour. Often pleasantly removed from major traffic routes and reached by specially designated scenic highways, the growth of such towns has been stunted by distance from major urban centres allowing the preservation of their early-1900s Downtown areas.

Cattle and mineral excavation also provided a commercial base, the latter's decline contributing to the large number of attractive lakes filling what were once ugly open-cast mines. For 67 years, Cypress Gardens was the area's major tourist destination but failed to recover from the visitor downturn that followed September 11, 2001 and closed. Nonetheless, many one-of-a-kind affairs survive, such as the whimsically-designed Chalet Suzanne, whose home-made soups have been consumed in space, beautiful Bok Tower Gardens, its immense carillon one of the few things to disturb the peace of this lovely and under-visited part of Florida, while Fantasy of Flight is pure joy for would-be aviators.

AVON PARK*

ⓘ Avon Park Chamber of Commerce *28 E Main Street, Avon Park; tel: (863) 453-3350; email: apcc@apfla.com; www.apfl.com. Open Mon–Fri 0900–1630.*

ⓘ Avon Park Museum *3 N Museum Avenue; tel: (863) 453 3525. Open Tue–Fri 1000–1400. Free.*

Set amid rolling hills and citrus groves, Avon Park could well be the sunkissed Florida retirement community on which all others are based. Golf courses and shuffleboard courts predominate in and around a community that labels itself 'city of charm'. The founder of the town, Marvin Crosby, intentionally created a community without the rowdy dancehalls and saloons that flourished in other Florida boom towns. Crosby is accorded due prominence by the **Avon Park Museum**. The town's name, meanwhile, derives from the birthplace of the first white woman to settle here, one Mary King from England's Stratford-Upon-Avon.

Bok Tower Gardens***

Bok Tower Gardens $
1151 Tower Boulevard, Lake Wales; tel: (941) 676-1408; email: info@boksanctuary.org; www.boktower.org. Open daily 0800–1700. Carillon recitals 1500 daily. Pinewood, visit by guided tour only; telephone number as for gardens, separate fee $.

Bok Tower Gardens reveal a side of Florida that few first-time visitors believe exists – 130 acres of bucolic serenity spread over the highest point (295ft above sea level) in the Florida peninsula. Shady trails lined by palms, pines and live oaks draped with Spanish moss chart a meandering course through the gardens passing colourful seasonal displays of azaleas, camellias and magnolias, and a host of other plant life.

Inquisitive squirrels and a colony of wood ducks are often sighted in the gardens; the resident racoons, bobcats and foxes tend to be more secretive. More wildlife can be surreptitiously viewed at the **window-by-the-pond**, a concealed overlook revealing the egrets, herons and other birds that nest in pond-side vegetation.

Built of pink and grey Georgia marble and coquina, Bok Tower rises 205ft and houses a carillon of 57 bronze bells. The bells, some weighing 12 tons, resound through the gardens as they mark each half hour, and are heard to best effect in the afternoon recital.

Intended as a sanctuary for birds, animals and people, the gardens provide a fitting reminder of the ideals of their founder, Dutch-born publisher, editor, writer and philanthropist Edward Bok, who donated this land to the people of his adopted country. Much of the landscaping was the work of Frederick Law Olmsted, best known for New York's Central Park.

The garden's history is detailed in the visitors' centre, occupying a pioneer-era cracker cottage. By contrast, the grounds also hold **Pinewood**, a Mediterranean Revival mansion built in 1931 for steel magnate Charles Austin Beck. The luxury home cleverly blends into its natural setting displaying some of Beck's extensive antique collection.

FANTASY OF FLIGHT**

Fantasy of Flight $$
1400 Broadway Boulevard, Polk City; tel: (863) 984 3500; email: www.fantasyofflight.com. Open daily 0900–1700.

Compass Rose Restaurant, at Fantasy of Flight $–$$
1400 Broadway Boulevard, Polk City; tel: (863) 984 3500. Art Deco diner with burgers shakes and lots more including the only Spitfire sandwich served in Florida.

For aircraft enthusiasts, the big draw in central Florida is not Walt Disney World or Universal Studios but the well-signposted plot just outside Plant City that holds Fantasy of Flight. Essentially a very large private collection of aircraft from all eras of flight up to the 1950s, and from all around the world, **Fantasy of Flight** seeks to instil a sense of aviation awe even in those who arrive not knowing their Grumman Ducks from their Stinson Trimmotors.

Not only can the large array of biplanes, monoplanes, autogyros and seaplanes, plus the odd helicopter and balloon capsule, be inspected at close quarters but the wonders of restoration and more than most people would wish to know about the technicalities of aircraft performance can be gleaned on the Back Lot Tour (1130), the Restoration Shop Tour (1330), and the Aircraft of the Day demonstration (1500), the pilot of which is available for questions before and after the display.

There is also the chance to test your own piloting mettle with a simulated takeoff, landing and dogfight above the Pacific in a World War II vintage Corsair fighter and to soar for real (albeit only as a passenger) above the flatlands of central Florida in an open cockpit biplane.

FLORIDA SOUTHERN COLLEGE**

The Florida Southern College is a Methodist academic institution founded in 1885, of note for its Frank Lloyd Wright buildings – the 1930s campus forms the largest single grouping of the celebrated

Florida Southern College *111 Lake Hollingsworth Drive, Lakeland; tel: (863) 680-4597; www.flsouthern.edu. Open Mon–Fri 1000–1600, Sat 1000–1400, Sun 1400–1600; visitors' centre closed during college holidays.*

architect's work. Calling the project his 'Child of the Sun', Wright envisaged the campus growing in harmony with the citrus grove that occupied the site. He used local stone and employed the geometric forms that had become trademarks of the 'organic architecture' that made his reputation.

The campus fell short of Wright's vision, however, with only eight of the intended 18 buildings completed. None the less, the campus is well worth a visit; the architectural details are described by free leaflets distributed in boxes along the covered walkways linking the buildings. A visitors' centre displays some of Wright's original campus drawings and other items.

HIGHLANDS HAMMOCK STATE PARK❖❖

Highlands Hammock State Park $ *off Hwy-27 near Sebring; tel: (863) 386-6094; www.floridastateparks.org/ highlandshammock. Open daily 0800–sunset.*

One of Florida's oldest, biggest and best state parks, Highlands Hammock fills 4700 acres. A series of paved and boardwalk trails accesses damp and shady fern pockets, orange groves, pine flatwoods, scrubland and a cypress swamp. Florida scrub jays are among the frequently sighted birds; at ground level, white-tailed deer and alligators are abundant. A ranger-led tram tour visits the remoter reaches of the park.

The park was constructed in the 1930s by the Civil Conservation Corp, created during the Depression to provide work for unemployed young men. They are remembered, alongside natural history exhibits, in the park's museum.

LAKE WALES❖❖

Lake Wales Chamber of Commerce *340 W Central Avenue; tel: (863) 676-3445; www.info@ lakewaleschamber.com. Open Mon–Fri 0830–1700.*

Spook Hill *on North Avenue near junction with Burns Avenue (Hwy-17A), Lake Wales.*

The Depot $ *325 S Scenic Highway; tel: (863) 678-4209. Open Mon–Fri 0900–1700, Sat 1000–1600.*

Right
Chalet Suzanne

Little Lake Wales has a surprising number of unusual sights in and around it. Strangest is **Spook Hill**, an optical illusion (though some offer spiritual and scientific explanations) making cars appear to roll uphill. To experience this slightly unnerving phenomena, park at the signposted spot, take the vehicle out of gear and await the results.

A more orthodox place is **The Depot**, where a 1927 railroad station has been turned into a historical museum and cultural centre, forming part of an attractively restored Downtown area. Among an extensive array chronicling the town's growth is a mesmerising display of citrus crates and labels. Railroad links are maintained with an elegant 1920s Pullman carriage and a 1944 locomotive.

Founded by a gourmet cook seeking to make ends meet during the Depression, **Chalet Suzanne** acquired its present form – the pink walls, turrets and towers conceal an insane conglomeration of rooms spread across 14 different levels – when a stable, rabbit hutches and chicken houses were knocked together in the 1940s. The chalet is now a Florida landmark and famed for its fine cuisine, including soup, which is available in tins and was carried to the moon by Apollo 15 astronauts in 1973. It makes an entertaining visit – there's an excellent gift shop and the chance to peep into the luxurious room.

Accommodation and food in Lake Wales

All Star Grill $–$$ *2019 State Road 60 E; tel: (863) 679-9689; www.allstargrill.com.* Local chain of sports bar diners with reliable sandwiches, burgers, chicken wings, and steaks of substance.

Chalet Suzanne $$$ *3800 Chalet Suzanne Drive; tel: (941) 676-6011 or (800) 433-6011; www.chaletsuzanne.com.* Noted local landmark (*see above*) that offers some of Florida's best cuisine in a lovely setting. Stay overnight in whimsically furnished rooms beneath turrets and spires.

Crazy Cuban Cafe $ *120 E Park Avenue; tel: (863) 679 3934.* Simple and quick Cuban fare, with ham and pork taking centre stage, for breakfast and lunch on weekdays (closed Sat–Sun).

Noah's Ark Bed & Breakfast $$ *312 Ridge manor Road; tel: (863) 676 1613 or (800) 346-1613.* Four guest rooms, a plethora of antiques, and a remarkable collection of Noah's Ark memorabilia, just south of the town centre.

LAKELAND✢

Lakeland's appearance is greatly enhanced by the 13 lakes within its borders, including Lake Mirror which flanks the tastefully landscaped **Munn Historic District** where many 1910s and 1920s commercial

ⓘ Lakeland Chamber of Commerce
35 Lake Morton Drive; tel: (863) 688-8551; www.lakelandchamber.com. Open Mon–Fri 0830–1700.

ⓜ Folk Museum of Art *800 E Palmetto Street; tel: (863) 688-7743; www.polkmuseumofart.org. Open Tue–Sat 1000–1700, Sun 1300–1700. Free.*

☾ Relax Inn $ *1433 Lakeland Boulevard; tel: (863) 683 6745 or (888) RELAAXX; email: lakeland.motel@earthlink.net; www.relaxinnflorida.com.* For a short stay, this small, simple and clean motel does the job at an affordable price.

buildings now house antiques shops. A few blocks away, the **Polk Museum of Art** has small but strong permanent collections, mostly of American painting, photography and sculpture, and regularly brings good-quality travelling exhibitions to the town.

SEBRING✧

The main streets of Sebring follow an unusual circular pattern, spreading outwards from the oak tree planted in 1912 by the town's founder, a ceramics manufacturer from Ohio called George Sebring. Much of the once-commercially important old centre has been pleasantly restored and provides a setting for **Roaring Twenties Day**, which finds merchants donning 1920s attire and many related events taking place.

In total contrast, the **International Grand Prix Sports Car 12-hour Endurance Race** brings nationwide attention to Sebring each March.

Suggested tour

Length: Main tour 40 miles, 95 miles with detours.

Duration: Main tour, 4 hours; add 2–3 hours for the Bok Tower Gardens or Avon Park detours.

Links: This tour is accessed from I-4 and Hwy-27 and links easily with Tampa (*see pages 134–43*) and Orlando and its theme parks (*see pages 180–91*).

Exit I-4 heading south on Hwy-98, which becomes Florida Avenue and continues for 3.2 miles into the historic centre of **LAKELAND** ❶. After exploring the immediate area, continue south on Florida Avenue, turning left on to McDonald Street after half-a-mile and immediately right on to Johnson Street, where the **FLORIDA SOUTHERN COLLEGE** ❷ sits prettily on the north bank of Lake Hollingsworth.

Leave Lakeland on Hwy-92 and travel 9.5 miles east before turning right on to Route 544. After 3.2 miles, turn right on to Hwy-17, where you will quickly be passing the rows of motels and restaurants that dominate the small town of **Winter Haven**, once serving visitors to Cypress Gardens, a long-serving attraction that closed in 2003.

Detour: Shortly before the junction with Route 544, Hwy-92 from Lakeland passes through Auburndale (*see below*). Turning left, Route 559 continues north towards Polk City, on the way crossing I-4 and the entrance to **FANTASY OF FLIGHT** ❸.

Continue on to Route 542, which after 6.2 miles crosses the busy Hwy-27 to reach the hamlet of **Dundee**. Turn right here for Hwy-27A (Route 17), a quieter, scenic alternative to Hwy-27. **LAKE WALES** ❹ is 9 miles ahead on a route that passes **Chalet Suzanne**.

BOK TOWER GARDENS ❺ occupy one of the highest section of the Florida Ridge (a limestone bulge forming the 'spine' of the Florida peninsula). Two miles north of Lake Wales on Hwy-27A, turn right on to Burns Avenue (Hwy-17A) where the gardens lie at the end of a signposted 5-mile route.

Detour: Continue south from Lake Wales on Hwy-27A, after 14 miles passing through **Frostproof**, a little settlement whose name signalled the ability of the local citrus crop to survive the winter. Six miles ahead, Hwy-27A joins Hwy-27; continue south for 6.5 miles, turning left for **Avon Park** on Route 64 (Main Street). Look for the right turn on to Hwy-17, which charts a scenic 10-mile course passing the lakes, citrus groves and golf courses that characterise the area, before reaching **SEBRING** ❻. Leave Sebring on Lakeview Drive, skirting the edge of Lake Jackson before briefly joining Hwy-27 and making a left turn on to Route 634 (Hammock Road). This continues for 5.5 miles to **HIGHLANDS HAMMOCK STATE PARK** ❼.

Below
Downtown Sebring

Also worth exploring

Between Lake Wales and I-4, Hwy-27 is crossed by Hwy-92. Travel 5 miles west on Hwy-92 to **Lake Alfred**, a village filled with an impossibly large number of antiques shops and self-consciously quaint tearooms. The shops deal in everything from vintage neon signs and moose heads to fine china, jewellery and silver. A slightly smaller number of similar shops can be found in **Haines City**, 2.5 miles east on Hwy-92. Another small town, **Auburndale**, 5 miles west of Lake Alfred may be unable to match its neighbours for antiques shops but can boast one of Florida's best inland beaches on the banks of Lake Ariana.

Orlando and its theme parks

Ratings

Children	●●●●●
Nightlife	●●●●●
Theme parks	●●●●●
Nature	●●●○○
Shopping	●●●○○
Museums	●●○○○
History	●○○○○
Scenery	●○○○○

Much of the Orlando area is Florida as first-time visitors usually imagine the whole state to be: a mass of freeway interchanges, gigantic billboards, chain hotels and the theme parks that provide the world's most technologically advanced entertainment. Filling an area twice the size of Manhattan, Walt Disney World opened its first park here in 1971 and made Florida a pacesetter in international tourism. Disney continues to develop new parks, as does Universal Studios, and both vie fiercely for visitor attention along with other major draws such as SeaWorld.

Be it in accommodation, dining or daytime activities, competition for the tourist dollar is fierce and Orlando, while not always cheap, offers excellent value for money. Away from the razzle-dazzle of theme parks, Orlando has several intriguing neighbourhoods and engaging minor museums, ranging from a centre for injured birds to displays of Tiffany glasswork and the proof that Orlando really did exist long before the arrival of Mickey Mouse.

DISNEY'S ANIMAL KINGDOM✧✧

ⓘ **Visitor Center** 8723 *International Drive;* tel: (407) 363-5872; www.orlandoinfo.com. *Open daily 0800–1900.*

Kissimmee/St Cloud Convention & Visitors Bureau *1925 E Hwy-192, Kissimmee;* tel: (407) 847-5477 or (800) 333-5477; www.floridakiss.com. *Open daily 0800–1700.*

Ⓗ **Disney's Animal Kingdom** $$$ *Walt Disney World, Lake Buena Vista;* tel: (407) 824-4321; disneyworld.com. *Open 0900–1800, later in summer holidays.*

Turning a flat and featureless chunk of central Florida five times the size of the Magic Kingdom into a landscape of vine-covered crags and waterfalls, Animal Kingdom opened in 1998, promising a 'new species of theme park'. The animals that roam the varied sections include gorillas, hippos, zebra, rhinos, giraffes, miniature deer and tree kangaroos; they are joined by Disney-created dinosaurs.

Animal Kingdom radiates outwards from the 14-storey-high **Tree of Life**, intended to symbolise the connectedness of all life with animal forms carved into its gnarled trunk. The park will certainly thrill young children and probably please all who visit, although the mixture of ecology, zoo and theme park, complete with the usual parades and fireworks, sometimes seems an uneasy combination.

Maitland Art Center/
Historical and Telephone Museums

Audubon House

Lake Avenue

Lake
Maitland

Park Avenue

Palmer Avenue

Lee Road

Lake
Osceola

Aloma Avenue

Winter Park

Morse Museum of
American Art

Park Avenue

Lake Killarney

Avenue Osceola

Lake
Mizell

Avenue Fairbanks Hwy-426

Rollins College

Little Lake
Fairview

Lake
Virginia

Lake
Berry

Orange Avenue Hwy-527

Par Street

Orlando Avenue

Lake Sue

Edgewater Drive

Orlando Science Center

Lake Rowena

Corrine Drive

Henry P Leu
House and Gardens

Lake
Ivanhoe

Orange Avenue

Virginia Drive

Bennet Road

Lake
Concord

East Colonial Drive

To theme
Parks

Downtown Orlando

Orange County
Regional History
Center and Heritage Square

Lake
Eola

East Robinson Street

0   1 km
0   1/2 mile

DISNEY-MGM STUDIOS✦✦✦

🅳 **Disney-MGM
Studios $$$** Walt
Disney World, Exit 26B from
I-4; tel: (407) 824-4321;
www.disney.go.com. Open
daily 0900–1900, until 2200
or 2400 from mid-June–mid-
Aug.

Smallest of the main Disney Parks, Disney-MGM Studios combines top-notch rides and shows based on American film and TV, with informative behind-the-scenes tours of the company's film and TV production facilities. The special effects and stunt shows are excellent, and if you have ever wondered how a Disney animation evolves, this is the place to find out.

This is the best Disney park for visitor involvement in shows. Participation ranges from being an extra on the Indiana Jones Epic Stunt Spectacular to appearing – through the magic of video editing – alongside Lucille Ball or the cast of *Cheers* at SuperStar Television. To become involved, be at the head of the queue outside the particular show when volunteers are requested. Be ready to spend time being made up and rehearsed before facing an audience or going on air, and do not volunteer if you are easily embarrassed.

Throughout the day along **Hollywood Boulevard**, a cast of Disney actors create 'Streetmosphere', adding to the illusion of being in Hollywood during its heyday. On **Sunset Boulevard**, Mickey Mouse and other Disney characters can often be spotted, ready to pose for photos and sign autographs. Save for the **Honey, I Shrunk The Kids Movie Set Adventure**, a play area with oversized objects and creatures, and some shows based on recent Disney film releases, there is little in the park specifically to appeal to small children.

The park has some of Disney's best rides. Combining film, sound and plenty of heart-stopping swerves and bumps, **Star Tours** takes visitors on a flight-simulator trip to the Moon of Endor with the characters of the *Star Wars* films. Equally effective, **The Twilight Zone Tower of Terror** traps participants in a spooky Hollywood hotel in an elevator that makes a dizzying 13-floor plunge in two seconds. The **Rock 'n' Roller Coaster** offers a hell-for-leather limo ride with rock band Aerosmith. The less frenetic **Great Movie Ride** passes a series of classic movie scenes with AudioAnimatronic robots playing celebrated actors.

Of the shows, the **Indiana Jones Epic Stunt Spectacular** demonstrates stage explosions, fights, and general stunt work; the riotous **Jim Henson's Muppet 3D Vision** has great 3D effects; and **SuperStar Television** pitches audience volunteers into classic TV shows with hilarious results. Audience participation also features at **Monster Sound Show and SoundWorks**, entertaining and informative looks at the making of sound effects.

The nuts and bolts of film-making are revealed on the **Backlot Tour**, taking visitors through genuine Disney sound stages, sometimes with filming in progress, to **Catastrophe Canyon** which brings first-hand experience of simulated floods, explosions and other dramatic movie effects. The calmer **Magic of Disney Animation** describes the processes involved in cartoon creation and peeks at Disney's own animators working on new productions.

DOWNTOWN ORLANDO✢

The surprisingly few square blocks that comprise Downtown Orlando are studded with the architecture that recalls the city's slow but steady pre-Disney growth as a citrus and cattle centre. The rampant commercial expansion seen across the area since the major theme parks opened has had relatively little impact here, as a daytime walk around the pleasant park-lined **Lake Eola** and nearby **Heritage Square** will prove.

Right
Downtown Orlando

EPCOT✢✢

🏢 **EPCOT $$$** *Walt Disney World, Exit 26B from I-4; tel: (407) 824-4321. Open daily 0900–2100, until 2200 or 2400 from mid-June–mid-Aug.*

EPCOT, the most ambitious Disney park, was intended to present a vision of tomorrow's world today and to celebrate the cultures of the world's nations. It is the toughest Disney park to explore within a day and the least interesting for children. The park divides into two sections, Future World and World Showcase, each housing a series of pavilions.

Future World explores the wonders of science and the natural world with a few rides and numerous exhibits. **Wonders of Life** includes EPCOT's best special-effects ride, *Body Wars*, replicating a bloodcell's journey through the human body. Less nerve jangling is the amusing *Cranium Command*, exploring the workings of the brain of a 12-year-old schoolboy through a typical day. *The Making of Me* is a child-aimed explanation of the human reproductive process.

Another Future World highlight, **Journey Into Imagination** has a 3D film, *Honey, I Shrunk The Audience*, with innovative effects making visitors feel they have been reduced to a fraction of their normal size. *The Image Works*, likely to occupy young teens for long periods, is a large collection of user-friendly, interactive creative games including the Electronic Philharmonic, an entire orchestra ready to play to your command.

The most exciting section of Future World is **Test Track**, with its simulated high-speed car test, while the most impressive is **The Living Seas**, which begins with a simulated descent to Sea Base Alpha, a deep-sea research centre. A range of exhibits and displays inform on the mysteries of ocean life, many examples of which inhabit the gigantic tank holding 6 million gallons of sea water and 6000 creatures.

Beside a large lagoon, World Showcase features the cultures of 11 nations with a film or ride focusing on the particular country, and a supposedly typical collection of its shops and restaurants. Highlights are **China**, with its *Wonders of China* film displayed across nine screens showing historic sites and landscapes.

Right
EPCOT's Moroccan Pavilion

The **Norway** pavilion has a stave church, fishermen's cottages and a medieval castle, and World Showcase's best ride, *Maelstrom*, a longboat journey in the company of Viking raiders. A more restful voyage, along *El Rio del Tiempo* in the **Mexico** pavilion, finds events in Mexican history re-enacted life by AudioAnimatronic characters. The

United Kingdom has a collection of façades in British architectural styles and a re-created traditional pub, the *Rose & Crown*, selling imported beer and Cornish pasties.

FLORIDA AUDUBON CENTER FOR BIRDS OF PREY✣

Florida Audubon Society 1101 Audubon Way, near Maitland; tel: (407) 644-0190; www.audubonofflorida.org. Open Tue–Sat 1000–1600.

A down side to the great expansion of Orlando has been the injuries to ospreys, bald eagles, owls, vultures and other birds of prey caused by increased human settlement. Several hundred are brought here annually, receiving treatment at one of the state's longest-running conservation centres. The aviary provides a glimpse of many feathered creatures usually only fleetingly spotted in the wild.

HARRY P LEU HOUSE AND GARDENS✣✣

Harry P Leu House and Gardens $ 1920 N Forest Avenue, Orlando; tel: (407) 246-2620; www.leugardens.org. Open daily 0900–1700. House open 1000–1600.

Green-fingered visitors will relish a trip to this gorgeous 50-acre array of roses, azaleas, camellias and other plants, that began with the botanical collection of a local businessman, Henry P Leu, in the 1930s. Should your visit coincide with the start of a guided tour of the Leu House, take the opportunity to see inside the 19th-century farmhouse that Leu and his wife made into a comfortable home.

MAITLAND✣

Maitland Art Center 231 W Packwood Avenue; tel: (407) 539-2181; www.maitartcenter.org. Open Mon–Fri 1000–1630, Sat–Sun 1200–1630.

Maitland Historical & Telephone museums 221 W Packwood Avenue; tel: (407) 644-1364; www. maitlandhistory.org. Open Thur–Sun 1200–1600. Free.

Maitland became an unlikely artists' colony during the 1930s when André Smith bought six lakeside acres and raised the striking stucco and concrete complex of **Maitland Art Center**, arranged around a central courtyard and decorated with Aztec and Mayan motifs. Although changing art exhibits fill the small galleries, it is the centre's striking design that steals the show.

Next door, the adjoined **historical** and **telephone museums** display a rich clutter relating to the early days of Maitland, including the bulky switchboards and wind-up devices through which its residents once communicated.

MORSE MUSEUM OF AMERICAN ART✣✣✣

Morse Museum of American Art $ 445 Park Avenue N, Winter Park; tel: (407) 645-5311; www.morsemuseum.org. Open Tue–Sat 0930–1600, Sun 1300–1600.

This small but excellent collection displays many examples of the decorative glasswork of Louis Comfort Tiffany. Pioneering the use of coloured glass, he became a legend for his lamps and stained-glass windows that decorated the homes of the rich and famous. A highlight is the *Four Seasons Window*, made in 1900 for a Paris exposition which established Tiffany's reputation at the forefront of art nouveau design.

ORANGE COUNTY REGIONAL HISTORY CENTER✢✢

Orange County Regional History Center $$ *65 E Central Boulevard, Orlando; tel: (407) 863-8500; www.thehistorycenter.org/home.html. Open Mon–Sat 1000–1700, Sun 1200–1700.*

It is easy to forget that Orlando existed before the arrival of Walt Disney World and easier still to forget that before even Orlando existed the area was inhabited by the Timucua, a people remembered here by a dugout canoe, tooled animal bones and other items. Orlando's subsequent periods are engagingly documented by exhibits on the cattle and citrus industries that provided its early growth, and on the arrival of Walt Disney World that powered its emergence as a global tourism centre.

ORLANDO SCIENCE CENTER✢✢

Orlando Science Center $$ *777 E Princeton Street; tel: (407) 514-2000; www.osc.org. Open Mon–Sat 0900–1700, Sun 1200–1700.*

Informing and entertaining young minds on the natural world through interactive exhibits spread across 207,000sq ft, the Orlando Science Center is an ideal place for children on rainy days. The adjoining planetarium reveals some of the mysteries of the star-filled sky, while the Crosby Observatory houses telescopes for night sky viewing.

ROLLINS COLLEGE✢

Rollins College *1000 Holt Avenue, Winter Park; tel: (407) 646-2000; www.rollins.edu*

Founded in 1885, Rollins College was the first officially recognised college in Florida. The 67-acre campus is studded with Mediterranean Revival buildings set along palm-lined walkways in a lakeside setting. The architecturally accomplished **Knowles Memorial Chapel** is the venue of a springtime Bach Festival.

SEAWORLD✢✢✢

SeaWorld $$$ *7007 SeaWorld Drive, south of Orlando off I-4; tel: (407) 351-3600 or (800) 4-ADVENTURE; www.seaworld.org. Open daily 0900–1900, open later during summer.*

With its dolphin and whale shows, and state-of-the-art exhibits on marine life, SeaWorld educates and entertains as well as carries out research and conservation work. Recently, it has broadened its appeal by introducing theme park-style thrill rides.

A simulated helicopter trip through an arctic blizzard begins **Wild Arctic**; the journey concludes at a re-created, 150-year-old exploration ship from which visitors can admire polar bears, walruses, beluga whales and other creatures who enjoy the very low temperatures on the other side of the glass. The other major ride, **Journey to Atlantis**, takes passengers on a high-speed water ride in the company of mythical sirens to the lost city of Atlantis.

Of SeaWorld's marine shows, the most popular are those featuring the five killer whales, each called Shamu, of **Shamu – World Focus**. More marine skills are demonstrated by the dolphins participating in **Key West Dolphin Fest**.

Exhibits include **Manatees: The Last Generation?** with interactive displays on and underwater views of manatees as they swim in a 300,000 gallon tank; **Pacific Point Preserve**, a re-creation of the rocky coast of the US's northwest, with South American seals and California sea lions gliding in and out of the water; **Penguin Encounter** where 200 penguins inhabit a replicated Antarctica; and **Terrors of the Deep**, a rogues' gallery of dangerous sea dwellers including sharks, barracudas and some very ugly green moray eels.

UNIVERSAL STUDIOS✦✦✦

Universal Studios
$$$ 1001 Universal Studios Plaza, Exit 29 from I-4; tel: (407) 363-8000; www.uescape.com. Open Mon–Fri 0900–1800, Sat–Sun 0900–1900, later during summer and holidays.

Universal Studios is a combined theme park and TV and film production facility with the emphasis very much on fun. Universal has the best special-effect rides of any Orlando theme park and appeals chiefly to adults and older children, although several areas are intended for the very young.

The park divides into **Hollywood**, **San Francisco/Amity** and **New York**, each with replicated streets and buildings; **Production**, where most of the film-technique shows are located; and **Expo Center**, a mixture of kids' entertainments and rides. Throughout the day, speedboats and jet-skiers perform daredevil manoeuvres on the lagoon, also the setting for the **Dynamite Nights Stuntacular**, performed just before closing time.

For thrills and spills, three rides stand out: **Back To the Future**, a four-minute trip through time with such incredible special effects the ride carries a health warning; **Men In Black Alien Attack**, a chance to pursue aliens through New York streets; and the **Revenge of the Mummy**, with a deviously planned surprise at every turn. Almost as good are **Twister**, a five-storey-high tornado complete with driving wind and rain, and **Terminator 2 3D**, with 3D effects, live actors and impressive stunts. Older rides include **Earthquake – the Big One**, putting visitors into a San Francisco underground train when a major earthquake strikes.

Below
Face to face with 'Jaws', Universal Studios

The **Gory, Gruesome and Grotesque Horror Make-Up Show** reveals some of the secrets of the blood and guts of horror films; try not to be the volunteer who has their throat cut.

Of the major rides, only **ET's Adventure**, taking visitors to ET's home planet aboard intergalactic bicycles, is calm enough for small children. Youngsters may also enjoy **Fieval's Playland**, with the oversized props of the animated mouse, **Woody Woodpecker's Nuthouse Coaster**, an easy-going roller-coaster through a nut factory and **A Day In The Park With Barney**, based on TV's *Barney & Friends*, a dinosaur-hosted musical show. Likely to appeal to adults as well as children are **Animals Actors Stage**, describing the training of animal actors, and the tour of the Nickelodeon TV studios, the children-orientated TV channel.

UNIVERSAL ISLANDS OF ADVENTURE❖❖

**Universal Islands
of Adventure $$$**
As Universal Studios.

Islands of Adventure very cleverly and effectively packs five separate sections into a single easily-walkable park with a focus that really is on adventure: the rides bring every opportunity for visitors to be tossed, turned, thrilled, and spilled. Almost the only respite comes with the calmer amusements designed for smaller children at the brightly-coloured **Seuss's Landing**. Water rides, where even spectators and those in the queue are liable to be drenched, include **Dudley's Do-Right's Ripsaw Falls**, where a berth on a log brings a relatively calm ride until the scream-inducing finale; and the white-knuckle climax of **Jurassic Park River Adventure**, where the attentions of angry velociraptors are nothing compared to the boat's final 85-ft plunge.

Away from the water but no less hair-raising are **Duelling Dragons**, a pair of roller coasters on separate tracks that perform a series of high-speed near misses; and the gravity defying twists, turns and dips of the **Incredible Hulk Coaster**, which includes a stomach churning 'weightless inversion' 110ft up, and **Doctor Doom's Fearfall**, a nice ride up followed by a faster-than-gravity drop down.

WALT DISNEY WORLD: THE MAGIC KINGDOM❖❖❖

Based on Disneyland in Los Angeles, the Magic Kingdom is the Disney park that everyone expects. Mickey and Minnie Mouse really do live here, and complementing the sense of fun and fantasy based around Disney films and creations are some genuinely thrilling rides.

The Magic Kingdom's 100 acres divide into four major areas: **Adventureland, Tomorrowland, Frontierland** and **Fantasyland**; and three minor ones: **Liberty Square, Mickey's Toontown Fair** and **Main Street USA**, which is where you will enter the park after being given a map and list of the day's special events. The latter includes the parades that find Disney characters marching through the park alongside floats and music from old-time bands. On late-opening nights, the park's closure is marked by Fantasy in the Sky, an elaborate firework display.

Although many of the entertainments are aimed at adults, this is the best Disney park for young children for whom **Mr Toad's Wild Ride, Peter Pan's Flight**, and **Snow White's Adventures** have tremendous appeal. Also relished by infants are **Mickey's Country House**, home of Mr Mouse, and **The Barnstormer at Goofy's Wiseacre Farm**, a gentle roller coaster.

Of the cleverly conceived and occasionally genuinely frightening adult-aimed rides, **Space Mountain** offers a warp-speed trip through

Magic Kingdom
$$$ Walt Disney World, Exit 25B from I-4; tel: (407) 824-4321. Open daily 0900–1900, until 2200 or 2400 from mid-June–mid-Aug.

space, **Splash Mountain** boat ride climaxes with a hair-raising drop, **Big Thunder Mountain Railroad** is a runaway train ride of white-knuckle jumps and bumps, the **Haunted Mansion** conceals a selection of ghoulish special effects, while **Buzz Lightyear's Space Ranger Spin** plots a course through a comical cosmos.

Three water-borne rides make for a relaxing interlude. The **Jungle Cruise** passes through a replicated jungle as the boatman provides an entertaining commentary; **Liberty Square Riverboat** charts a course through a Revolutionary-era US; while **It's A Small World** passes groups of dolls dressed in the national costumes of various countries and singing for world peace.

Best of the Magic Kingdom's shows are **The Time Keeper**, a sweep through world history from the dinosaur-era using a 360-degree screen, and the **Country Bear Jamboree**, a song-and-dance show performed by remarkably life-like AudioAnimatronic bears. Very popular, despite its sentimentality, the **Hall of Presidents** finds more AudioAnimatronic creations, this time replicating US presidents, and a 20-minute tour through US history in the company of Abraham Lincoln.

Accommodation and food

Every hotel and motel chain worth its salt is represented in and around Orlando, particularly on International Drive and along Hwy-192 in Kissimmee. Within Walt Disney World are several hotels, every bit as imaginatively themed as the parks themselves. Each theme park also offers a choice of dining, from cafeteria lunches to semi-formal dinners; the area also holds several 'show restaurants'.

Ayothaya $$ *7555 W Sand Lake Road, Orlando; tel: (407) 345-0040.* Good range of tasty Thai cuisine in a cosy setting.

Café Tu Tu Tango $$ *8625 International Drive; tel: (407) 248-2222; www.cafetututango.com.* Florida delights such as conch fritters and bite-sized chunks of alligator are offered along with brick-oven pizzas, Cajun-style chicken and lots more.

Cracker Barrel $–$$ *5859 Caravan Court, Kissimmee; tel: (407) 248-2460; www.crackerbarrel.com.* Meatloaf and catfish fillets are among the homely delights served in generous portions.

Ming Court $$–$$$ *9188 International Drive; tel: (407) 351-9988; www.ming-court.com.* Not the cheapest but probably the best Chinese food for miles, served in a serene setting.

Rain Forest Café $$ *Downtown Disney, 1670 Buena Vista Drive; tel: (407) 827-8500; www.rainforestcafe.com.* A replicated rainforest with talking banyan trees is the setting for this usually crowded Disney-owned eatery. The food is regular American fare given strange names.

Nightlife

Arabian Nights $$ *6225 W Hwy-192; Kissimmee; tel: (407) 239-9223 or (800) 533-6116; www.arabian-nights.com.* Thoroughbred horses and their riders perform in the world's latest indoor equestrian arena.

CityWalk Universal Studios $$ *tel: (407) 224-2600 Open 1100–0200. www.citywalkorlando.com.* Universal's nightlife complex includes venues for reggae, jazz and rock music, a variety of restaurants and endless shopping opportunities. Free admission to the complex and separate charges for each venue (or buy a Party Pass to visit them all).

Disney West Side *Walt Disney World, signposted from I-4; tel: (407) 824-4321.* A complex of first-run cinemas, restaurants and music venues; adjacent to Pleasure Island.

Medieval Times $$ *4510 Hwy-192, Kissimmee; tel: (800) 299-8300 or (888) WEJOUST; www.medievaltimes.com.* Knights joust and sword fight as dinner is served in a mock 11th-century castle.

Pirate's Dinner Adventure $$ *6400 Carrier Drive; near International Drive; tel: (407) 248-0590 or (800) 866-2469; www.piratesdinneradventure.com.* After being sworn-in as a pirate, guests board a ship floating in a 300,000-gallon lagoon; swashbuckling adventures ensue.

Pleasure Island $$ *Walt Disney World, signposted from I-4; tel: (407) 939-42648.* New Year's Eve is celebrated nightly in variously themed music and comedy clubs; one admission fee provides entrance to all and there are free shows from an open-air stage; adjacent to Disney West Side.

Show Restaurants The Orlando area has several show restaurants offering a multi-course dinner, usually with unlimited drinks, for a set fee, plus spectacular entertainment:

Sleuth's Mystery Dinner Show *7508 Republic Drive; near International Drive; tel: (407) 363-1985 or (800) 393-1985; www.sleuths.com.* Diners meet and cross-examine the cast to find out whodunnit in an Agatha Christie-like setting.

Orientation

Filling a vast tract of central Florida well beyond the city whose name it bears, the Orlando area is an often unprepossessing mixture of road junctions and petrol stations, with the 43 square miles of Walt Disney World (WDW) making a bucolic contrast to the west.

The 8-mile long **International Drive**, a purpose-built tourist base, lies close to Universal Studios and SeaWorld, 9 miles southwest of Downtown Orlando and 12 miles northeast of WDW. The other major tourist area is **Kissimmee**, spread along Hwy-192 with a seemingly endless line of motels, restaurants and souvenir shops, 20 miles south of Downtown Orlando and 10 miles east of WDW.

Initially confusing, the area soon becomes familiar and easy to travel around, though always carry one of the free maps, readily distributed by hotels and TICs.

Also worth exploring

Along with its four major theme parks, Walt Disney World also has several smaller parks. There are few better places to cool down on a hot Florida day than **Typhoon Lagoon**, a water park with a wave pool, river and replicated coral reef, where snorkellers can meet real but non-dangerous sharks. The relaxing **River Country** re-creates a water hole surrounded by a wood; visitors can river raft and tackle white-water rapids. **Discovery Island** has flamingos, toucans, tortoises, swans, pelicans and alligators lurking amid 11 acres of exotic foliage. Ski fanatics who chose the wrong holiday can seek solace at **Blizzard Beach**, where the slopes of a replica Alpine mountain are covered by fake snow and the buildings are hung with icicles.

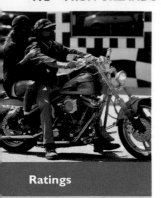

From Orlando to Daytona Beach

Ratings

Beaches	●●●● ○
Motorsports	●●●● ●
Nature	●●●● ○
Children	●●● ○○
Food	●●● ○○
Museums	●●● ○○
Scenery	●●● ○○
History	●● ○○○

Only 54 miles separate Orlando from the world-famous sands of Daytona Beach, making one of Florida's most popular coastal destinations an easy day-trip from the world's theme park capital on the swift I-4. Revealing the best of Daytona Beach, including the racetrack that has done as much as the beach to give the town an international reputation and the lesser-known reaches of the coastal strip, this drive also uncovers some of the less-visited attractions that lie amid the citrus groves, scrubland and golf courses that dominate the view from the Interstate.

Two of the area's natural springs are protected as state parks, one of them as popular with manatees as it is with people, and both allow ample opportunity to enjoy natural Florida at its best. Also within easy reach of I-4 is DeLand, where the creator of the stetson hat funded the university whose campus fills half the town, and the other-worldly community of Cassadaga.

BLUE SPRING STATE PARK*

Blue Spring State Park $ 2100 W French Avenue, off Hwy-92; tel: (386) 775-3663; www.floridastateparks.org/ bluespring. Open daily 0800–sunset.

The crystal-clear waters of a natural spring make this park popular for swimming, scuba diving and canoeing. Humans are not permitted to swim with the manatees who frequent the park in winter, but the creatures can be observed from the park's boardwalks as they enjoy the warmth of the 72°F waters. In prehistoric times, sandbanks here held the snails that provided food for native people. The discarded shells formed a mound that subsequently provided a foundation for the 1872 **Thursby House**, inside which are mementoes of the paddle-steamers that once travelled on the St John's River, fed by the spring.

CASSADAGA*

Inhabited almost entirely by spiritualists who offer half-hour consultations, Cassadaga was founded by George Colby, a New York-born travelling medium who chose the 35-acre site in 1875 with the

ⓘ Cassadaga
Information Center
112 Stevens Street; tel: (386)
228-2880;
www.cassadaga.org.
Open Mon–Sat 1000–1700,
Sun 1130–1700.

help of a Native American spirit guide. A large number of the simple wood-framed cottages of the 1920s, built when many believers settled here, remain and create a slightly spooky first impression. This is quickly dispelled by the helpful staff of the information centre inside the Andrew Jackson Davies Building and the realisation that all who practise here are sincere in what they do.

DAYTONA BEACH✦✦✦

ⓘ Daytona Beach
Area Convention &
Visitors Bureau *126 E*
Orange Avenue; tel: (386) 255-
0415 or (800) 854-1234;
www.daytonabeach.com. Open
Mon–Fri 0900–1700.

🄷 Daytona USA $
1801 W International
Speedway Boulevard;
tel: (386) 947-6800;
www.daytonausa.com. Open
daily 0900–1900.

Halifax Historical
Society Museum $
252 S Beach Street;
tel: (386) 255-6976;
www.halifaxhistorical.org.
Open Tue–Fri 1000–1600,
Sat 1000–1200.

Museum of Arts and
Science $ *1040 Museum*
Boulevard; tel: (904) 255-
0285; www.moas.org. Open
Tue–Fri 0900–1600, Sat
1200–1700.

Daytona Beach, probably the most famous and certainly one of Florida's biggest expanses of sand, is 18 miles long and 500ft wide at low tide. This is one of the few Florida beaches where driving on the sand is possible and permitted, from marked access points and with a strictly enforced speed limit of 10mph.

Cars have been driven on Daytona Beach since 1902, a period when the firm sands offered a better and straighter surface than most roads for auto designers such as Henry Ford, Ransom Eli Olds and Louis Chevrolet to put their latest vehicles to the test. Speed records were frequently set, the last in 1935 by Malcolm Campbell who achieved 276mph.

Away from the endless motels and souvenir shops lining the beach strip, Daytona is a surprisingly small city with a nicely restored Downtown area and two commendable museums (*see below*) occupying the mainland area, divided by the Halifax River from the beach.

When motor racing on the beach was deemed unsafe, the completion of **Daytona International Speedway** in 1959 enabled the city to retain its money-spinning links with speed. The stadium, which holds 150,000 people, hosts eight major race meetings annually, the biggest being the Daytona 500. The track can be toured aboard a minibus which makes an informative if disappointingly slow navigation of the circuit, allowing close-up views of the 30-degree bank beds and some of the burn marks produced by champion racers as they brushed the wall at 190mph.

The tours begin from **Daytona USA** which also holds a multimedia exhibition charting the history of auto racing at Daytona Beach. Other computer-aided displays allow visitors to design their own racing car, participate in a timed pit stop and add their own commentary to a race.

Proof that there has been life in and around Daytona even before its beach brought the area international renown is provided by the well-stocked **Halifax Historical Society Museum** inside the ornate *beaux arts*-style Merchants Bank building. Native American relics include a 800-year-old dugout canoe; other items document Florida's Spanish and British periods when sugar and cotton plantations were established locally, and entertaining photographs and exhibits chart Daytona Beach's motor-racing legacy.

The natural history section of Daytona Beach's **Museum of Arts and Science** has plenty to appeal to children, not least the skeleton of

Above
Daytona USA

a locally found 13-ft-high giant ground sloth, 130,000 years old and striking an angry pose. Adjacent exhibits are designed to provide an introduction to the delights of fossils and Florida ecosystems. A planetarium adjoins the museum, whose arts section includes a major collection of pre-revolution Cuban painting, much of it from the collection donated by the country's one-time dictator General Batista who was ousted in 1959 and spent his exile near Daytona Beach. The works explore the rise of Cuban art from the colonial-era through independence to the modernism that blossomed in 1950s Havana.

The Arts in America Wing documents the US's artistic heritage from the Pilgrim Fathers to Victorian times. The cache includes Philadelphia cabinets, Chippendale chairs, decorative glass and silverware, and art from influential figures such as portraitist Gilbert Stuart and landscape painter George Inness.

Accommodation in Daytona Beach

Atlantic Dunes $–$$ *1993 S Atlantic Avenue; tel: (386) 255-7501 or (800) 292-7501; www.atlanticdunesmotel.com.* Choice of regular rooms and cottages sleeping up to eight people and free internet access.

Capri Motel $–$$ *832 N Atlantic Avenue; tel: (386) 252-2555 or (800) 874-1820; www.ocean-villa.com.* Small, friendly beachside motel with a games room and coin-operated laundry.

Coquina Inn $$ *544 S Palmetto Avenue; tel: (386) 254-4969 or (800) 805-7533; www.coquinainndaytonabeach.com.* This beautifully furnished 1912 home with just four guest rooms makes a perfect escape from the crowds and motels of Daytona's beach strip.

DeLand*

ⓘ DeLand Chamber of Commerce 336 N Woodland Boulevard; tel: (386) 734-4331; www.delandchamber.org. Open Mon–Fri 0830–1700.

ⓗ Henry A DeLand House 137 W Michigan Avenue; tel: (386) 740-6813; www.deland.org/parks/ henrydeland.htm. Open Tue–Sat 1200–1600. Free.

Gillespie Museum of Minerals Stetson University, 234 E Michigan Avenue; tel: (386) 822-7330; www. gillespiemuseum.stetson.edu. Open Tue–Fri 1000–1600. Closed during university vacations.

In 1876, Henry A DeLand founded what he hoped would become the 'Athens of Florida'. Despite falling short of its founder's vision, DeLand is an agreeable place with a nicely restored centre and the Greek Revival **Henry A DeLand House**, built in 1886 and furnished in period style.

To attract settlers, Henry DeLand founded the private college that evolved into **Stetson University**, in recognition of the financial contribution made by his friend, hat-maker John Stetson. Spread across 150 acres, the campus has many attractive century-old buildings and with the **Gillespie Museum of Minerals** boasts one of the world's largest privately owned mineral collections.

Food in DeLand

Hontoon Landing Resort & Marina $$ 2317 River Ridge Road; tel: (904) 734-2474 or (800) 248-2474; www.hontoon.com. In a rural setting beside the St John's River offering a choice of motel-type rooms, kitchen-equipped cottages and houseboats.

DeLeon Springs State Recreational Area***

ⓗ DeLeon Springs State Park $ off Hwy-17; tel: (386) 985-4212; www.floridastateparks.org/ deleonsprings. Open daily 0800–sunset.

Canoeing and swimming are offered in this 600-acre park built around a natural spring. From the early 1800s, the spring powered a waterwheel used to grind sugar cane. Still in use, the machinery now grinds the flour used in the breads and biscuits made at the park's Sugar Mill Restaurant, where customers can also bake their own pancakes at the griddle-equipped dining tables.

Ormond Beach**

ⓗ The Casements $ 25 Riverside Drive; tel: (386) 676-3216. Open Mon–Fri 1000–1430, Sat 1000–1130.

Ormond Memorial Art Museum and Gardens 78 E Granada Boulevard; tel: (386) 676-3347; www.ormondartmuseum.org. Open Mon–Fri 1000–1600, Sat–Sun 1200–1600.

Connection to the railway in the 1880s made Ormond Beach a favoured winter base of the rich and famous. One who took a shine to the place was millionaire oil baron John D Rockefeller who from 1918 to his death in 1937 spent his winters at the elegant mansion known as **The Casements**. A small collection of furnishings and other items record Rockefeller's occupancy, although the building now houses a Hungarian Culture Centre as well as somewhat incongruous displays of Italian ceramics and boy scout paraphernalia.

Close by, the art exhibitions of the **Ormond Memorial Art Museum** are of less interest than its 4-acre **gardens**, a profusion of tropical trees and plants set along shady walkways that lead to a pleasant gazebo and a turtle-inhabited pond.

Food in Ormond Beach

Atlantic Diner $–$$ *790 S Atlantic Boulevard, tel: (386) 615-6860.* Enjoyable beachside diner that offers home-made soups and a variety of other dishes, for breakfast, lunch and dinner, seven days a week.

PONCE DELEON INLET*

Ponce deLeon Inlet Lighthouse $
4931 S Peninsula Drive; tel: (386) 761-1821; www.ponceinlet.org. Open May–Labor Day, daily 1000–2100; rest of year daily 1000–1700.

Right
Ponce deLeon Inlet
Lighthouse

Ponce deLeon Inlet was known as Mosquito Inlet until 1927 when the name was deemed a deterrent to would-be settlers. At the southern extremity, the restored outbuildings of the 1887 **Ponce deLeon Inlet Lighthouse** provide an intriguing history of Florida's lighthouses and record some of the many shipwrecks they failed to prevent. The reward for clambering up 203 steps is a coastal view from 175ft high.

Food in Ponce Inlet

Down the Hatch $–$$ *4849 Front Street; tel: (386) 761-4831.* A riverside location and an impressively lengthy menu that includes oysters, lobster tails and grouper sandwiches amid mostly fish-based lunches and dinners.

SUGAR MILL GARDENS*

Sugar Mill Gardens
Old Sugar Mill Road, Port Orange; tel: (386) 767-1735; www.dir.gardenweb.com. Open daily dawn–dusk. Free.

Footpaths weave through the magnolia and holly trees of this 12-acre park to the substantial ruins of the buildings at the heart of an 1804 sugar plantation. The plantation produced molasses (using the juice of crushed sugar cane) and during the Civil War was used by Confederate troops to extract salt from seawater. During the 1950s, the grounds made an unlikely setting for a dinosaur theme park, a few bizarre remnants of which remain.

Suggested tour

Length: Main tour 115 miles; detours: Ponce Inlet, 22 miles; DeLand and DeLeon Springs State Recreation Area, 25 miles; Cassadaga, 4 miles; Blue Springs State Park, 22 miles.

Duration: Main tour 3 hours; detours: Ponce Inlet, 1 hour; DeLand and DeLeon Springs State Recreation Area, 40 minutes; Cassadaga, 20 minutes; Blue Springs State Park, 45 minutes.

Links: Orlando and its theme parks (*see pages 180–91*).

This is designed as a day-long tour but if your preference is to sunbathe at the beach then there will be little time left for detours, although Ponce Inlet makes a simple and worthwhile excursion from Daytona Beach. For wildlife and nature, take one of the state park detours, and for sheer strangeness do not miss Cassadaga.

Leave Orlando heading east on I-4, after 48 miles joining Hwy-92. As it reaches the outskirts of **DAYTONA BEACH ❶**, Hwy-92 passes the **Daytona International Speedway**. Continue east on Hwy-92. A right turn 3 miles ahead along Nova Road leads to the **Museum of Arts and Sciences**. From the museum, return to Hwy-92 and turn right. At the junction with Hwy-1 (Ridgeway Avenue), turn right for the heart of mainland Daytona Beach and the **Halifax Historical Society Museum,** two blocks east on Beach Street.

Return to Hwy-92 to cross the Halifax River. Directly ahead is the **Pier**, the focal point of Daytona Beach. A concrete boardwalk running three blocks north from the pier provides a chance to sample the seaside atmosphere without getting sand between your toes. Drive north along the hotel-lined Atlantic Avenue for 3 miles to reach **ORMOND BEACH ❷**.

Detour: One of the area's nicest oceanside drives runs 11 miles south from the Daytona Beach pier. Tourist-dominated areas give way to quiet residential communities and the sands become steadily less crowded. At the end of the route is **PONCE DELEON INLET ❸** and its redbrick **lighthouse**. Returning north, turn left on to Dunlawton Avenue, after 5.5 miles reaching the mainland at **Port Orange**. Turn right on to Nova Road and shortly after right into Herbert Road. Old Sugar Mill Road forks to the left and holds the entrance to **SUGAR MILL GARDENS ❹**.

Detour: The placid and welcoming town of **DELAND ❺** is reached on Route 44, off I-4, and by Hwy-92 from Daytona Beach. Seven miles north of DeLand, **DELEON SPRINGS STATE PARK ❻** is at the end of a signposted turning off Hwy-17.

Detour: The spiritualists' community of **CASSADAGA ❼** can be reached using Exit 54 from I-4, 35 miles from Orlando and 25 miles

Tomoka State Park $ *2099 N Beach Street; tel: (386) 676-4050. Open daily 0800–sunset; museum daily 0930–1630.*

from Daytona Beach. Continue by turning right on to Route 4139. Nestled in undulating hillsides, the village lies 1.75 miles ahead.

Detour: BLUE SPRING STATE PARK ❽ is close to the aptly named citrus-producing community of **Orange City**, 5.5 miles south of DeLand on Hwy-92 and 4 miles from I-4 using Route 472. The signposted park lies 2.6 miles west of the town, off W French Avenue, reached with a right turn 1.5 miles south of the Hwy-92 and Route 472 junction.

Also worth exploring

Occupying an oak and magnolia-studded peninsula at the meeting point of the Halifax and Tomoka rivers, **Tomoka State Park** lies 4 miles north of Ormond Beach off Route 5A (Old Dixie Highway). The verdant park makes an appealing spot for a picnic and ramble along its trails, and also has a small **museum** remembering the Timucuan people, the pre-European inhabitants of the area, and Fred Dana Marsh.

Although an award-winning painter, Marsh made his name with art deco murals depicting working people and in the 1920s designed a striking modernist house for himself and his wife in Ormond Beach. Photographs of the house, his murals and other items from his life are displayed. The park also holds Marsh's sculpture, *Legend of Tomokie*, completed in 1957 four years before his death.

The Space Coast

Ratings

Beaches	●●●●●
Science	●●●●●
Children	●●●●○
Nature	●●●●○
Scenery	●●●●○
Museums	●●●○○
Surfing	●●●○○
History	●●○○○

It was from Florida's Space Coast that the first moon landings were launched and it is here that the space shuttle lifts off and returns to earth. Even for locals, the excitement of watching a launch, be it the shuttle or satellite-carrying rockets, never pales and this predominantly flat area has endless vantage points for doing so. The pivot of the Space Coast is the Kennedy Space Center, its exhibition areas illustrating NASA's greatest achievements and its future aspirations.

Strangely, though, nature rather than technology is likely to be your lasting impression of the Space Coast. NASA's launch pads rise from the alligator-patrolled fringes of one the nation's largest wildlife refuges and the Space Center marks one end of a series of barrier-island beach communities. Some, such as Cocoa Beach, are heavily developed while others are set amid lush rows of pine trees with small beach parks often used more by residents than tourists.

ASTRONAUT MEMORIAL PLANETARIUM & OBSERVATORY*

Astronaut Memorial Planeterium & Observatory $ BCC Cocoa Campus, 1519 Clearlake Road; tel: (321) 634-3732; www.brevardcc.edu/planet. Open Wed 1330–1630, Fri–Sat 1830–2230.

Florida's largest planetarium, located in Cocoa on the campus of Brevard Community College, features star shows, an Iwerks movie theater and laser shows. The building also houses a fully accessible observatory, a hands-on demonstration hall and museum honouring space explorers from around the world.

CANAVERAL NATIONAL SEASHORE**

Canaveral National Seashore $ off Hwy-1 near Titusville; tel: (321) 267-3036; www.nps.gov.cana. Open May–Oct, 0600–2000; rest of the year open daily 0600–1800.

Between the Atlantic and Mosquito Lagoon (aptly named, especially so in summer) and overlooked by the launchpads of the Kennedy Space Center, the Canaveral National Seashore comprises 24 miles of pristine protected beaches walled by sand dunes. Roads reach **Apollo Beach** and **Playalinda Beach** between which the 12-mile-long **Klondyke Beach** can only be explored on foot. Swimming is not advised due to strong currents, and walkers should be wary of high tides.

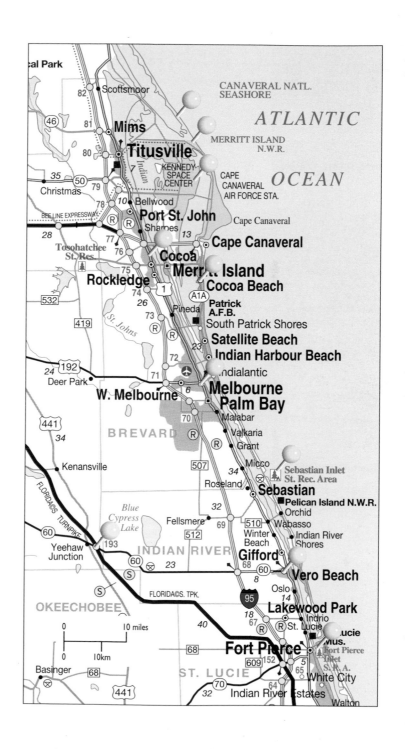

COCOA*

ⓘ Brevard Museum of History and Natural Science $ *2201 N Michigan Avenue; tel: (321) 632-1830; www.brevardmuseum.com. Open Oct–Apr, Tue–Sat 1000–1600, Sun 1300–1600. Closed Sun rest of the year.*

Cobbled streets, small parks and restored buildings largely occupied by antique shops and cafés, fill the four-block **Old Cocoa Village**. The Olde World atmosphere makes a welcome contrast with the predominantly ultra-modern Space Coast. The village lies at the heart of the sprawling settlement of Cocoa, founded in the 1860s in the hope of exploiting the commercial potential of the Indian River. The town's past is cogently documented by the **Brevard Museum of History and Natural Science**.

COCOA BEACH*

ⓘ Cocoa Beach Area Chamber of Commerce *400 Fortenberry Road, Merritt Island; tel: (321) 459-2200; www.cocoabeachchamber.com. Open Mon–Fri 0900–1700.*

ⓘ Cocoa Pier *401 Meade Avenue; tel: (321) 783-7549; www.cocoabeachpier.com*

◖ Ron Jon Surf Shop *4151 N Atlantic Avenue; tel: (321) 799-8888; www.ronjons.com. Open 24 hours daily.*

Cocoa Beach, the major beach community of the Space Coast, is a long and narrow strip of beach shops and motels, with 8 miles of splendid sands sometimes buffeted by the powerful waves that make this one of the few Florida locations renowned for surfing. The pulse of the community is best felt at the 800-ft-long **Cocoa Pier** which holds several bars and restaurants, and is one of the region's best places to view space launches. The other local landmark is the **Ron Jon Surf Shop**, a vividly decorated store offering outrageously kitsch beach accessories alongside its staple stock of top-class surfboards.

Accommodation and food in Cocoa Beach

Atlantic Ocean Grille $–$$ *Cocoa Beach Pier, 401 Meade Avenue; tel: (321) 783-7459; www.cocoabeachpier.com.* Enjoying a perfect setting on the area's most popular pier, with good-value daily specials often featuring freshly-caught seafood.

Bernard's Surf $$–$$$ *2 S Atlantic Avenue; tel: (321) 783-2401; www.bernardssurf.com/contact.html.* Family owned since 1948 and a favourite of locals and astronauts for its fresh seafood and steaks in a friendly atmosphere. The adjoining Rusty's Raw Bar offers inexpensive lunches.

Grills Seafood Deck & Tiki Bar $–$$ *505 Glen Creek Drive, Cape Canaveral; tel: (321) 868-2226; www.visitgrills.com.* Watch cruise ships and occasional space launches while tucking into a fish sandwich or a Spanish Armada omelette.

The Inn at Cocoa Beach $$–$$$ *4300 Ocean Beach Boulevard, tel: (321) 799-3460 or (800) 343-5307; www.theinnatcocoabeach.com.* All rooms have patios or balconies, fresh breads and fruit are served for breakfast, and the resident parrot enjoys a chat.

Luna Sea Bed & Breakfast Motel $$ *3185 N Atlantic Avenue; tel: (321) 783-0500 or (800) LUNA SEA; www.lunaseacocoabeach.com.* Restfully appointed rooms with minifridges; serves a fairly simple breakfast.

South Beach Inn on the Sea $–$$ *1701 S Atlantic Avenue; tel: (877) 546-6835; www.southbeachinn.com.* Sunbathe and view shuttle launches from kitchen-equipped rooms a few steps from the beach.

FORT PIERCE INLET STATE RECREATION AREA✧✧

Fort Pierce Inlet State Recreation Area $ *905 Shorewinds Drive; tel: (561) 468-3985; www.floridastateparks.org/ fortpierceinlet. Open daily 0800–sunset.*

This 340-acre park, a mix of ocean beach, sand dunes and coastal tree hammock, marks the southern end of the pine-lined Hutchinson Island. Park activities include swimming, surfing, picnicking and walking the marked nature trails. Birdwatchers will find more to their liking by crossing the 300-ft concrete bridge leading to **Jack Island State Preserve**, a mangrove-dominated area abutting the Intracoastal Waterway with a mile-long trail and an observation platform likely to bring sightings of herons, ospreys and other birds.

KENNEDY SPACE CENTER✧✧✧

Kennedy Space Center (bus tours $$); *Merritt Island; tel: (321) 452-2121; www.ksc.nasa.gov. Open daily 0900–1730; bus tours every 15 mins 1000–1415, lasting 2 to 2¹/₂ hours.*

The undisputed highlight of the Space Coast is the Kennedy Space Center, where NASA puts its past and present on show, exhibited in and around the visitor centre and on bus tours that access the far-flung reaches of this enormous complex. Complementing the displays are powerful IMAX films on themes of space travel and exploration.

The **Visitor Complex** is a cornucopia of space flight memorabilia, with real and replica space craft from the Mercury, Gemini and Apollo programmes, a lunar rover, assorted space suits, moon rock and many other items accompanied by a photographic record of manned space flight. Outside, the **Rocket Garden** demonstrates how small the early space rockets were, particularly when compared to the monstrous

Right
Saturn rocket, Kennedy Space Center

Saturn V and the full-sized space shuttle replica adjacent to the interactive exhibits of the **Launch Status Center**, which highlights the craft's pre-launch routines.

Further afield and only accessible on a bus tour, the **Apollo/Saturn V Center** focuses on the Apollo programme that used the immense power of the Saturn V rocket to reach speeds of 25,000mph to escape the earth's atmosphere on the way to the exploration of the moon. The **Firing Room Theater** effectively re-creates the launch, including the shuddering blast of Apollo 8, the craft that carried the first astronauts to orbit the moon with footage of the event shown on towering screens. The momentous first moon landing is re-created inside the **Lunar Surface Theater**.

Also on the bus tour, the **LC39 Observation Gantry** provides an unobstructed view of the space shuttle's two launch pads, previously used by the Apollo missions, and of the 525-ft-high Vehicle Assembly Building where the shuttle is put together. Exhibits and a narrated film describe the extraordinarily complex task of simply moving the shuttle, at 1mph, to its launch site.

Other tours visit the **International Space Station Center**, with exhibits on the current multinational space station project and teasing tasters of NASA's plans for the exploration of Mars, and the **Cape Canaveral Air Force Station**, launch site for military and commercial rockets, and home to the **Air Force Space Museum** with its enormous collection of missiles.

MELBOURNE*

Spick and span but rather soulless, Melbourne was originally settled by freed slaves and given its name by the Australian proprietor of the local post office. The small economic boom it enjoyed when linked to the railroad in 1894 was greatly surpassed in the 1960s when NASA's expansion brought thousands of new settlers. Across the Indian River, **Melbourne Beach** is a pleasantly low-key alternative to the busier Cocoa Beach.

MERRITT ISLAND NATIONAL WILDLIFE REFUGE**

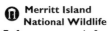 **Merritt Island National Wildlife Refuge** *eastern end of Route 402; tel: (321) 861-0677; www.merrittisland.fws.gov. Open daily dawn–dusk; some roads closed during space launches. Free.*

The Merritt Island National Wildlife Refuge fills 220 square miles around the Kennedy Space Center and holds more endangered species than any other refuge in the US. Within a landscape dominated by marshes but studded with hardwood hammocks and pine woods are alligators, bobcats, otters, marsh rabbits and even a few wild pigs among a long list of regularly sighted creatures.

Above the refuge, particularly during winter migrations, the skies teem with herons, gulls, terns and pelicans, while wading birds such as wood storks and ibis are often spotted feeding at the water's edge. Majestic bald eagles and colourful roseate spoonbills make less frequent appearances. Also occasionally sighted overhead, the space shuttle uses a landing strip adjacent to the refuge.

The 6-mile **Black Point Wildlife Drive** provides an excellent introduction to the refuge and is lined by marked stops with displays highlighting aspects of the landscape, be they bald eagle habitats or mudflats. The drive also accesses the **Cruickshank Trail**, a 5-mile foot trail with an observation tower a few minutes' walk from the car park.

The salt marsh mosquitoes that gave Mosquito Lagoon its name and prevented human settlement of the area can still make summer visits very unpleasant. The best time to spot wildlife is during the winter, in the early morning and as dusk approaches.

SEBASTIAN INLET STATE RECREATION AREA✦✦

Sebastian Inlet State Recreation Area $ 9700 S Hwy-A1A, between Melbourne Beach and Vero Beach; tel: (321) 984-4852; www.floridastate parks.org/sebastianinlet. Open daily 0800–sunset.

McLarty Treasure Museum $ 1380 N Hwy-A1A, between Melbourne Beach and Vero Beach; tel: (772) 589-2147. Open daily 1000–1630.

Spanning both sides of Sebastian Inlet, where the Indian River meets the Atlantic Ocean, this 587-acre park is much admired by anglers for the snook, redfish and Spanish mackerel that surrender themselves to hooks, and by surfers for the powerful breakers that make this Florida's premier wave-riding location.

Also in the park, the **McLarty Treasure Museum** tells the dramatic story of the Spanish fleet that floundered in Sebastian Inlet during a hurricane in 1715 and the attempts by the 1500 survivors to salvage the gold and silver, essential to the economy of Spain, that had gone down with the ships. Some of the recovered booty was subsequently raided by British pirates.

VERO BEACH*

Center for the Arts *3001 Riverside Drive; tel: (561) 231-0707; www.vbmuseum.org. Open Mon–Sat 1000–1630, Sun 1300–1630. Possible charge for special exhibitions, otherwise free.*

Although it has little to detain visitors, Vero Beach is among Florida's most attractive small coastal towns and has compounded its affluent and culturally aspiring image with the $2.5 million **Center for the Arts**, an art museum and teaching facility that is the largest of its kind in the state. Despite its ramshackle form, a longer-standing structure of note is the splendid **Driftwood Inn**, constructed from odd bits of timber during the 1930s and serving as a hotel until being converted to apartments.

YEEHAW JUNCTION*

At dot-on-the-map Yeehaw Junction, the **Desert Inn** can trace its roots to the 1880s when it became a supply stop for timber-carrying trains and cattle-driving cowboys. The inn's bar and dining room is a wonderful evocation of bygone Florida, and also serves traditional Florida food (*see below*). If asked nicely, the owner will lead guided tours of the upper floor, giving customers a glimpse of the state's only restored bordello.

Accommodation and food in Vero Beach and Yeehaw Junction

Desert Inn $ *5570 S Kenansville Road, Yeehaw Junction; tel: (407) 436-1054; www. desertinnrestaurant.com.* A genuine slice of old Florida that offers gator tail and frogs' legs among more common delights.

Disney's Vero Beach Resort $$$ *9250 Island Grove Terrace, Vero Beach; tel: (561) 224-2000; www.dvc.disney.go.com.* Disney fans who love the beach will relish this luxurious Disney-owned oceanside property, styled as an old Florida resort complete with replica Spanish galleon.

Left
Vero Beach

NASA and the Space Coast

In May 1961, President Kennedy's pledge that the US would land a man on the moon and return him safely to earth by the end of the decade sparked a massive influx of technicians, engineers, astronauts and other NASA (National Aeronautics and Space Administration) personnel into a thinly populated citrus and cattle-farming area around the Air Force missile base of Cape Canaveral, soon to become known as the Space Coast.

Through the 1960s, the Apollo programme, climaxing with the first manned moon landing in 1969, brought world attention to the region. Declining public enthusiasm and a reduction in NASA's funding prompted the development of the reusable space shuttle, its success tempered by the *Challenger* disaster of 1986. With the current International Space Station project and a long-term objective of a manned Mars landing, NASA continues to be a major employer in a region where developments in space exploration are perhaps more keenly observed than in any other place in the world.

Suggested tour

Space launch information

Almost any section of the Space Coast makes a good vantage point for watching shuttle launches from the Kennedy Space Center and the satellite-carrying rocket lift-offs from the nearby Cape Canaveral Air Force Base. NASA's anticipated launch dates and times are obtainable by calling *(321) 867-4636* and given on the web: *www.ksc.nasa.gov*

Length: Main tour 162 miles; Merritt Island detour, 20 miles; Sebastian Inlet detour and return to Orlando, 150 miles.

Duration: Main tour 3 hours; Merritt Island detour, 45 minutes; Sebastian Inlet detour and return to Orlando, 3.5 hours.

Links: Orlando and its theme parks (*see pages 180–91*).

Designed as a day tour from Orlando but with the option of spending a night on the coast, this tour focuses on the Kennedy Space Center and explores the surrounding communities with a scenic drive along a portion of the coast. The first detour is the unspoilt beaches and wildlife areas adjacent to the Kennedy Space Center. The second extends the idea of coastal touring but also branches inland to one of Florida's more unusual places of interest.

The Bee Line Expressway is the most direct route from Orlando to the **KENNEDY SPACE CENTER ❶**, 50 miles east. Exit on to Route 407 and after 6.6 miles join Route 405 following the well-signposted route that continues across the Indian River. From the Kennedy Space Center, head south from Route 405 on Hwy-1, continuing for 13 miles to **COCOA ❷** with its **Astronaut Memorial Planetarium & Observatory** and its atmospheric historic area, Old Cocoa Village. This is on the banks of the Indian River, just south of the junction with Route 520.

Return to Route 520, which becomes the Merritt Island Causeway as you turn right and cross the Indian River and a section of Merritt Island before sweeping over the broad Banana River. After 7 miles, the route reaches the ocean-hugging Hwy-A1A and **COCOA BEACH ❸**. This expansive beachside community extends for many miles along Hwy-A1A, though its spiritual centre is the **Cocoa Pier**, half a mile ahead after turning north on to Hwy-A1A.

Below
Ron Jon Surf Shop, Cocoa Beach

From the pier, head south along Hwy-A1A, passing myriad motels, beach accessory and souvenir shops, and oceanside small parks. Possessing a lengthy runway and the laboratories where military rocket technology was developed, the **Patrick Air Force Base**, 6.5 miles south of Route 520 junction, provides the first major variation in the view. The route continues through shoulder-to-shoulder beach towns such as **Satellite Beach** and **Indian Harbour Beach**, each with their own small beach parks.

Four miles south of Indian Harbour Beach, turn right on Hwy-192 and re-cross the Banana River to reach **MELBOURNE ❹**, 2.8 miles ahead. Continue on Hwy-192 to return to Orlando, 60 miles further.

Detour: Turn right turn on to Hwy-1 after leaving the Kennedy Space Center. After 6.5 miles, this passes through **Titusville** where there's a right turn on to Route 406 leading to the **MERRITT ISLAND NATIONAL WILDLIFE REFUGE ❺**. Within the refuge, Route 402 branches from Route 406 to provide access to **Playalinda Beach** marking the southern edge of the **CANAVERAL NATIONAL SEASHORE ❻**.

Detour: Instead of turning inland off Hwy-A1A towards Melbourne, continue on the scenic coast course for 19 miles, reaching the **SEBASTIAN INLET STATE RECREATION AREA ❼**. The route continues across the inlet and after a further 16 miles meets the junction with Route 60, which heads inland to **VERO BEACH ❽**. Continue inland on Route 60 from Vero Beach for 31 miles and the tiny crossroads settlement of **YEEHAW JUNCTION ❾**. The **Desert Inn** stands by the junction of Route 60, Hwy-441 and the Florida Turnpike. Travel north on the latter (toll) for 84 miles to reach Orlando.

Also worth exploring

Overlooking cruise and cargo ships and the launch pads of the adjacent Cape Canaveral Air Force Base, **Jetty Park** is a 35-acre patch of sand-dune-lined greenery in Port Canaveral, immediately north of Cocoa Beach off Hwy-A1A. Popular with anglers and surfers, the park also makes an excellent picnic stop and is a fine place to view space launches.

Ratings

History	●●●●●
Ambience	●●●●○
Architecture	●●●○○
Children	●●●○○
Museums	●●●○○
Arts and crafts	●●○○○
Beaches	●●○○○
Nature	●○○○○

St Augustine

St Augustine is a pocket-sized town that speaks volumes about Florida's colonial past. It's an immediately welcoming place and one of the few towns in the state that can be comprehensively explored on foot. The short, narrow streets are lined by palm trees and 200-year-old houses whose plaster-coated walls and wooden verandas would evoke an atmosphere akin to a sleepy Mediterranean village were it not for the many tourists who flock to this deservedly popular destination.

Founded by the Spanish in 1565, St Augustine is the oldest permanent European settlement in the US. Swapping Havana, Cuba, for Florida in 1763, the British arrived here and stayed for 20 years until Florida returned to Spanish rule, prior to being ceded to the US in 1821. From the town's oldest house to the old county jail, it showcases all these periods with the kind of authenticity that Walt Disney World might spend a fortune trying to re-create.

Sights

ⓘ St Augustine Visitor Information Center *10 Castillo Drive; tel: (904) 825-1000; www.ci.st-augustine.fl.us. Open June–Labor Day, daily 0800–1930; Apr, May, Sept and Oct, daily 0830–1830; rest of the year 0830–1730.*

ⓝ Castillo de San Marcos $ *1 Castillo Drive; tel: (904) 829-6506; www.nps.gov/casa. Open daily 0845–1645.*

Castillo de San Marcos***

If a single feature symbolises St Augustine's battled-scarred past, it is Castillo de San Marcos. The castle was completed around 1695, with pointed triangular bastions at each corner, and is the oldest masonry fort in the US. The 12-ft-thick coquina (limestone formed by compacted sea shells) walls were able to resist a 27-day British bombardment in 1740 by absorbing the arriving cannon balls.

The 35-ft-high ramparts provide a good view over the town and many of the castle's atmospheric rooms carry historical displays. Free guided tours and the periodic 'living history' demonstrations by period-attired volunteers explain much more about the castle's history and architecture.

0   300m
0   300 yards

Ribera Street

Old Jail

Williams Street

Fountain of Youth
Archaeological Park

San Marco Avenue

Magnolia Avenue

Myrtle Avenue

Sebastian Avenue

Ocean Avenue

Mission de Nombre Dios

Old Mission Avenue

Pine Street

Rhode Avenue

Water Street

5

Shenandoah Street

Matanzas
River

Castillo Drive

Ripley's Believe
It or Not!

Old City Gate

Castillo de San Marcos

Orange Street

Ponce De Leon Boulevard

Riberia Street

Oldest Wooden Schoolhouse

Cordova Street

Sevilla Street

Cuna Street

St George Street

Charlotte Street

Spanish Quarter
Museum

Avenida Menendez

Riberia Street

Treasury Street

Peña-Peck House

Plaza de la Constitución

A1A

Flagler
College

Sevilla Street

Cordova Street

Cathedral Place

Bridge of Lions

Valencia Street

King Street

Spanish Military Hospital

King Street

Malaga Street

Lightner Museum

Granada Street

Ximenez-Fatio
House

Avila Street

Cadiz St

St George Street

Cordova Street

Avenida Menendez

Marine St

Charlotte Street

Riberia Street

M L King Avenue

Bridge Street

San
Sebastian
River

Tovar House

Oldest House

St Francis Street

Flagler College◆◆

Flagler College occupies the former Ponce de León Hotel, opened by oil and transportation magnate Henry Flagler in the 1880s to accommodate the wealthy vacationers brought to St Augustine by his railway.

Named for the first European to land in Florida and intended to be the last word in luxury lodgings, the hotel sought to replicate the grandeur and elegance of the finest European architecture with a profusion of spires, masses of terracotta ornamentation and two bell towers. The renowned Louis Comfort Tiffany provided stained-glass windows and lampshades in a design overseen by fledgling architects, Carrere & Hastings, later to find fame with the New York Public Library.

Flagler College 74 King Street; tel: (904) 829 6481; www.flager.edu. Free guided tours daily in summer 1000–1600 and winter college vacation.

The extension of the Flagler railroad to create the new resort of Palm Beach contributed to the decline of the hotel, which became a college in the 1970s, although many interior features can still be admired on guided tours.

Fountain of Youth Archaeological Park $
155 Magnolia Avenue; tel: (904) 829-3168; www. fountainofyouthflorida.com. Open daily 0900–1700.

Fountain of Youth Archaeological Park◆

When Ponce de León and his crew made the first European landing in Florida in 1513, their agenda included discovering gold and silver, converting natives to Catholicism and finding the secret of eternal life which modern-day visitors are led to believe consists of drinking the slightly sulphurous water issuing from the well around which this park is built. The park has greater significance, however, for the archaeological excavations which have yielded evidence of the Timucuan settlement, thought to have been the first point of contact for Spanish Pedro Menéndez de Avilés, who landed in the vicinity in 1565 having been appointed first governor of Florida.

Lightner Museum $
75 King Street; tel: (904) 824-2874; www.lightnermuseum.org. Open daily 0900–1700.

Lightner Museum◆◆◆

Only slightly less posh than the Ponce de León (see Flagler College, above), the Alcazar was another Flagler-owned hotel with an exuberant Spanish-Moorish design. Many of the original architectural features have been maintained and create an impressive backdrop for the outstanding collection of mostly 19th-century decorative arts amassed by publisher Otto Lightner, who bought the dilapidated hotel as a home for his collection in 1948.

Over three copiously-filled floors are Tiffany windows, crystal glass, Meissen porcelain, musical instruments, furnishings, clocks, paintings, stamps, buttons, dolls and dolls' houses, and all manner of objets d'art, mostly acquired from the estates of wealthy Chicagoans as they sought to raise money during the Depression. On a lower level, once the site of the world's largest indoor swimming pool, is an antiques mall.

Mission de Nombre Dios *San Marco Avenue; tel: (904) 824-3045. Open daily 0800–sunset. Free.*

Old Jail $ *167 San Marco Avenue (tickets from 1 King Street); tel: (904) 826-4281. Open Mon–Sat 1000–2100, Sun 1000–1800.*

Oldest House $ *14 St Francis Street; tel: (904) 824-2874. Guided tour only, daily 0900–1700.*

Oldest Wooden School House $ *14 St George Street; tel: (888) 653-7245. Open daily 0900–1700.*

Useful website Information on St Augustine's historical sites, tours, accommodation and restaurants can be found at *www.visitoldcity.com*

Mission de Nombre Dios*

The first Mass in what became the US was held on these grounds in 1565. The fact is marked by a 208-ft stainless steel cross rising above the Tolomato River, marking the alleged landing site of the ship carrying first Florida governor Pedro Menéndez de Avilés and Father Lopez de Mendoza Grajales, who conducted the Mass in front of Timucuan villagers. A re-creation of the original chapel makes an atmospheric addition to the pleasant, tree-filled grounds where the US's first Spanish mission was erected and which now hold an uninteresting modern church.

Old Jail**

This county jail and sheriff's quarters was built in 1892 and remained in service until 1953. Now a museum, the jail gives surprisingly intriguing insights into Florida's one-time penal system, not least the fact that the prisoners, segregated by race as well as gender, ate food cooked by the sheriff's wife (some inmates apparently considered this part of their punishment). Assorted weapons, a gallows and an electric chair complete the picture.

Personal items belonging to Flagler and the story of his railway form the best sections of the **Florida Heritage Museum**, in a building adjoining the jail.

Oldest House***

The strongest evocation of daily life in early St Augustine is provided by this inauspicious dwelling, the oldest parts of which are the coquina walls, built around 1702. A tabby floor and spartan furnishings suggest the deprivations of artilleryman Tomás González and his family who lived here during the first period of Spanish rule. The British takeover of Florida in 1763 saw an increase in comfort, with glass windows and fireplaces, plus the addition of an upper storey complete with balcony.

Operated for a time as a tavern and occupied by Joseph and Maria Peavett (inspiration for the main character in Eugenia Price's best-selling novel, *Maria*) until being sold at auction in 1790, the house spent the second period of Spanish rule and the early years of US control under the ownership of Gerónimo Alvarez and his descendants. These years are remembered by the Alvarez family dining room and the four-poster bed once occupied by General Joseph Hernández, a leader in the US's war against the Seminoles.

Oldest Wooden School House*

This rickety-looking structure was probably built in the mid-1700s, its cedar and cypress planks held together by wooden pegs and handmade nails. Classes were conducted on the ground floor, the teacher and family living above.

ℹ Peña-Peck House $
143 St George Street;
tel: (904) 829-5064. Guided
tour only, daily 1230–1600.

**Cathedral-Basilica of
St Augustine** *Plaza de
la Constitución; tel: (904)
824-2806. Open daily
0900–1700.*

**Ripey's Believe It or
Not! $$** *19 Marco Avenue;*
tel: (904) 824-1606;
www.staugustine-ripleys.com.
Open Sun–Thur 0900–1900,
Fri–Sat 0900–2000.

**Spanish Military
Hospital $** *(entrance free
with Spanish Quarter
Museum ticket) 3 Aviles
Street; tel: (904) 827-0807.
Open daily 0900–1700.*

**Spanish Quarter
Museum $** *33 St George
Street; tel: (904) 825-5035.
Open daily 0900–1730.*

Tovar House $ *(included
with Oldest House admission;
shared entrance) 14 St
Francis Street; tel: (904)
824-2874. Guided tour only,
daily 0900–1700.*

Below
Blacksmith working in the
Spanish Quarter Museum

Peña-Peck House✦✦

Originally the residence of Juan de Peña, St Augustine's Spanish royal treasurer, and probably built in the 1740s, this house has an elegant appearance accentuated by a second storey added after its purchase by Seth Peck, a doctor from New England, in 1837. Peck, his wife and their descendants amassed the fine collection of paintings, antiques and furnishings that now fill the house.

Plaza de la Constitución✦

The Spanish influence in St Augustine is compounded by this tree-studded plaza, laid out in 1589 to provide the settlement with an administrative and business centre. On the west side of the plaza, **Government House**, restored to its 1764 appearance, marks the site from where St Augustine has been run since the 16th century. A small **museum** uses archaeological finds and other items to document the town's history.

On the plaza's north side, the **Cathedral-Basilica of St Augustine** dates largely from 1887 when the transept and bell tower were added, although there are a few items, such as the marble altar, that survived the fire that destroyed the 1790 original.

Ripley's Believe It or Not!✦✦

Wherever tourists gather so too, it seems, does a Ripley collection of oddities. This was, in 1950, however, the first Ripley's collection to go on permanent public show and Ripley himself, cartoonist, traveller and collector of curios, sometimes stayed as a guest at this 1887 mock-Moorish castle which for a time served as a hotel. From the story of a six-legged cow to a gigantic ferris wheel made from Meccano, the exhibits are sometimes pointless but never dull.

Spanish Military Hospital✦✦

This 1960s reconstruction depicts the apothecary's office and a ward of the Spanish-built hospital erected here in the late 1700s. The hospital's rules and records, surgical instruments and a selection of medicinal herbs, strongly suggest that 18th-century St Augustine was not a good place in which to fall ill.

Spanish Quarter Museum✦✦

The St Augustine of the 1740s is kept alive in this series of restored homes, gardens and workshops in which period-attired guides take the roles of locals and craftspeople, such as blacksmiths, weavers and carpenters, and go about their chores with period tools. Describing and demonstrating the ups and downs of everyday life in the Spanish colony, the quarter is entertaining and extremely informative, and a good place to keep children amused.

Tovar House*
Occupied by infantryman José Tovar from 1763 and subsequently by a Scottish merchant, this two-storey house now contains the **Museum of the Florida Army**, with displays of uniforms worn by Florida soldiers during the Spanish and British periods, and through the Seminole and Civil wars to the present day.

Ximenez-Fatio House
$ 20 Aviles Street; tel: (904) 829-3575; www.ximenezfatiohouse.org. Guided tour only, Mon–Sat 1100–1600.

Ximenez-Fatio House**
This inviting coquina house was built around 1798 for Spanish merchant Andres Ximenez, and has a typically St Augustine blend of Spanish and British architecture. It gained a second storey after being purchased in 1830 by an American, Margaret Cook.

Cook ran the extended property as a boarding house and, prior to the arrival of Flagler's railway and his luxury hotels, it became one of the town's most popular lodgings for wealthy and adventurous northerners. Guided tours tell the story of the house, its design and its owners, and pass through the rooms maintained in the style that Florida tourists enjoyed in the mid-1800s.

Accommodation and food

Cedar House Inn $$–$$$ *79 Cedar Street; tel: (904) 829-0079 or (800) 233-2746; www. cedarhouseinn.com.* Each of the five rooms in this bed-and-breakfast inn is named after the owner's grandparents.

Columbia Restaurant $$ *98 S George Street; tel: (904) 824-3341; www.columbiarestaurant.com.* Local branch of a respected Florida chain specialising in classy Spanish and Cuban dishes.

Coquina Gables $$$ *1 F Street, St Augustine Beach; tel: (904) 461-8727; email: gables@aug.com; www.coquinagables.com.* Ocean-facing bed and breakfast in a plushly furnished 1920s house.

Creekside Dinery $–$$ *160 Nix Boatyard Road, off Hwy-1; tel: (904) 829-6113; email: fiddlers@aug.com; www.creeksidedinery.com.* This out-of-the-way magnolia-shrouded eatery beside the Intracoastal Waterway is worth a stop for the unusual Southern-style dishes.

Harry's Seafood Bar & Grill $$ *46 Avenida Menendez; tel: (904) 824-7765; www.hookedonharrys.com.* New Orleans-style cuisine, including jambalaya and shrimp remoulade, and live entertainment.

Old City House $$$ *115 Cordova Street; tel: (904) 826-0184; www.oldcityhouse.com.* Highly regarded for its creative menu and subdued setting; dinner only.

Suggested tour

Oldest Store Museum $ 4 Artillery Lane; tel: (904) 829-9729. Open Mon–Sat 0900–1700, Sun 1200–1700; open at 1000 on Sun June–Aug.

St Augustine Lighthouse and Museum $ Old Beach Road, Anastasia Island; tel: (904) 829-0745. Open daily 0900–1800.

Length: Main tour, 0.7 miles; 1 mile with American era detour and 2.5 miles with the Fountain of Youth Archaeological Park detour.

Duration: Main tour, 30 minutes' walk; 45 minutes with American era detour; 1.5 hours with Archaeological Park detour.

Begin at the **Old City Gate** ❶, the only access to the city after the British bombardment of 1702. To the left is the **CASTILLO DE SAN MARCOS** ❷; directly ahead is the palm-lined and pedestrianised St George Street with the **OLDEST WOODEN SCHOOLHOUSE** ❸ on the right. The main entrance to the homes and workshops of the **SPANISH QUARTER MUSEUM** ❹ is ahead on the left.

Cross the junction with Treasury Street for the **PENA-PECK HOUSE** ❺, then continue along St George Street to reach **PLAZA DE LA CONSTITUCION** ❻. East of the plaza, the decorated 1926 **Bridge of Lions** ❼ carries traffic across Mantanzas Bay toward the beaches.

On the south side of the plaza, the **SPANISH MILITARY HOSPITAL** ❽ is to the left on Aviles Street. Ahead on the right is Artillery Street holding the **Oldest Store Museum** ❾, a well-stocked general store in early-1900s style. Return to Aviles Street where the **XIMENEZ-FATIO HOUSE** ❿ is ahead on the right. From here, turn left on to Cadiz Street then right on to Charlotte Street, walking south for St Francis Street and the neighbouring **TOVAR HOUSE** ⓫ and **OLDEST HOUSE** ⓬.

Detour: To discover the key sights of St Augustine's American era walk west along King Street from Plaza de la Constitución. The strikingly ornate forms of **FLAGLER COLLEGE** ⓭, to the right, and the **LIGHTNER MUSEUM** ⓮, to the left, loom across Cordova Street.

Detour: A contrast to the narrow and mostly traffic-free streets of the old centre, busy San Marco Avenue runs north from the Old City Gate. Immediately ahead is **RIPLEY'S BELIEVE IT OR NOT!** ⓯. Half-a-mile further is the **MISSION DE NOMBRE DIOS** ⓰. Continue north, along Myrtle and Magnolia avenues to reach the **FOUNTAIN OF YOUTH ARCHAEOLOGICAL PARK** ⓱. From the park, Williams Street runs west and meets San Marco Avenue directly opposite the **OLD JAIL** ⓲.

Also worth exploring

Cross the Bridge of Lions and the ocean is just 2 miles distant on Anastasia Boulevard, a local section of the coastal route, Hwy-A1A, which continues along the slender and scenic **Anastasia Island**. The 11-mile-long island is flanked by a glorious beach. For a bird's-eye view of the island and St Augustine itself, climb the 214 steps to the top of the **St Augustine Lighthouse** on Old Beach Road.

0   300m
0   300 yards

18 Old Jail
Dufferin Street
Williams Street

17 Fountain of Youth Archaeological Park
Magnolia Avenue

San Marco Avenue

Sebastian Avenue
Myrtle Avenue
Ocean Avenue

16 Mission de Nombre Dios

Old Mission Avenue

Pine Street

Rhode Avenue

Water Street

5

Shenandoah Street

Castillo Drive

15 Ripley's Believe It or Not!

Matanzas River

Ponce De Leon Boulevard

Riberia Street

1 Old City Gate

2 Castillo de San Marcos

Orange Street

3 Oldest Wooden Schoolhouse

Cordova Street

Cuna Street

St George Street

4 Spanish Quarter Museum

Charlotte Street

Avenida Menendez

Sevilla Street

Riberia Street

Valencia Street

Cordova Street

Treasury Street

5 Peña-Peck House

13 Flagler College

Cathedral Place

7 Bridge of Lions   A1A

6 Plaza de la Constitución

King Street

8 Spanish Military Hospital

9 Aviles St

Malaga Street

King Street

Sevilla Street

Granada Street

14 Lightner Museum

10 Cadiz St

Ximenez-Fatio House

Avenida Menendez

Marine Street

San Sebastian River

M L King Avenue

Bridge Street

Cordova Street

St George Street

Charlotte Street

St Francis Street

Tovar House **11** **12** Oldest House

Riberia Street

Amelia Island and the northeast corner

Ratings

Beaches	●●●●●
Nature	●●●●○
Scenery	●●●●○
History	●●●○○
Sport	●●●○○
Surfing	●●●○○
Children	●●○○○
Museums	●●○○○

Florida first-timers can be forgiven for being unaware of the charms of the state's northeast corner. A glance at the map suggests the area is consumed by sprawling Jacksonville and an enormous naval air force base. Old hands know better, however, and this tour makes a point of showing why many of them make repeated visits to the area, happy in the knowledge that much of it remains secret from the vacationing hordes.

From commercially developed surfer-friendly beach communities, the route strikes into less developed areas of old shrimping villages and state parks that consume entire islands. With Fernandina Beach, the end of the road is literally reached in a time-locked port town of hundred-year-old homes and dune-lined beaches. Throughout are echoes of earlier times: from the pre-European Timucua people and a 16th-century French Huguenot settlement to a slave-worked plantation and a dramatic re-creation of life in a Civil War fort.

AMELIA ISLAND✦✦✦

ⓘ **Amelia Island Chamber of Commerce** *102 Centre Street, Fernandina Beach; tel: (904) 261-3248 or (800) 226-3542; www.aifby.com. Open Mon–Sat 1100–1600, Sun 1200–1600.*

☾ **Amelia Island Plantation** *$$$ 3000 First Coast Highway; tel: (904) 261-6161 or (888) 261-6161; www.aipfl.com. A sybaritic retreat embracing faultless rooms and service, golf courses, tennis courts and several miles of beach.*

Mixing verdant greenery with 12 miles of sparkling beaches, Amelia Island is the gem of Florida's northeastern corner. Although its perfectly contoured golf courses and champion-frequented tennis courts attract many regular visitors, this is still one of the few places in Florida where horses can be ridden bareback along the sands.

The peace and tranquillity of the present day conceal the island's lively past. Becoming the Atlantic terminal of a cross-state railway to Cedar Key made Amelia a transit point for slaves and liquor. The decline of the railway left the island high and dry, particularly as newer railways carried tourists to more southerly sections of the state. The largest settlement, Fernandina Beach (*see opposite*) is a wonderfully preserved Victorian town; the excellent Fort Clinch State Park (*see page 221*) marks the island's northern tip.

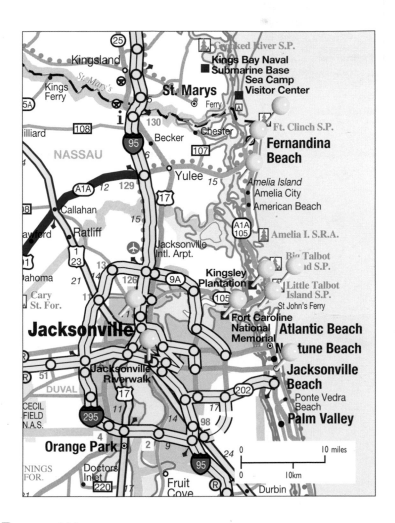

FERNANDINA BEACH❖❖❖

Amelia Island
Museum of History
$ 233 S 3rd Street; tel:
(904) 261-7378;
www.ameliaisland.com.
Guided tour only, Mon–Sat
1100 and 1400.

A sheltered estuary and the US's ban on foreign shipping in 1807 helped Fernandina Beach (then under Spanish control) become a multinational port with merchants, pirates and smugglers all looking to exploit illicit trade routes into the US. The outlaw days were ended by US rule in Florida and Fernandina's relocation to a site adjacent to the cross-state railway, which boosted the local economy as it brought the first major influx of American tourists and settlers.

Remarkably, some 450 structures dating mostly from the last quarter of the 19th century still remain in the heart of Fernandina Beach, forming part of a 50-block **historic district** on and around Centre

Eight Flags Shrimp Festival The first weekend in May finds 100,000 people heading to Fernandina Beach to eat shrimps in familiar and unfamiliar ways and watch a variety of strange shrimp-related events. Information on the festival can be found at *www.shrimpfestival.com*

Street. The predominantly Queen Anne and Italianate architectural features of the carefully maintained homes, such as bay windows, corner turrets, wraparound porches and all manner of decorative carpentry, bring considerable charm to the town.

The island's eventful past is outlined at the **Amelia Island Museum of History**, housed in a former gaol. The museum also details the shrimping industry that developed on the Amelia River in the 1850s and is still among the most important in the US, celebrated each May with the **Eight Flags Shrimp Festival** around the docks at the west end of Centre Street.

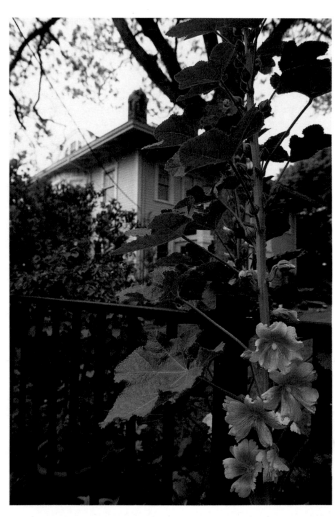

Accommodation and food in Fernandina Beach

The Bailey House $$ *28 S 7th Street; tel: (904) 261-5390 or (800) 251-5390; www.bailey-house.com.* One of the most photographed homes in the historic district offers bed and breakfast in antique-filled rooms with a wealth of period features, not least the claw-foot baths.

Beech Street Grill $$–$$$ *801 Beech Street; tel: (904) 277-3662; www.beechstreetgrill.com.* Offers an enticing range of imaginatively prepared seafood from the blackboard's daily specials.

Florida House Inn $$ *20 & 22 S 3rd Street; tel: (904) 261-3300 or (800) 258-3301; www.floridahouseinn.com.* Dating from 1857 and one of Florida's oldest hotels, this 11-room bed-and-breakfast inn has handmade quilts and rugs; the pricier rooms have fireplaces and Jacuzzis. The restaurant serves black-eye peas, catfish, mashed potato, pork chops, meatloaf and other staples of Deep South cuisine from help yourself bowls.

FORT CAROLINE NATIONAL MEMORIAL*

Fort Caroline National Memorial 12713 Fort Caroline Road, Jacksonville; tel: (904) 641-7155; www.nps.gov/foca. Open daily 0900–1700. Free.

This reconstructed fort faces a mile-wide section of the St John's River and remembers one of the bloodiest episodes in colonial-era Florida: the Spanish decimation of the 300-strong French Huguenot settlement here in 1565. After storming the triangular earthen and timber fort, built a year earlier, the Spanish soldiers pursued the fleeing French to the coast off St Augustine where, despite being unarmed and having surrendered, they were attacked and killed.

A visitors' centre describes the rise and fall of the French colony, the subsequent French revenge mission, and much more of the human and natural history of an area that now forms part of the National Park-run Timucuan Ecological and Historic Preserve.

FORT CLINCH STATE PARK**

Fort Clinch State Park $ 2601 Atlantic Avenue, Fernandina Beach; tel: (904) 277-7274; www.floridastateparks.org/fortclinch. Park open daily 0800–sunset; fort open daily 0900–1700; candle-lit tours (separate fee $) May–Labor Day, Fri–Sat, phone for reservations and times.

Fort Clinch, started in 1849, was used by both sides during the Civil War although the cannons mounted on its ramparts saw little action: Confederate forces took the fort without opposition in 1861 and abandoned it to the Union a year later. The Union occupation is convincingly portrayed with candle-lit re-enactments led by guides dressed as soldiers who act in character as they lead visitors around the restored outbuildings.

Aside from the fort, the 1100-acre park has sand dunes, tidal marshes, maritime hammocks and an alligator-inhabited pond to be explored on marked trails. A beach lines the park's eastern edge, while directly across the Cumberland Sound to the north are views of Georgia.

JACKSONVILLE*

Jacksonville and the Beaches Convention & Visitors Bureau 3 Independent Drive; tel: (904) 798-9111 or (800) 733-2668; www.jaxcvb.com. Open Mon–Fri 0830–1700.

Jacksonville is named after Andrew Jackson, governor of Florida before becoming the US's seventh president. It is the state's largest city in terms of area and one of its major financial centres. High-rise glass and steel offices reflect its commercial importance while visitor attention focuses on the Riverwalk and the city's beaches (see below).

JACKSONVILLE BEACH**

Adventure Landing $$ 4825 Blanding Boulevard; tel: (904) 771-2803; www.adventurelanding.com. Mon–Thur 1000–2300, Fri–Sat 1000–0100, Sun 1100–2300.

A 983-ft-long **pier** lined by snack stands and anglers encapsulates the seaside mood of Jacksonville Beach, one of a string of oceanside communities that form the city's eastern edge. While the beach itself is the main point of note, much more diversion, such as go-karting, navigating a futuristic laser-illuminated maze, and a wide selection of arcade games and simulations, can be found at **Adventure Landing**.

JACKSONVILLE RIVERWALK❖

Skyway monorail $
tel: (904) 743-3582;
www.ridejta.net/services/
skyway.aspx. Mon–Fri
0600–2300, Sat
1000–2300, Sun special
events only.

**Museum of
Science and
History $** 1025 Museum
Circle; tel: (904) 396-7062;
www.themosh.org. Open
Mon–Fri 1000–1700,
Sat 1000–1800, Sun
1300–1800.

**River City Brewing
Company $–$$**
835 Museum Circle;
tel: (904) 398-2299;
www.rivercitybrew.com.
Usefully placed beside the
Riverwalk with steak and
seafood dishes, a river
view and quality beers
brewed on the premises.

The heart of Downtown Jacksonville, including the St John's River, which runs through it, can best be appreciated from the **Skyway monorail**. At ground level, the **Riverwalk** runs for 1.2 pleasant miles along the river's south bank, passing on the way the large but uninspiring **Friendship Fountain**, where jets of water reach 100 feet.

The **Museum of Science and History** has interactive exhibits aimed at youngsters and covers topics such as Florida's pre-European inhabitants and the coast's endangered marine life. An adjoining planetarium has space and laser shows. Crossing the river to the north bank by bridge or river taxi leads to **Jacksonville Landing**, a popular conglomeration of shops and restaurants with live open-air entertainment.

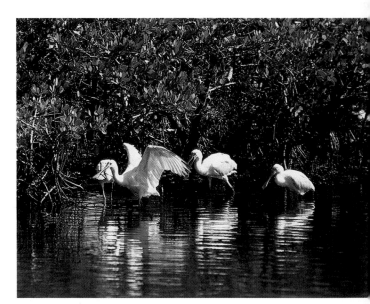

Right
Local marine life: roseate
spoonbills

KINGSLEY PLANTATION❖❖

**Kingsley
Plantation $** 11676
Palmetto Avenue, King
George Island; tel: (904)
251-3537;
www.cr.nps.gov/nr/travel/geo-
flor/21.htm. Open daily
0900–1700.

Set on 25 acres beside the Fort George River, the Kingsley Plantation flourished in the early 1800s producing sugar and cotton. The plantation was owned by Zephaniah Kingsley, a Scots-born member of Florida's legislative council during its territorial period (prior to full statehood). Kingsley's belief that slaves should be treated well, if only to make them more efficient workers, made him a thorn in the side of his slave-owning peers and he defied convention still further by marrying an African woman.

Florida's oldest extant plantation home, Kingsley's nine-room house dates from 1817 and has furnishings typical of the time. The adjacent kitchen, barn and 23 slave cabins have also been restored. Exhibits detail many aspects of plantation life and Kingsley's pioneering agricultural work.

LITTLE TALBOT ISLAND STATE PARK❖

Little Talbot Island State Park $ *11435 Fort George Road; tel; (904) 251-2320; www.floridastateparks.org/ littletalbotisland. Open daily 0800–sunset.*

Long and narrow Little Talbot Island is entirely consumed by a 2500-acre state park. Five miles of dune-lined beach marks the ocean side, woods of holly, oak and magnolia fill much of the interior, while tidal creeks and salt marshes define the island's mainland-facing edge. Wildlife spans river otters, bobcats and rabbits, and the multitude of shore birds that bring legions of birdwatchers during spring and autumn migrations. There are picnic areas and an excellent nature trail weaving through the park's diverse terrain.

ST JOHN'S FERRY❖

Jacksonville River Taxi ($) *makes a 10-minute trip across the St John's River linking the Riverwalk and Jacksonville Landing; crossings are continuous throughout the day and early evening. Tel: (877) 222-5873.*

Launched in November 1950 to carry cars and pedestrians across the St John's River between Fort George Island and the shrimp-fishing village of Mayport, this ferry *(tel: (904) 241-9969)* earned such local affection that attempts to end the service in the 1990s were successfully resisted. The diminutive size of the craft makes a vivid contrast with the cargo ships and naval vessels that regularly use the river.

Jacksonville Beach Pier *Eastern end of 6th Avenue, Jacksonville Beach; tel: (904) 249-3868. Open daily 0600–2000; extended hours in summer.*

Suggested tour

Length: Main tour 65 miles; 97 miles with detours.

Duration: Main tour 1.5 hours; 3 hours with detours.

Links: This route assumes you arrive in the Jacksonville area on I-95, although it can also, and far more scenically, be joined by using the coastal Hwy-A1A north from St Augustine *(see pages 210–17)*.

Take any route to **JACKSONVILLE BEACH ❶**, its effervescent mood contrasting with that of the commercially important city of Jacksonville 12 miles inland. Dotted by high-rise hotels and beach accessory shops, and with the **pier** at the foot of 6th Avenue South, Jacksonville Beach is the most popular and lively of a string of beach communities. The waves close to the pier often draw surfers.

Third Street, the local section of Hwy-A1A, is the main traffic artery parallel to the beach. Follow this north through **Neptune Beach**. Just ahead, turn left on to Atlantic Boulevard then very shortly right on to

ℹ Pablo Historical Park 425 Beach Boulevard, Jacksonville Beach; tel: (904) 246-0093. Open Mon–Sat 1000–1600, Sun 1300–1600.

⛰ Horse Riding $ Situated 25 minutes drive from downtown Jacksonville, **Country Day Stable** offers activities for both groups and individuals. They include horse riding and organised picnic treks. Tel: (904) 879-9383; www.countrydaystable.com

Mayport Road. For 5 miles Mayport Road skirts the tidal marshlands of the St John's River and then reaches the 300-year-old shrimping village of **Mayport**.

The still-thriving shrimping fleet is dwarfed by the aircraft carriers, frigates, destroyers and other craft commonly seen in and around the vast **Mayport Naval Station**, one of the US's largest naval bases. From Mayport, the **St JOHN'S FERRY ②** carries cars on to Fort George Island.

Using Hwy-A1A, the 52-mile route from Fort George Island to Amelia Island is among the most scenic coastal drives in the US, officially called the **Buccaneer Trail**. After 2.4 miles, a signposted turn-off leads to the **Huguenot Memorial Park**, an oceanfront park ideal for a picnic stop. Directly north, Hwy-A1A crosses **LITTLE TALBOT ISLAND ③** passing the entrances to the state park of the same name before reaching Big Talbot Island.

Winding through forests and beside wildlife-rich marshes, Hwy-A1A crosses Nassau Sound to reach **AMELIA ISLAND ④**, first passing the Amelia Island Plantation, a sprawling luxury resort which occupies much of the island's southern tip. Eleven miles ahead is the island's largest settlement, **FERNANDINA BEACH ⑤**.

Detour: On Fort George Island, look for the signposted left turning for **KINGSLEY PLANTATION ⑥**, on Hwy-A1A 5 miles north of the Mayport Ferry crossing. The approach to the plantation is a 3-mile course along a bumpy, gravel road. Rows of stately sabal palms mark the entrance to the plantation.

Detour: When leaving Jacksonville's beaches, keep to Atlantic Boulevard rather than turning right for Mayport. Ten miles ahead is **Downtown Jacksonville**. Follow signs for the **JACKSONVILLE RIVERWALK ⑦** on the river's south bank. Alternatively, cross the river and park on the north bank at Jacksonville Landing. Between the beaches and the city, the **FORT CAROLINE NATIONAL MEMORIAL ⑧** can be reached on a signposted 5-mile loop off Atlantic Boulevard.

Also worth exploring

Prior to 1925, Jacksonville Beach was known as San Pablo and it grew around a railway network that formed part of Henry Flagler's East Coast Railroad. At the **Pablo Historical Park**, the railroad days are remembered inside the 1880s station building and outside with a 28-ton steam locomotive. Exhibits also document the almost forgotten aviation achievement of Army Air Corps Lieutenant James 'Jimmy' Harold Doolittle, who in 1922 took off from San Pablo and 21 hours 28 minutes later landed in San Diego, California, completing the US's first single-day, coast-to-coast flight.

Amelia Island's eight flags

Much is made locally of Amelia Island's unusual past which has seen it under the rule of eight different flags. After it was landed by French Huguenots in 1562, control of the island switched between Spain and Britain (Amelia takes its name from the daughter of King George II) as did the rest of Florida. The island also saw the one-day reign of the Patriots of Amelia Island (locals who overthrew the Spanish), the raising of the Green Cross of Florida (a more sustained overthrow of Spanish rule) and a Mexican rebel flag hoisted by a Scotsman and French pirate. In 1821, Amelia came under US control, subsequently joining the Confederacy at the start of the Civil War.

Tallahassee

Ratings

History	●●●●●
Architecture	●●●●○
Art	●●●○○
Museums	●●●○○
Scenery	●●●○○
Sport	●●○○○
Children	●○○○○
Nature	●○○○○

Staples of the Sunshine State such as theme parks and crowded beaches seem far removed from Tallahassee, a small city easily explored on foot that has been the seat of Florida's government since 1823. With its streets lined by oak and magnolia trees and everything, including local accents, moving at subdued pace, Tallahassee's mood and manners are much more akin to the US's Deep South than the brash Florida epitomised by Orlando and Miami.

Many early Tallahassee fortunes were earned from plantations, the owners sinking some of their wealth into elegant homes in fashionable areas in what was still very much a frontier settlement. Their neighbours were the financiers and politicians who shaped Florida through its early years of US rule. Two restored historic areas and several museums keep Tallahassee's past on view, while the contrasting old and new capitol buildings illustrate the gulf between the state's rough-and-ready past and modern Florida's power and influence.

Sights

Black Archives Research Center and Museum *FAMU Campus, junction of Martin Luther King Boulevard and Gamble Street; tel: (850) 599-3020; www.taltrust.org/blkarchv.htm. Currently closed for renovation of building. Free.*

Calhoun Street Historic District *On and around Calhoun Street between Tennessee and Georgia streets.*

Black Archives Research Center and Museum⁕⁕
Housed in the 1907 Carnegie Library, the oldest building on the FAMU (Florida Agricultural and Mechanical University) campus, this museum's collection spans half-a-million manuscripts, paintings, photos, taped oral histories and many other artefacts relating to the history of Black people in Florida and beyond. The regularly changing exhibitions focusing on topics as diverse as African-American slavery and the tribal art of Ethiopia are imaginatively constructed and invariably thought-provoking.

Calhoun Street Historic District⁕⁕
In 1840s Tallahassee, the discerning professional lived in or around Calhoun Street, dubbed 'gold dust row' for its wealthy reputation. Surviving a road-widening scheme in the 1940s and social decay in the 1970s, the area is now a designated historic district where oak-lined streets hold some of the finest gatherings of antebellum and territorial-period homes in Florida.

ℹ Tallahassee Chamber of Commerce *100 N Duval Street; tel: (850) 224-8116; www.talchamber.com. Open Mon–Fri 0900–1700. Free.*

Tallahassee Visitor Information Center *106 E Jefferson Street; tel: (850) 413-9200 or (800) 628-2866; email: vic@mail.co.leon.fl.us; www.seetallahassee.com. Open Mon–Fri 0800–1700, Sat 0900–1200. Free.*

FSU Campus *Visitor Information Center, 100 S Woodward Avenue; tel: (850) 644-3246; www.fsu.edu. Open Mon–Fri 0800–1700; extended hours during summer semester. Free.*

🏠 Brokaw-McDougall House *$ 329 N Meridian Street; tel: (850) 891-3900; www.taltrust.org/brokaw.htm. Open Mon–Fri 0900–1500.*

The Columns *100 N Duval Street; tel: (850) 224-8116. Open Mon–Fri 0900–1700. Free.*

FSU Museum of Fine Arts *Fine Arts Building, junction of Tennessee and Copeland streets, FSU Campus; tel: (850) 644-6836. Open Mon–Fri 1000–1600, Sat–Sun 1300–1600. Closed Sat–Sun May–Aug. Free.*

Governor's Mansion *700 N Adams Street; tel: (850) 488-4661. Open Mar–May, 1000–1200; closed rest of the year. Free.*

The only example open to the public is the excellent **Brokaw-McDougall House**, completed in 1860 for a livery stable owner. Mixing Italianate and Classical Revival styles, a full-width second-floor porch supported by six Corinthian columns adds elegance to the exterior, as does the cupola which crowns the house. Inside, tall ceilings and period furnishings evoke the well-heeled Florida lifestyle of a time when much of the state was still swamp.

The Columns✦

Now occupied by the Chamber of Commerce, the Columns is the oldest extant house within Tallahassee's original boundaries, built around 1830 for prominent banker William 'Money' Williams. At the heart of high finance and political intrigue in Florida's formative years, the Columns, named for the four two-storey high columns supporting its porticoed entrance, spent many ignominious decades serving as a boarding house and a restaurant before being restored and furnished in the style of the 1840s.

FSU Campus✦

The array of collegiate Gothic (the architectural style pioneered at Princeton University and adopted by US academic institutions during the early decades of the 1900s) buildings that dominate the eastern section of the 347-acre campus of FSU (Florida State University) can be admired from shady pathways lined by oak, palm, pine, dogwood and azalea trees.

Founded in 1857 as a womens' college, the university now has 30,000 students, two of the world's most powerful computers, and an alumni that includes actor Burt Reynolds. The **Museum of Fine Arts** features work by top names in temporary exhibitions and holds end-of-year student art shows.

Governor's Mansion✦

One of the perks of being elected governor of Florida is you get to use this redbrick official residence, built in the 1950s on the site of

Knott House Museum $ *301 E Park Avenue; tel: (850) 922-2459; www.taltrust.org/knott.htm. Open Wed–Fri 1300–1600, Sat 1000–1600. Guided tours on the hour.*

the 1907 governor's mansion. The antebellum home of Andrew Jackson (Florida's first governor, later US president) in Tennessee provided the design inspiration for the house whose front door bears the state seal. Inside, guided tours pass through formal rooms decorated with a disparate collection of paintings and antiques.

Knott House Museum✦✦✦

Knott House, built around 1843, is deeply entwined with Tallahassee's history. The emancipation proclamation freeing Florida's slaves was read from its steps in 1865, and its occupants included several Supreme Court judges and Tallahassee's first Black physician. While successive owners steadily enlarged the original house, it was the arrival of newly appointed state treasurer William Knott and his wife, Luella, in 1928 that added the Classical Revival portico and most of the Victorian furnishings that the sumptuous dwelling retains.

The restored house evokes both luxury living and the trials and tribulations of the turbulent 1920s and 1930s, when William Knott became one of Florida's most influential politicians. Luella, meanwhile, was a leading Tallahassee society figure, a campaigner in

Below
Knott House Museum

the Temperance Movement (her efforts led to a 50-year alcohol ban in Tallahassee), and author of the twee poems that are attached to pieces of furniture and other domestic items, earning the dwelling a nickname of 'the house that rhymes'.

Why Tallahassee?

In colonial times, Pensacola to the west and St Augustine to the east enjoyed periods as Florida's centre of government. When Florida became part of the US in 1821, both contested for the honour of becoming capital of the new territory. The result was a compromise: representatives from both sides agreed that they would meet halfway. Tallahassee, then an empty plot of land accessed by dirt track, was chosen in 1823 and a log cabin erected for the meetings of the legislature.

🏛 **Museum of Florida History**
500 S Bronough Street;
tel: (850) 245-6400;
www.flheritage.com/museum.
Open Mon–Fri 0900–1630,
Sat 1000–1630, Sun
1200–1630. Free.

Museum of Florida History**

The proof that Florida existed before Walt Disney World arrived is contained within this comprehensive but very easily toured museum which charts the region's development from uninhabited swamp to one of the US's fastest-growing states.

The exhibits, from a 12,000 BC mastodon skeleton (sporting a ferocious set of tusks) to temporary displays on contemporary themes outline Florida's geology and chart the lifestyle and customs of its native cultures, particularly the Paleo-Indian peoples of the Panhandle. The native decline was largely due to the European diseases that arrived with the Spanish, whose expeditions and first settlements are described and colonial exploits illustrated with an array of early maps, cannons, nautical paraphernalia and gold and silver coins recovered from sunken galleons.

Florida's brief period under British rule and subsequent acquisition by the US is covered, and the state's role in the Civil War is described with a mock-up of a Confederate camp. The wars between the US and the Seminoles are told beneath a series of portraits of the Seminole chiefs who frequently outwitted their opponents but were ultimately unable to outgun them.

The removal of the Seminoles (many to Oklahoma, some to the Everglades) cleared the way for the exploitation of Florida as a cattle and citrus producing region, and as a vacation destination for newly mobile car-owning Americans, nicknamed the 'tin can tourists' during the 1920s and remembered here with photos and early Florida travel souvenirs.

ⓘ New Capitol
S Adams Street; tel:
(850) 488-6167. Open
Mon–Fri 0800–1700,
Sat–Sun 0900–1500.

Old Capitol *S Monroe*
Street; tel: (850) 487-1902.
Open Mon–Fri 0930–1600;
Sat 1000–1630; Sun
1200–1630.

Old City Cemetery
Corner of Park Avenue and
Martin Luther King
Boulevard; tel: (850) 488-
3901; www.taltrust.com.
Open daily sunrise–sunset.

Park Avenue Historic
District *Park Avenue*
between Meridian and
Macomb streets.

Lewis House *316 E Park*
Avenue; tel: (850) 488-
7100.

New Capitol✦

The site of Florida's legislature and executive, the remarkably unattractive 307-ft-high New Capitol building has been a concrete blot on the city's skyline since 1977. The best way to experience the building is by escaping to its interior where, from the 22nd-floor observation deck there are wonderful views across Tallahassee and the tree-filled hillsides that surround it. Paintings and murals on Florida themes are found throughout the building. From March to May, the Florida legislature can be seen in action from public galleries.

Old Capitol✦✦

Ugly though it may be, the New Capitol was a necessary replacement for the Old Capitol, completed in 1845 to mark Florida's acquisition of statehood but since 1911 lacking the space to keep the expanding state's organs of government under one roof. The Old Capitol's copper dome that brings considerable gravitas was added in 1902, as were the wings and the distinctive red-and-white striped awnings protecting the interior from excessive sunlight.

Stepping inside reveals the splendidly restored interior, where a grand staircase rises toward the stained-glass dome and rooms such as the dainty Supreme Court, the governor's office and the legislative chambers.

Several side rooms are packed with absorbing memorabilia, among it the documents and weapons with which Florida's leaders sought to steer a course through the traumatic years of the Civil War, Reconstruction, and the 'Bourbon era' from the 1870s which re-defined the politics and economies of the southern states.

Old City Cemetery✦

Florida was still in its pre-statehood territorial phase when this 11-acre cemetery was laid out in 1829. The graves are arranged on a grid-style system, adopted following a yellow fever outbreak that claimed several hundred lives in 1841 and providing a simple method for racial segregation: Whites being buried in the eastern half, Blacks in the west. The full roll-call includes an ex-state governor, the dead from both sides in the Civil War (buried in separate sections), and many more who are described in the walking tour leaflet available from a kiosk near the entrance.

Park Avenue Historic District✦✦

Once marking the northern edge of the city, Park Avenue began as a dirt track probably intended to deter Indian attack. When the dirt was re-shaped into a series of small parks, Park Avenue evolved into an address favoured by the city's social élite during the 1840s.

Noted residences include the Columns (*see page 227*) and Knott House (*see page 228*); the **Lewis House**, bought by the founder of the Lewis State Bank and periodically open for public tours of its restored interior;

First Presbyterian Church *110 N Adams Street; tel: (850) 222-4504. Usually closed except for services.*

Federal Courthouse *110 W Park Avenue.*

and the **First Presbyterian Church**, dating from the 1830s and Tallahassee's oldest extant church, now restored to its neo-classical form after being gothicised during the late 1800s. A more recent addition to the street is the 1930s **Federal Courthouse**, a WPA (Works Project Administration, a Depression-era government body intended to create employment) initiative, decorated with murals depicting Florida's history.

On Park Avenue's south side, the 1838 **Murphy House** is said to have been a billet for government troops during the Reconstruction period, while legend has it that the 1841 **Chittenden House** was financed by winnings on the Louisiana state lottery.

St John's Episcopal Cemetery North side of Call Street, facing Old City Cemetery; tel: (850) 222-2636. Open daily dawn–dusk.

Union Bank Building 219 Apalachee Parkway; tel: (850) 561-2603. Open Mon–Fri 0930–1630. Free.

The Old City Cemetery (*see page 230*) anchors the district's west side. Behind it is **St John's Episcopal Cemetery**; its graves include that of Prince Murat, exiled son of the King of Naples and a nephew of Napoleon Bonaparte, and his wife, Catherine, a great-grandniece of George Washington. Murat owned a 100-acre plantation north of Tallahassee and his writings have provided valuable information about 1820s Florida.

Union Bank Building**

Florida's oldest commercial structure, the Union Bank Building, dates from 1841, but the financial institution it housed, one of the most important of the time, failed a few years later due to crop failure and the Seminole wars. Beneath its vaulted ceiling the restored bank now carries exhibits on Florida banking and remnants from its time as a National Freedmen's bank, set up during Reconstruction to financially assist freed slaves, and less distinguished periods when it served as a shoe factory and beauty parlour.

Accommodation and food

During the March to May sitting of the Florida legislature and home games of the FSU's well-supported football team, the Seminoles, accommodation can be scarce in Tallahassee. At any other time, the few centrally located properties and scores of hotels and motels on the periphery offer good-priced lodgings.

Barnacle Bill's $–$$ *1830 N Monroe Street; tel: (850) 385-8734; www.barnaclebills.com.* Generous portions of smoked, steamed, boiled and fried seafood and other dishes, to eat inside or out.

Bonefish Grill $$ *3491-7 Thomasville Road, tel: (850) 297-0460; www.bonefishgrill.com.* Fresh grilled fish with a variety of styles and toppings is the main attraction, but the restaurant also offers beef, pork and pasta dishes.

Chez Pierre $$$ *1215 Thomasville Road; tel: (850) 222-0936; www.chezpierre.com.* Fits the bill for a special event, established since 1976 as Tallahassee's leading French restaurant.

Dutch Inn $ *2997 Apalachee Parkway, tel: (850) 877-7813 or (800) 328-782; email: info@dutch-inn.com; www.dutch-inn.com.* Not very Dutch, but the good sized rooms, amenities and coin-op laundry, make this a more than serviceable base.

El Chico $–$$ *2225 N Monroe Street; tel: (850) 386-1133; www.elchico.com.* A cut above the average Mexican restaurant with tasty, well-prepared dishes.

Governor's Inn $$–$$$ *209 S Adams Street; tel: (850) 681-6855 or (in Florida) (800) 342 7717; www.thegovinn.com.* Much loved by visiting politicians for its luxurious rooms and suites named after Florida governors; serves a complimentary breakfast.

The McFarlin House $$–$$$ *305 E King Street, Quincy; tel: (850) 875-2526 or (877) 370-4701; www.mcfarlinhouse.com.* An atmospheric bed-and-breakfast inn in the small town of Quincy, 23 miles north of Tallahassee on Hwy-90, offering a choice of individually furnished rooms.

Silver Slipper $$$ *531 Scotty's Lane; tel: (850) 386-9366; www.thesilverslipper.com.* A favourite of Florida legislators for its steaks, seafood and Greek specialities, all served in a sophisticated atmosphere.

Right
Florida State University, Tallahassee

Suggested tour

Length: Main tour 1 mile; Calhoun Street Historic District and Governor's mansion detour 0.75 mile; Museum of Florida History and Black Archives Research Center and Museum detour, 2 miles.

Duration: Tallahassee is compact and its streets very easy to walk, though crossing them can be slow especially during rush hours. Main tour walking time is 40 minutes. The Calhoun Street Historic District and Governor's Mansion detour will add a further 40 minutes; the detour to the Museum of Florida History will add only an additional few minutes; but continuing to the Black Archives Research Center and Museum is best done by car and will take 10 minutes driving time.

Links: Around Tallahassee: the Old South (*see pages 236–43*) and Tallahassee to the Forgotten Coast (*see pages 244–53*).

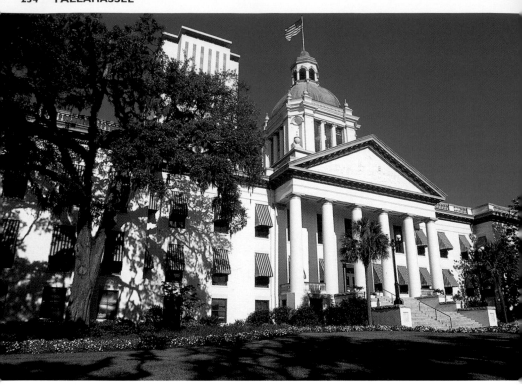

Above
Tallahassee's Capitol complex

The **NEW CAPITOL ❶** is far and away the tallest building in Tallahassee, and is easy to find as it lies at the heart of the Capitol Complex, a grouping of state administrative offices that occupies a large chunk Tallahassee's compact centre. The main entrance is on Duval Street, and in the lobby is a useful tourist information centre. Adjacent is the elevator to the 22nd-floor observation level.

Directly east stands the **OLD CAPITOL ❷**, recognised by its dome and stripped awnings, its entrance facing Monroe Street. A block further east, on the right side of Apalachee Parkway, a major traffic route into the city, stands the **UNION BANK BUILDING ❸**. To the right on Monroe Street, the 40-ft-high black marble pylons of the **Vietnam Veteran's Memorial ❹** are etched with the names of Floridians dead or missing in the Vietnam War.

Walk north along Monroe Street to the junction with Park Avenue. Formerly McCarthy Street, Park Avenue gained its name in 1905 for the series of parks in its centre and the wish of a local resident for a 'more sophisticated' address for her son's wedding invitations. This section forms the **PARK AVENUE HISTORIC DISTRICT ❺**. Turn right, passing the 1903 **Walker Library ❻** and crossing Calhoun Street, for the **KNOTT HOUSE MUSEUM ❼**, neighboured by the **Murphy ❽** and **Chittenden ❾** houses. Cross to the north side of

Mission San Luis
*2020 W Mission Road;
tel: (850) 487-3711;
www.dhr.dos.state.fl.us/bar/
san_luis. Open Tue–Sun
1000–1600.*

Festival For four
weeks over March
and April, the Springtime
in Tallahassee Festival finds
parades, concerts and
many other special events
throughout the city, one of
the southeast US's largest
annual events; *www.
springtimetallahassee.com*

Park Avenue and walk west for five blocks. This route passes the **Lewis House ⑩**, the **Federal Courthouse ⑪**, the **First Presbyterian Church ⑫** and the **Columns ⑬**.

Directly ahead across Copeland Street is the **OLD CITY CEMETERY ⑭**, created five years after Tallahassee formally became a city. Behind it across Call Street is **St John's Episcopal Cemetery ⑮**, with graves dating from 1840. Further west along Park Avenue are the fraternity and sorority houses lining the approach to the **FSU CAMPUS ⑯**, its eastern side marked by early-1900s collegiate Gothic buildings.

Detour: If Park Avenue stimulates a thirst for more historic buildings, walk two blocks north along Adams Street, turning right along Tennessee Street and left on to Calhoun Street. Ahead is the oak- and magnolia-lined heart of the **CALHOUN STREET HISTORIC DISTRICT ⑰**. The **Brokaw-McDougall House ⑱** stands two blocks east facing Virginia Street, surrounded by a small park. Rejoin Adams Street and continue north to the **GOVERNOR'S MANSION ⑲**.

Detour: Housed in the Gray Building, which also stores the state archives, is the **MUSEUM OF FLORIDA HISTORY ⑳**, two blocks west of the New Capitol and entered from Bronough Street. Martin Luther King Junior Boulevard is the most direct route to the FAMU campus, a mile south, site of the **BLACK ARCHIVES RESEARCH CENTER AND MUSEUM ㉑** (currently closed for renovation).

Also worth exploring

Remnants of a Spanish mission, established in 1567, are steadily being excavated at the 60-acre **San Luis Archaeological and Historic Site**. The mission was among the most important of the hundred established in Florida and, at its peak, housed 1400 Spanish and natives. Exhibitions and finds displayed at the visitors' centre provide a vivid picture of mission life. Children will enjoy the monthly 'living history' days, when period-attired guides take the roles of mission dwellers and describe their daily routines.

Around Tallahassee: the Old South

Ratings

History	●●●●●
Nature	●●●●○
Scenery	●●●●○
Architecture	●●●○○
Crafts	●●●○○
Food	●●●○○
Museums	●●○○○
Children	●○○○○

Some of the most relaxing routes in Florida lie close to Tallahassee, the roads draped with Spanish moss and passing through hamlets where the silence is broken only by the hum of insects and the drone of farm machinery in nearby fields. Tallahassee developed as a centre for cotton and other crops grown on the many plantations that exploited the rich and fertile soils in its vicinity. The population shift to southern Florida has left much of this farmland intact, still crossed by the winding roads that once linked the plantations and provided access to the city's markets.

Many of the area's larger towns, such as Monticello and Thomasville, maintain a fine stock of 19th-century buildings. Others, like Havana, have become filled with antiques shops. Elsewhere, the area holds evidence of major prehistoric settlements, the sites of battles between White settlers and natives, and a celebrated store where devoted locals have been buying their sausages for years.

BRADLEY'S COUNTRY STORE*

 Bradley's Country Store *Route 3, Centerville Road, 12 miles from Tallahassee; tel: (850) 893-1647; www.bradleyscountrystore.com. Open Mon–Fri 0800–1800.*

Promising the 'best country smoked sausage money can buy', Bradley's Country Store has been in business since 1927. The tin-roofed, wood-framed building was erected to capitalise on the fame of Grandma Bradley's sausages, which were first cooked, smoked and

sold from her kitchen in 1910. The sausages, seasoned with black and red pepper, sage and salt to a recipe handed down through the generations, have no artificial preservatives and are sold alongside other rural Florida specialities such as hog's head cheese, liver pudding, cane syrup and grits. Each November, the Bradley Farm Days festival, based here, celebrates rural craft and cuisine.

HAVANA❖

Like the Cuban capital after which it is named, Havana once enjoyed a flourishing cigar industry and was noted for producing a broad-leafed tobacco used in the cigars' production. Nowadays, the concentration of antiques shops set in the compact turn-of-the-century Downtown district is the reason Havana's 2000-strong permanent population is swamped every weekend by a mixture of serious collectors and casual browsers. Havana's dainty size and its setting amid pine forests brings a measure of rural charm although there is little to savour beyond the antique outlets.

Accommodation and food in Havana

Market Cafe $–$$ *206 N Main Street; tel: (850) 539-9797.* Good assortment of well-priced lunches and something of a locals' meeting place.

Nicholson Farmhouse $$–$$$ *Route 12, 3 miles west of Havana; tel: (850) 539-5931; www.nicholsonfarmhouse.com.* Beef is the speciality and it comes in large portions at this former farmhouse complex; chicken and seafood are also on offer.

Slack Key Café $ *206 NW First Street; tel: (850) 539-6716.* Eatery thinly disguised as an art gallery, with a pleasing menu of snacks, light meals and tasty desserts.

LAKE JACKSON INDIAN MOUNDS**

Lake Jackson Indian Mounds *3600 Indian Mounds Road, Tallahassee; tel: (850) 922-6007; www.floridastateparks.org/ lakejacksonmounds/history.asp. Open daily dawn–dusk. Free.*

One of Florida's most important archaeological sites occupies a quiet setting on the banks of Lake Jackson. From AD 1000 to 1500, the site is believed to have been a religious and administrative centre of the Apalachee culture. Native inhabitants of the Panhandle, the agriculture-based Apalachee people had an advanced political system and spiritual beliefs that included the building of temple mounds. Three such mounds, the tallest 26ft-high, are visible at the site and once formed part of a large village built around a central plaza.

Copper breastplates, badges and axes decorated with elaborate ritual figures are among the finds that indicate the historic significance of the site and also suggest the Apalachees' links with other native groups across the Southeast: part of the 'Southern Cult', at its height around 1200. Other discoveries reveal trading links with native peoples as distant as the Great Lakes and Oklahoma. For unknown reasons, the Apalachee abandoned the Lake Jackson area around 1500; by the early 1800s it was occupied by a cotton plantation.

MACLAY STATE GARDENS***

Maclay State Gardens $ *3540 Thomasville Road, Tallahassee; tel: (850) 487-4556; www.floridastateparks.org/ maclaygardens. Gardens open daily 0800–sunset.*

In 1923, New York financier Alfred B Maclay purchased 1900 acres on the shores of Lake Hall as a winter retreat and set aside 28 acres for formal gardens, designed to be in bloom from December to April. With pines and oaks set alongside dogwoods and redbuds, the gardens mix native and exotic flora, and include 150 types of camellia and 50 azalea species. Among the gardens' wildlife is the flying squirrel, a nocturnal species born with a loose fold of skin that enables it to glide through the air.

Overlooking the gardens, the **Maclay House** dates from 1905 and holds many of the Maclay family's furnishings and personal items.

Though the house is only open when the gardens are at their best, from January to April, the gardens and the lakeside area are worth a visit at anytime. There are designated swimming and picnic areas, and the **Big Pine Nature Trail**, which picks a short course trail through wooded hillsides.

MICCOSUKEE❖

The village of Miccosukee was inhabited by Miccosukee people until 1818 when it was attacked by 3000 US troops under Andrew Jackson, who arrived from Georgia without official sanction ostensibly to repel a British incursion into Spanish-ruled Florida, but actually setting in place the events that would culminate in the US takeover of the region and the removal of its natives. Burning the village to the ground, Jackson became known as 'Sharp Knife' among the Miccosukee, who fled to central and southern Florida. The village was subsequently occupied by White settlers.

MONTICELLO❖

ℹ️ **Monticello Chamber of Commerce** 420 W Washington Street; tel: (904) 997-5552; www. monticellojeffersonfl.com

Monticello thrived on the cotton trade from the 1820s but was later by-passed by the rail routes that opened up the rest of Florida. As a result, 27 central blocks are made up almost exclusively of 19th-century buildings, a mixture of wood-framed homes in Classical Revival and Italianate style, and brick-built commercial buildings.

The most eye-catching structure, however, is the 1909 **Jefferson County Courthouse**, modelled after Thomas Jefferson's home,

Monticello, in Virginia, around which the main traffic arteries flow. Close by, the splendidly restored **Opera House** was built in the 1890s and made Monticello the cultural centre of northern Florida. The Chamber of Commerce offers a free guide detailing walking and driving tours of the town.

Accommodation in Monticello

John Denham House $$ *555 W Palmer Mill Road; tel: (850) 997-4568; email: pat@johndenhamhouse.com; www.johndenhamhouse.com.* In an acre of land despite being in the centre of town, this 1872 house offers bed and breakfast and makes a point of welcoming children.

Palmer Place $–$$ *625 W Palmer Mill Road; tel: (850) 997-5519; www.palmerplace.com.* Extremely comfortable and well-priced bed and breakfast in a restored antebellum home; one of the five guest rooms is a two-bedroom suite.

PEBBLE HILL PLANTATION❖❖

ℹ Pebble Hill Plantation $
Thomasville Road (Hwy-319), south of Thomasville; tel: (229) 226-2344; www.pebblehill.com. Open Oct–Aug, closed Sept; Tue–Sat 1000–1700, Sun 1300–1700.

Around the Florida-Georgia border is the US's largest concentration of plantation homes. One of the few open to the public is Pebble Hill, where lanes of live oak and magnolia lead to the two-storey, 40-room mansion occupied, until her death in 1978, by Elisabeth Ireland Poe, better known to her staff as Miss Pansy.

Although the plantation was founded as a working cotton farm in 1820, it became a winter home for the affluent Cleveland-based Hanna family for whom the present mansion was erected in 1936, replacing a less opulent home destroyed by fire. Antiques, silverware, porcelain and crystal decorate the house, as do an extraordinary number of hunting and wildlife paintings including several valuable Audubon bird study prints.

The former cow barn serves as a visitors' centre with exhibits on family and farm history; other outbuildings include the log cabin school for the children of plantation workers.

THOMASVILLE❖❖

ℹ Thomasville Welcome Center
401 S Broad Street; tel: (229) 228-7977 or (866) 577-3600. Open Mon–Fri 0830–1700, Sat 0900–1200.

Situated 330ft above sea-level, Thomasville earned a reputation during Victorian times as a health resort, its comparatively high elevation sparing it the disease-carrying mosquitoes common to lower-lying marsh areas. Wealthy northerners wintered in the town's hotels while some built the 'winter cottages' that lie within a few blocks of Thomasville's enjoyable commercial centre, the well-preserved Broad Street.

The only such cottage open for tours is the Queen Anne-style **Lapham-Patterson House.** This yellow-painted structure was completed

ⓗ Lapham-Patterson House $ *626 N Dawson Street; tel: (229) 226-0405; www.gastateparks.org/info/lapham. Open Tue–Sat 0900–1700, Sun 1400–1730.*

Thomas County Museum of History $ *725 N Dawson Street; tel: (229) 226-7664; www.rose.net/~history. Open Tue–Sat 1000–1200, 1400–1700.*

in 1885 and has 26 windows and 19 rooms but not a single right angle due to a superstition of its owner, a Chicago shoe merchant.

The **Thomas County Museum of History** records Thomasville's health resort era with photographs and assorted memorabilia, stocks a formidable display of ladies' fashions from 1825 to 1947, and has a pioneer-era log cabin and, oddest among many odd exhibits, a single-lane bowling alley from 1893.

Accommodation and food in Thomasville

Jameson Inn $$ *1670 Remington Ave; tel: (229) 227-9500; www.jamesoninns.com.* A white colonial-style property with swimming pool. Room rates include complimentary southern-style breakfast.

Linda Gail's Southern Kitchen $ *420 W Jackson Street; tel: (229) 225-9533.* Groaning buffet of southern-style fare; lunch only. Closed Sat.

The Market Diner $$ *502 Smith Avenue; tel: (229) 225-1777.* Fresh produce is a certainty at this friendly restaurant which shares the site with the local farmers' market.

Serendipity Cottage $$ *339 E Jefferson Street; tel: (229) 226-8111 or (800) 383-7377; email: goodnite@serendipitycottage.com; www.serendipitycottage.com.* Decorated with antiques, wicker furniture and potted ferns, the three guest rooms include modern features such as VCRs and cable TV.

Suggested tour

Length: Main tour 83 miles. If driving a rental car, ensure that crossing from Florida into Georgia is permitted. Detours 25 miles each.

Duration: Main tour 2.5 hours. First detour 45 minutes; second detour 1 hour.

Links: Tallahassee (*see pages 226–35*), Tallahassee to the Forgotten Coast (*see pages 244–53*).

Take Hwy-319 (Thomasville Road) north from Tallahassee. A mile north of the junction with I-10, the entrance to **MACLAY STATE GARDENS ❶** is on the left. Continue north for 14 miles, crossing the state border into Georgia, where the winding two-lane route becomes appreciably straighter and wider. After 13 miles, the entrance to **PEBBLE HILL PLANTATION ❷** is on the left and 3 miles further is **THOMASVILLE ❸**.

Leave Thomasville heading south on Hwy-19, re-entering Florida and after 31 miles reaching **MONTICELLO ❹**. Hwy-19 (called Jefferson

The route is intended as a day-trip from Tallahassee but there are a number of distinctive bed-and-breakfast inns in the area, often offering accommodation for much lower prices than more heavily touristed areas.

Street locally) passes through the centre of this largely Victorian-era town; the junction with Hwy-90 forms the commercial centre and holds the unmistakable **Jefferson County Courthouse.**

West from Monticello, much of the 25-mile length of Hwy-90 to Tallahassee is known as **Fred Mahan Drive**, remembering the local nursery owner who donated some 40,000 plants to beautify highways, churches and cemeteries during the 1930s. For 30 cents an hour, labourers spent eight years planting the palms, arbor vita, crape myrtle and other flowering vegetation whose summertime blooms bring colour to the edge of the highway.

Detour: Looping off Hwy-90 between Tallahassee and Monticello, this detour explores the quiet, moss-draped roads along which horse-drawn wagons once transported cotton from local plantations to Tallahassee. From Monticello, Hwy-90 skirts the southern edge of Lake Miccosukee and, just under 5 miles ahead, is the junction with Route 59. Route 59 heading north passes through the hamlet of **Concord** and reaches **MICCOSUKEE ❺** at the junction with Route 151. Turn right here, left at the next junction and right again soon for **Reeve's Landing**, a popular fishing and picnic spot on the edge of tranquil **Lake Miccosukee.**

Return to Miccosukee and continue west on Route 151. After 5 miles, this tree-lined route bends to the south and passes **BRADLEY'S COUNTRY STORE ❻**. A further 5 miles ahead on the left, a gravel driveway leads to the white wooden form of **Old Pisgah United Methodist Church**, built in 1858. Route 151 continues into Tallahassee forming one of the city's celebrated 'canopy roads', overhung by Spanish moss from the branches of live oaks.

Detour: A better detour for antique seekers is to return to Tallahassee from Monticello on Hwy-90, joining I-10 east of the city and continuing to the Hwy-27 exit. Follow Hwy-27 north for 12 miles until it reaches **HAVANA ❼**. The town's antiques shops line the highway and adjoining streets. If browsing takes less time than expected, stop on the way back to Tallahassee at the **LAKE JACKSON INDIAN MOUNDS ❽**, signposted from Hwy-27 on the approach to Tallahassee.

Also worth exploring

Nine miles west of Monticello, Hwy-90 passes the southbound Route 59. After dipping beneath I-10 Route 59 reaches **Lloyd**, a tiny settlement with a disproportionately large brick-built railway station. The station was raised in 1858 during a period when the town enjoyed prominence for its connection to the Seaboard Coast Line Railroad. The building is now restored and much fussed over by the county historical society.

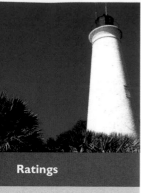

Tallahassee to the Forgotten Coast

Ratings

Beaches	●●●● ○
Food	●●●● ○
History	●●●● ○
Nature	●●●● ○
Architecture	●●● ○ ○
Scenery	●●● ○ ○
Children	●● ○ ○ ○
Museums	● ○ ○ ○ ○

The area between the state capital and the Gulf of Mexico, one of Florida's least known but most rewarding corners, is a landscape rich in natural sights: freshwater springs, forests of oak and pine, and numerous rivers around which the lack of modern development allows the sense of history to be strong, bolstered by the remnants of a 16th-century Spanish fort and the site of the Civil War battle that kept Tallahassee in Confederate hands.

At the coast, too, the scenery has changed little in decades. The so-called Forgotten Coast is studded with once-thriving towns whose growth was stunted as transport patterns changed (in one case, a town was simply abandoned), leaving behind Victorian-era wood-framed buildings and local economies more dependent on oysters than tourism. For good measure, the region has some of the least crowded beaches in the state and unpretentious eateries serving the best seafood for miles.

APALACHICOLA✦✦✦

❶ Apalachicola Chamber of Commerce and Visitors Center 99 *Market Street; tel: (850) 653-9419; email: info@baynavigaor.com; www.baynavigator.com. Open Mon–Fri 0930–1600, Sat 1000–1500.*

It's hard to believe on first sight, but in the early 1800s Apalachicola was a thriving port and rivalled New Orleans as a transportation centre, sending cotton to New England and Europe. Many of the elegant homes of cotton merchants still stand in the now sleepy and thinly populated town, as do those of the 1920s lumber barons who moved in following the decline of cotton, staying until the local cypress forests were decimated.

When railway travel surpassed ships, Apalachicola turned to the 6000 acres of oysters beds that lie in the nearby estuaries to the shore and now produce 10 per cent of all oysters consumed in the US. The estuaries and the broad Apalachicola River make fruitful territory for nature-orientated river trips, many of which operate from the small marina.

The most instantly noticeable of the town's many historic buildings is the 1907 **Gibson Inn**, complete with wraparound veranda. Through the 1980s, the inn set the trend for the stylish restoration that is

John Gorrie State Museum $ *Corner of 6th Street and Avenue D; tel: (850) 653-9347; www.floridastateparks.org/ johngorriemuseum/ default.asp. Open Thur–Mon 0900–1700.*

River Trips Apalachicola makes a good base for excursions on the river of the same name. Nature-watching trips are operated by **Eco Ventures Inc** *tel: (850) 653-2593; www.apalachicolatours.com;* **Bay & Bayou Excursions** *275 Magnolia Bay, Eastpoint, tel: (850) 670-1529; email: rsharris@gtcom.net; www. bayandbayouexcursions.com;* and, along with a host of fishing and other watery trips, **Journeys of St George Island** *240 E Third Street, St George Island; tel: (850) 927 3259; email: info@sgislandjourneys.com; www.sgislandjourneys.com*

Festivals The only time of year when accommodation may be at a premium in Apalachicola is during the November Seafood Festival, when the local oysters, shrimps, clams and other succulent marine creatures are consumed by the bucketful.

steadily rejuvenating many local buildings. A useful free walking tour map is provided by the Chamber of Commerce.

A prominent figure in 1840s Apalachicola was John Gorrie. At times post master, treasurer and bank director, Gorrie is best remembered as a physician. Seeking a way of cooling his patients' rooms during an outbreak of yellow fever in 1841, he developed an ice-producing machine that formed the basis of modern air conditioning. His work is remembered in the one-room **John Gorrie State Museum**, where a replica of the ice machine takes pride of place.

Accommodation and food in Apalachicola

The Boss Oyster Bar $–$$ *123 Water Street; tel: (850) 653-9364; www.apalachico/ariverinn.com/boss.html.* Oysters are what Apalachicola is famous for and this rustic dockside eatery is among the most enjoyable places to sample them served in a variety of styles. Shrimp, scallops, clams and other fare is also offered.

Brigitte's Romantic Retreat $$ *101 6th Street; tel: (888) 554-4376; email: ken@bryanthouse.com; www.romantic-retreat.com.* Exceedingly cosy bed and breakfast in a wonderfully furnished house, complete with friendly hosts.

Coombs House Inn $–$$ *80 6th Street; tel: (850) 653-9199; email: coombstaff@coombshouseinn.com; www.coombshouseinn.com.* The largest of several antique-filled old homes offering bed-and-breakfast accommodation, this three-storey 1905 dwelling also offers free bicycles for local exploration.

Tamara's Cafe Floridita $–$$ *17 Avenue E; tel: (850) 653-4111.* Well-priced lunch and dinner fare featuring seafood and meat dishes given a Latin-American twist.

That Place on 98 $$ *500 Highway 98, Eastpoint; tel: (850) 670-9898; www.thatplaceon98.net.* Dine overlooking Apalachicola Bay on local oysters, grouper, shrimp or crabcakes.

Apalachicola's oysters

Seafood of many kinds is plentiful throughout Florida but Apalachicola can justly claim to have the region's best oysters; the local waters yield 90 per cent of all the state's oysters and 10 per cent of those harvested in the entire US. Offered raw, steamed and in numerous other styles, oysters are a mainstay of many restaurants in the area and are popularly consumed with ample quantities of beer. Occasionally oysters take second place to scallops, which appear roughly every seven years as thick, floating 'islands' off the coast.

Above right
Black-crowned night heron

Apalachicola National Forest❖

Apalachicola National Forest tel: (850) 523-8500; www.southernregion.fs.fed. us/florida

Spanning 565,000 acres, Apalachicola National Forest is easily the largest of Florida's three federally protected forests. The canoe-friendly rivers, swamps, savannahs, pine woods and glades of cypress, oak and magnolia within it are all accessed by walking and horse-riding trails. Among the more popular sections is the **Silver Lake Recreation Area** with boating, swimming and a small beach.

Natural Bridge Battlefield Site❖❖

Natural Bridge Battlefield Site Natural Bridge Road, tel: (850) 922-6007; www.floridastateparks.org/ naturalbridge. Open daily 0800–sunset. Free.

Its present-day peace interrupted only by birdsong, the 7-acre Natural Bridge area made an unlikely setting for the battle in March 1865, shortly before the end of the Civil War, which enabled Tallahassee to become one of the few Confederate capitals not to fall to the Union. In a five-day battle that claimed 24 lives, some 500 advancing Union soldiers were forced back towards the coast by 700 Confederate troops made up of teenage students (who required their mothers' permission to fight) and elderly men. Displays beside a monument indicate the progress of the conflict, re-enacted on its anniversary.

PORT ST JOE✦

Constitution Convention State Museum $ *200 Allen Memorial Way; tel: (850) 229-8029. Open Thur–Mon 0900–1200, 1300–1700.*

Whispering Pines $$ *1177 Cape San Blas Road, Port St Joe; tel: (850) 227-7252; www.capesonblas.com/ whispine. Cottages enclosed by oak, pine and palm trees with views of St Joseph's Bay, just a few minutes' walk from the beach; guests have free use of canoes and, in season, can scoop their own scallops from the nearby shoreline.*

Hard-working Port St Joe, set on a sheltered bay, is noted for its paper mills and scallop fishing, and occupies the site of the vanished city of St Joseph. Flourishing as a port during the 1830s, St Joseph enjoyed a brief period as Florida's capital but was abandoned when it lost its political role to Tallahassee and was decimated by disease and hurricane. Its houses were destroyed or reassembled in Apalachicola and only the town cemetery remained.

The strange story of St Joseph is outlined at the **Constitution Convention State Museum**, which also details the 34-day convention that led to the drafting of the first Florida constitution in 1839, a step on the road to statehood that was acquired six years later. The convention delegates are rather unflatteringly represented by speaking mannequins.

Right
Wetland egrets

ST GEORGE ISLAND✦✦✦

St George Island State Park *1900 E Gulf Beach Drive; tel: (850) 927-2111.*

St George Island is one of three barrier islands that protect Apalachicola Bay and allow its oyster beds to thrive, and is the only one accessible by road. At the eastern end, **St George Island State Park** protects 9 miles of beaches, dunes, pine woods and live oak hammocks. The park is the best place to spot the island's abundant birdlife, particularly the ospreys which are frequently seen plucking fish from the water and whose nests adorn many pine trees. During spring and autumn the park provides an important stop for migratory birdlife. Besides swimming and picnic areas, the park has a 2.5-mile hiking trail and two observation decks providing excellent views of the island and beyond.

Accommodation and food in St George Island

Inn at Resort Village $$ *119 Franklin Boulevard; tel: (800) 824-0416; www.resortvillage.com.* This wood-framed hostelry is a long-serving local landmark; the simple but comfortable rooms open on to balconies with views of the bay or the Gulf.

Blue Parrot Oceanfront Café $$ *68 West Gorrie Drive, St George Island; tel: (850) 927-2987.* Boasts the largest deck and Po-Boy sandwich on the beach. Other dishes include grilled steaks and seafood.

ST JOSEPH PENINSULA STATE PARK❖❖

St Joseph Peninsula State Park $ *Eastern end of Cape San Blas Road, near Port St Joe; tel: (850) 227-1327; www. floridastateparks.org/stjoseph. Open daily 0800–sunset.*

Named for the long-gone city whose site is now occupied by Port St Joe (*see opposite*), this long and slender park has water on both sides and looms as a mirage-like string of white-sand dunes and beaches. The ocean beaches are used for swimming and fishing; the bay side has a picnic area and two nature trails.

ST MARCOS DE APALACHE HISTORIC SITE❖❖

St Marcos de Apalache Historic Site *148 Old Fort Road, near St Marks; tel: (850) 925-6216; www.floridastateparks.org/ sanmarcos. Open Thur–Mon 0900–1700.*

Sweet Magnolia Inn $$ *803 Port Leon Drive, near St Marks; tel: (850) 925-7670 or (800) 779-5214; www.sweetmagnolia.com. In an unlikely rustic setting, offering excellent seven-course dinners.*

This site, one of Florida's oldest reminders of its Spanish past, was chosen for a fort by Pánfilo de Narváez in 1528 because of its strategic importance at the confluence of the Wakulla and St Marks rivers. The series of wood and stone forts built here was regularly attacked by pirates and natives, and switched hands frequently as control of Florida passed from Spain to Britain and back again. Future Florida governor and US president Andrew Jackson occupied the fort during his illegal incursion into Florida in 1818.

Using stones from the Spanish-built foundations, a sailor's hospital was constructed here in 1857 and now holds a small **museum** outlining the fort's eventful past. A signposted **walking tour** links many of the main points of interest, including the thick-walled Spanish bombproof fort, the cemetery holding members of Jackson's expedition, and the hillock constructed by Confederate troops to hold a gunpowder magazine during the Civil War.

TORREYA STATE PARK❖❖

Torreya State Park $ *Near Bristol; tel: (850) 643-2674; www.floridastateparks.org/ torreya/default.asp. Open daily 0800–sunset.*

Hills of any kind are rare in Florida, which makes this park, set round the 150ft-high limestone bluffs that rise from dense forests above a bend in the Apalachicola River, seem all the more spectacular. The park is named after the torreya tree, a rare species of yew found only here.

From 1840 to the 1920s, the river was an important steamboat trading route and strategically significant during the Civil War. The remains of

Gregory House $
Guided tour only,
Mon–Fri 1000, Sat–Sun
1000, 1400 and 1600.

Confederate gun placements, dug into the bluffs to attack Union shipping, can still be seen on the dramatic **Apalachicola River Bluffs Trail**, which passes through a hardwood forest before emerging high above the river. Another walk, the **Weeping Ridge Trail**, explores one of the deep ravines carved by the river's tributaries over many centuries.

The importance of the river and the ups and downs of a cotton planter's life in the run-up to the Civil War are revealed during the guided tours of the **Gregory House**. The two-storey house, with its period fixtures and fittings, was built in 1849 for a successful planter and, perched above the river, enjoys one of the finest back garden views in Florida.

WAKULLA SPRINGS STATE PARK✦✦✦

**Wakulla Springs
State Park $ 550**
*Wakulla Park Drive; tel:
(850) 224-5950;
www.floridastateparks.org/
wakullasprings/default.asp.
Open daily 0800–sunset;
boat trips ($) operate when
water is clear.*

Lodge $ / *Spring
Drive; tel: (850) 224-
5950;
www.floridastateparks.org/
wakullasprings/lodge.asp.
Peace, quiet and a slice of
Florida history are all
provided by this 1930s
hotel where every room
has a marble bathroom
and fireplace.*

At the heart of this 2860-acre park is one of the world's largest and deepest freshwater springs. An average day brings 561 million gallons of crystal clear water from a source as yet undiscovered amid the intricate network of caves which lie hundreds of feet below the springs' deceptively calm surface.

The discovery of a fossilised mastodon skeleton here in 1850 prompted scientific interest in the springs. A few fossils can still be spotted, along with a multitude of colourful fish, on the glass-bottomed boat trips which provide a commentary on the mysteries of the spring and offer views reaching 100ft down.

A 6-mile hiking route penetrates the park but a less demanding form of exploration are the river trips venturing for 3 miles along the cypress-lined Wakulla River. Park wildlife includes alligators, turtles and deer, and a bird population of turkeys, herons, egrets, vultures, ospreys and the occasional bald eagle. The setting provided the backdrop for the 1954 film *Creature from the Black Lagoon* and several early *Tarzan* films.

Suggested tour

Length: Main tour 190 miles; St Joseph Peninsula State Park detour 50 miles; Torreya State Park detour 19 miles.

Duration: Main tour 4 hours. Taking one or both detours will require dropping something from the main tour unless it is spread over two days. If nature is preferred to history, ignore the St Marcos de Apalachee and Natural Bridge Battlefield sites in favour of Wakulla Springs and Torreya state parks (the latter adding 45 minutes' driving time). If isolated beaches appeal, be sure to include the St Joseph Peninsula State Park detour (30 minutes' driving time).

Links: Although designed as a day-trip from Tallahassee, stopping overnight in Apalachicola or nearby makes this an easy link with Crossing the Panhandle (*see pages 254–63*).

Above
Wakulla Springs State Park

Leave Tallahassee on Hwy-363. As it proceeds south, this route parallels the **Tallahassee-St Marks Railroad**, completed in 1837 and the first railway in Florida. The line, on which wagons were originally pulled by mules, saw 147 years of commercial use until being abandoned and redeveloped in the 1990s as a cycling, walking and skating route.

Six miles south of Tallahassee at **Woodville** is a left turn for Natural Bridge Road which, after 6.2 miles, reaches the **NATURAL BRIDGE BATTLEFIELD SITE ❶**. Just beyond the Battlefield Site are two natural springs. Return to Woodville and continue south for 6 miles on Route 363, to a far larger spring within **WAKULLA SPRINGS STATE PARK ❷**. The park's entrance is on Route 267, 4.8 miles from the junction with Route 363. Ahead on Route 363, **ST MARCOS DE APALACHE HISTORIC SITE ❸** is 3.5 miles from the Route 267 junction, close to the village of **St Marks**. The remains of the old fort enjoy a bucolic setting above the meeting point of the Wakulla and St Marks rivers.

The main coastal route, Hwy-98, crosses Route 363 2.5 miles north of the historic site. Join Hwy-98 heading west. The route is uneventful until, after 17 miles, it passes through **Panacea**, built around one of the many coastal inlets which now become a feature of the tour and here mark the start of the 'Forgotten Coast'. The road continues through numerous hamlets and the relatively large **Carrabelle**, from which **Dog Island**, accessible only by boat, is visible.

A further 16 miles along the coast, Hwy-98 passes the access road to the 5-mile bridge linking **ST GEORGE ISLAND ❹** to the

◐ **St Marks National Wildlife Refuge $**
Tel: (850) 925-6121;
email: saintmarks@fws.gov;
saintmarks.fws.gov. Open
daily dawn–dusk; visitors'
centre Mon–Fri 0815–1615,
Sat–Sun 1000–1700.

mainland. Cross the bridge into the heart of the island; the main beach is directly ahead. A left turn along Gulf Beach Drive continues for 11 miles into the sand-dune-dominated **St George Island State Park** and the island's eastern tip.

Back on the mainland, Hwy-98 continues west across the 5-mile-long John Gorrie Memorial Bridge, crossing a large bay fed by the Apalachicola River and touching ground at the time-locked town of **APALACHICOLA** ❺ with the stately **Gibson Inn** directly ahead. As it steers through the town, Hwy-98 passes the only traffic light in the county. Hwy-98 continues for 26 miles, bringing views of **St Vincent Island**, an offshore wildlife refuge, before passing the right turn to the **Constitution Convention State Museum** on the outskirts of PORT ST JOE ❻.

In the centre of Port St Joe, Hwy-98 forms a junction with Route 71. Take the latter north to return to Tallahassee. For 51 miles the route passes riverside hamlets and crosses bridges bringing views of cypress swamps before reaching Blountstown and the junction with Route 20. Turn right, heading east for 26 miles passing through **Bristol** and meeting the junction with Route 267. Continue on Route 20 for a direct 18-mile course to Tallahassee, or join Route 267 skirting the **APALACHICOLA NATIONAL FOREST** ❼ before meeting Hwy-319 near Wakulla Springs State Park, 12 miles south of Tallahassee.

Detour: Eight miles west of Apalachicola on Hwy-98 is a left turn on to Route 30A. The latter skirts the north bank of the Indian Lagoon and after 16 miles sweeps northwards along the slender arm of land that holds **ST JOSEPH PENINSULA STATE PARK** ❽.

Detour: From Bristol, head north on Route 12 for 6.5 miles, then take the left turn on to Route 271. After 5.5 miles, passing through tiny **Rock Bluff**, is the entrance road to the isolated **TORREYA STATE PARK** ❾.

Also worth exploring

Covering 66,000 acres of the marshy shoreline of Apalachicola Bay, the **St Marks National Wildlife Refuge** is studded with roadside wildlife lookout points from which patience and luck may result in sightings of racoons, white-tailed deer and otters. A visitors' centre documents the area and its denizens. Also within the refuge is the still-functioning **St Marks Lighthouse**, constructed in part with bricks from San Marcos de Apalache (*see page 249*) and completed in 1831. The adjacent **observation tower** brings views of the coastline and the wide variety of birdlife inhabiting it.

Reach the refuge by turning right on to Hwy-98 after leaving the San Marcos de Apalache Historic Site, passing through **Newport** and, after 2.5 miles, making a right turn on to Route 59, the only road into the refuge and one which continues to the lighthouse.

GULF OF MEXICO

Crossing the Panhandle

Ratings

Beaches	●●●●●
Architecture	●●● ○○
Fishing	●●● ○○
Nature	●●● ○○
Scenery	●●● ○○
Children	●● ○○○
History	●● ○○○
Museums	● ○○○○

As it crosses the central section of the Panhandle, this route encounters Florida beach towns of every kind. They range from Seaside, a planned community fresh off the designer's drawing board, to rustic hamlets such as Grayton Beach and the commercially excessive Panama City Beach. What they all share, however, is proximity to intensely white-sand beaches (due to the powdered quartz washed up here over thousands of years from the Appalachian Mountains) and a section of the Gulf of Mexico where the near-shore waters are a gorgeous emerald colour.

Deep-sea fishing is a major draw, particularly around Destin, where charter boats for novice anglers are as plentiful as the seafood restaurants that serve the best of the day's catch. Away from the coast, old Florida asserts itself in sleepy rural towns, often decorated by Confederate flags of which De Funiak Springs is by far the most distinctive.

DE FUNIAK SPRINGS✦✦

ⓘ Beaches of South Walton Visitors Center *junction of Hwy-98 and Hwy 399, Santa Rosa Beach; tel: (850) 267-1216 or (800) 822-6877; www. beachesofsouthwalton.com. Open daily 0800–1630.*

🏛 Walton-De Funiak Library *3 Circle Drive; tel: (850) 892-3624. Open Mon–Wed, Fri–Sat 0900–1500 or later.*

If local lore is to be believed, De Funiak Springs is set around one of the world's two naturally circular lakes. The beauty of the spring-fed lake, discovered in a forest by a railway survey party, encouraged the founding of the town as a transportation base in the 1880s and it gained *élan* as the winter base of the Chautaqua Alliance. Founded to promote educational values in rural areas, the alliance raised an imposing domed **auditorium** beside the lake in 1909 and made this small town one of the cultural hot spots of the southeastern US.

Ringed by live oaks and magnolias, the lake forms a magnificent centrepiece to the town and is overlooked by the best examples of the community's Victorian homes: a rich confection of turrets, dormer windows, gingerbread carpentry, fluted columns and two-storey verandas that line the mile-long and aptly named **Circle Drive**. Also on Circle Drive is the dainty 1886 **Walton-De Funiak Library**, among the oldest libraries in Florida and the only one to display medieval armour and weaponry alongside its books.

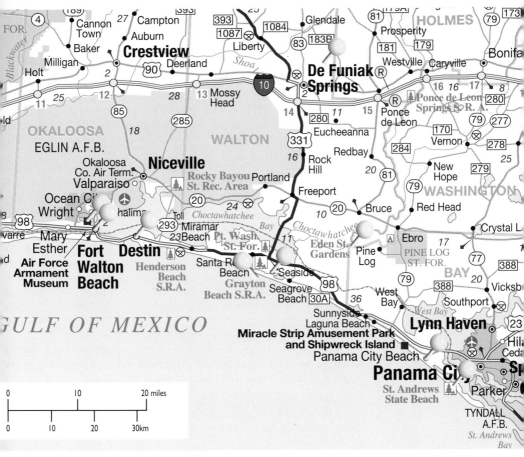

The Panhandle was more deeply involved in the Civil War than any other region of Florida and in 1871, having raised a collection of $250, De Funiak Springs became the area's first town to erect a monument to its Confederate dead. The **Confederate Monument** still stands outside the county courthouse beside Hwy-90.

Accommodation and food in De Funiak Springs

Hotel Defuniak $ *400 E Nelson Avenue, tel: (850) 892-4383; email: gm@hoteldefuniak.com; www.hoteldefuniak.com.* Raised in the 1920s and lovingly restored in the 1990s, this antique-filled hotel with three suites and eight rooms, oozes atmosphere.

Lake Room $ *at Hotel Defuniak 400 E Nelson Avenue, tel: (850) 892-4383; email: gm@hoteldefuniak.com; www.hoteldefuniak.com.* The hotel's dining room overlooks the lake and offers buffet style lunches and nightly dinners.

DESTIN*

ℹ **Destin Chamber of Commerce** *1021 Hwy-98; tel: (850) 837-6241; www.destinchamber.com. Open Mon–Fri 0900–1700.*

Destin began as a fishing village and is now a major centre for sports-fishing thanks to the 100-ft-deep De Soto Canyon – a lair of tuna, marlin, tarpon and other denizens of the deep that put up a fight when snagged by an anglers hook – which is within easy reach of the charter and private fishing boats berthed at the town's busy marina.

Unappealing high-rise condominiums diminish Destin's visual appeal, even though there is a very fine **beach** on its eastern edge. Otherwise, the core of the town is a functional but unattractive string of petrol stations and shopping malls. Fishing opportunities are endless and widely advertised; more ecologically sensitive might be dolphin and birdwatching voyages by **glass-bottomed boat** from Boogies Dock at the foot of the Destin Bridge (*tel: (850) 654-7787*) and the **Dolphin Cruise** on the Southern Star from *Harbor Walk Marina, by Highway-98; tel: (850) 837-7741; www.dolphin-sstar.com*

Food in Destin

Beachwalk Cafe $–$$ *2996 Scenic Highway, tel: (850) 650 7100; www.beachwalkcafe.com.* Sip wine, sample a dessert, or grapple with a full meal while gazing across the bright white sands stretching to the Gulf of Mexico.

Lucky Snapper Grill & Bar $–$$ *76 Hwy-98 E; tel: (850) 654-0900; www.luckysnapper.com.* Squid, shrimp fritters and gator tail are among the many options at this seafood eatery, with a menu as long as your arm.

EDEN STATE GARDENS**

🏛 **Eden State Gardens $** *Port Washington; tel: (850) 231-4214; www.floridastateparks.org/edengardens/default.asp. Gardens daily 0800–sunset; house by guided tour only Thur–Mon 1000–1500.*

Though his company laid waste to the Panhandle's forests from the 1890s, lumber baron William Henry Wesley made some amends by building this charming white-columned Greek Revival mansion in 1897. The architecture reveals some of the features of living in Florida in the days before air conditioning. Raised above ground level, the house allows air to circulate beneath while preventing flood damage; large windows embrace whatever breeze may appear during the humid summer and allows the air to flow through a lofty central hallway dividing the rooms on both floors of the two-storey structure.

The Wesley family occupied the house until the 1950s. Subsequently, New York journalist Lois Maxon expanded it and added the cornucopia of family heirlooms and antiques, among them a Chippendale cabinet and Louis XVI mirror, that remain. Even when the house is closed, the splendid gardens justify a visit. Moss-draped oaks fringe the lawns, while masses of camellias and azaleas blossom throughout the winter, reaching their colourful peak in mid-March.

EGLIN AFB ARMAMENT MUSEUM❖

Eglin AFB Armament Museum *Route 85, near Valparaiso; tel: (850) 651-1808; www.destin-ation.com/airforcearmamentmuseum. Open daily 0900–1630. Free.*

Within Eglin AFB (Air Force Base), which covers 720 square miles and dominates the economy of nearby Fort Walton Beach (*see below*), this collection of planes, missiles and other weaponry that has determined the course of history from World War I to the 1991 Gulf War will convince anyone of the US's technological superiority in global conflict. Among the planes that can be inspected at close quarters are a B-52 bomber, a F16 fighter and a SR17 spy plane.

Other exhibits include a replica of *Fat Boy*, the atomic bomb dropped on Nagasaki in 1945, a variety of cruise missiles, accounts of the Korean and Vietnam wars focusing on the role of the air force, and a collection of duelling pistols and early revolvers decidedly at odds with the high-tech implements of death arranged all around.

FORT WALTON BEACH❖

Greater Fort Walton Beach Chamber of Commerce *34 Miracle Strip Parkway; tel: (850) 244-8191; www.fwbchamber.com. Open Mon–Fri 0900–1700.*

The sand dune-lined beach that fringes Okaloosa Island is one reason to linger in Fort Walton Beach. Another is the engaging **Indian Temple Mound Museum $** (*139 Miracle Strip Parkway; tel: (850) 833-9595. Open Sept–May, Mon–Fri 0900–1600, Sat 0900–1600; June–Aug, Mon–Sat 0900–1630, Sun 1230–1630*) which documents the Native American cultures of the region over a period of 10,000 years. Facing the museum is an Indian-built mound, believed to date from 1400 and topped by a reconstructed temple.

Beside the Gulf of Mexico, the **Gulfarium $$** (*1010 Miracle Strip Parkway; tel: (850) 244-5169; www.gulfarium.com. Open spring and summer, daily 0900–1800; rest of the year daily 0900–1600*) is among the better of the Panhandle's marine parks with displays of dolphins and sea lions, and glass tanks full of sharks, eels, sea turtles and other creatures.

Florida in the Civil War

The Panhandle was Florida's most populated region during the Civil War (1861–5), when the state aligned with the Confederacy though most of Florida's coastal fortifications were occupied by Union forces. The battles that took place in Florida were mostly in the Panhandle, the largest being the Battle of Olustree (near Live Oak) in February 1864, which involved 10,000 men and left 300 dead. Overall, the conflict took the lives of a third of the 15,000 Floridians who fought in it.

GRAYTON BEACH❖❖❖

Despite its beach constantly being rated among the best in the US, Grayton Beach remains largely unspoilt and seemingly does little to encourage large-scale tourism. Unlike many of its neighbours where high-rise resort hotels are two-a-penny, this appealing place finds hammocks strung across porches, surfboards resting against garage doors, vibrant murals, and art galleries and small cafés lining its short main street.

The town's greatest asset is the **Grayton Beach State Recreation Area $** *(357 Main Park Road; tel: (850) 231-4210; www.floridastateparks.org/graytonbeach. Open daily 0800–sunset)* with a mile-long white-sand beach flanked by sea-oat-topped dunes. Swimming, sunbathing and surfing are all popular pursuits here, while a nature trail penetrates the scrub and pinelands beside a large brackish lake on the inland side.

Accommodation and food in Grayton Beach

Above
Grayton Beach

Hibiscus Coffee & Guesthouse $ *85 De Funiak Street; tel: (850) 231-2733; email: info@hibiscusflorida.com; www.hibiscusflorida.com.* Bed and a vegetarian breakfast in four simple rooms enclosed by gardens on the road into Grayton Beach. By day, it operates as a coffee-house serving gourmet blends and simple snacks.

Criolla's $$$ *North side of Hwy-30A, near junction with Route 283; tel: (850) 267-1267; email: staff@criollas.com; www.criollas.com.* Coffee-scented duck breast, wood-grilled swordfish and salmon steamed in bamboo are among the creative offerings that blend Creole and Caribbean cookery.

Panama City Beach*

Seascape Inn $–$$
15505 Front Beach Road; tel: (800) 874-2410; www.seascapeinnpcb.com. Located at the centre of the beach's miracle strip. All rooms come equipped with kitchenettes and private patio or balcony.

Panama City Beach is not a place to find peace and solitude. With every seaside amusement imaginable – go-karting, mini-golf, game arcades and lots more – plus an influx of 600,000 hedonistic students during the February to Easter Spring Break, the town is devoted to mass market tourism and earning as much revenue as possible from a powdery beach that stretches more than 20 miles.

The tackiness is so unrelenting that it almost becomes appealing in itself. The only escapes from the highly developed beach strip are diving and sports-fishing (both well provided for by boat trips from the local marinas) and visiting the unspoilt St Andrews State Beach (*see below*).

St Andrews State Beach**

St Andrews State Beach $ *4607 State Park Lane; tel: (850) 233-5140; www.floridastateparks.org/standrews. Open daily 0800–sunset.*

This deservedly popular park is a welcome antidote to the unrelenting commercialism of Panama City Beach and fills over 1200 acres on a finger of land that extends eastwards from the busy beach city. Facing the emerald-coloured Gulf of Mexico, a glorious sugar-sanded beach is ideal for swimming; other park areas offer snorkelling, diving, canoeing and kayaking. Many locals catch a fish dinner from the park's piers and jetties.

An inland nature trail leads to Gator Lake and a vantage point for gazing at wildlife that includes alligators, racoons, deer and a multitude of birds. Another trail explores the pine woods and marshlands of the park's northern section and passes a reconstructed pioneer-era turpentine still. The turpentine industry flourished here in the late 1800s and accounts for the scars still borne by some pine trees.

Another rewarding section of the park is 700-acre **Shell Island**, accessible only by boat (shuttle trips depart during spring and summer), with 7 pristine miles of beach coated with a fresh layer of shells with each tide.

SEASIDE**✧✧✧**

Looking at first glance like a New England coastal town, complete with picket fences and clapboard cottages, Seaside was created from scratch in the 1980s. With cottages for rent or purchase and a number of shops and restaurants linked by brightly painted porches, Seaside hoped to acquire an instant smalltown atmosphere and sense of community. Some find Seaside a sentimental, theme park-like creation, while others, such as those who return year after year, regard it as idyllic. Love it or loathe it, Seaside has won numerous architectural awards, provided a backdrop for the 1998 film, *The Truman Show*, and is definitely worth a look.

Suggested tour

Length: Main tour 64 miles; first detour 10 miles; second detour 70 miles.

Duration: The main tour is a scenic coastal route taking about 4 hours of driving time. The Eden State Gardens detour will add 30 minutes and should be ignored if you are taking the second detour to De Funiak Springs, which will add 90 minutes.

Links: Tallahassee to the Forgotten Coast (*see pages 244–53*), The Pensacola Area and its beaches (*see pages 272–81*).

From the east, the main coastal route, Hwy-98, passes through the industrial port town of **Panama City** before crossing Hathaway Bridge above St Andrews Bay and entering **PANAMA CITY BEACH** ❶. To check the pulse of this heavily developed vacation town, take the left fork on to Alt Hwy-98. This continues past 15 miles of restaurants, shopping malls and motels. To re-discover the coast as nature intended it, take the left turn on to Route 3031 (Joan Avenue) soon after crossing the bridge and follow signs for **ST ANDREWS STATE BEACH** ❷.

On the western edge of Panama City Beach, Alt-Hwy 98 rejoins Hwy-98. After 2.5 miles, take the left turn on to Route 30A at tiny **Inlet Beach**. This coast-hugging road brings views of dune-walled beaches and the emerald waters of the Gulf of Mexico; large brackish lakes appear on the inland side. The first community reached is **Rosemary Beach**, an architect-planned coastal village still under construction. After 7 miles, the route passes through **SEAGROVE BEACH** ❸ and then reaches the spick-and-span cottages of **SEASIDE** ❹.

In contrast to Seaside's award-winning but rather soulless appearance is the rustic beach community at **GRAYTON BEACH**. Reach it by passing through Seaside and turning left at the junction of Route 30A and Route 283. The latter proceeds into Grayton Beach, passing

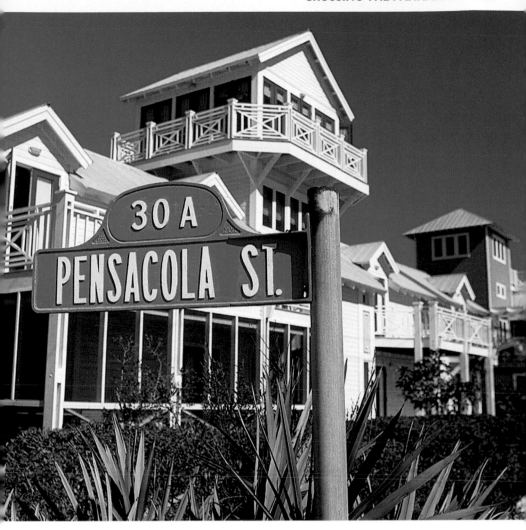

Above
Nouveau Victorian architecture
in the town of Seaside

wooden bungalows and expiring at the little beach town's main
street, parallel to an excellent and easily accessed beach. The main
entrance to **Grayton Beach State Recreation Area** is signposted on
Route 30A, just east of the Route 283 junction.

Nine miles west of Grayton Beach, having passed through the quiet
coastal villages of **Blue Mountain Beach** and **Dune Alley Beach**,
Route 30A rejoins Hwy-98. Take this route for 4.4 miles, passing
through the high-rise developments of Sandestin where the two-lane
road expands into a six-lane highway, and turn left on to Route 2378,
returning to the coast. For the next 7 miles, the route passes holiday
condos and high-rise hotels facing a commendable beach.

Chautauqua Vineyards *Hwy-331, 1 mile south of De Funiak Springs; tel: (850) 892-5887; www.chautauquawinery.com. Free tastings Mon–Sat 0900–1700, Sun 1200–1700.*

Ponce de Leon State Park $ *Route 181A, east of De Funiak Springs; tel: (850) 836-4281; www.floridastateparks.org/poncedeleonsprings. Open daily 0800–sunset.*

The route returns to Hwy-98 on the eastern edge of **DESTIN** ⑤. For 3 miles, the route passes through the commercialised section of the town with Destin Harbor to the left, lined by fishing boats and seafood restaurants. By bridge, the route crosses the **East Pass** that separates the vast Choctawhatchee Bay from the Gulf of Mexico.

Hwy-98 touches ground on **Okaloosa Island**, a slender strip of sand dune and beach owned by the US Air Force that stretches nearly 5 miles. Hwy-98 crosses the island and continues over a high bridge into the centre of **FORT WALTON BEACH** ⑥, where many residents are employed at the nearby Eglin Air Force Base. Look for the **Indian Temple Mound Museum** on the right beside this busy stretch of Hwy-98.

Detour: From Hwy-30A, turn right on to Route 395 at Seagrove Beach, crossing Hwy-98 and continuing towards the one-time logging community of **Port Washington**. After 4.8 miles is the entrance on the left to **EDEN STATE GARDENS** ⑦.

Detour: From Grayton Beach or Eden State Gardens, return to Hwy-98 and continue west to the junction with Hwy-331. This makes a 3.3-mile crossing of Choctawhatchee Bay, along which logs were floated during the late-1800s Florida timber boom. Some invitingly shaded picnic tables stand on the bridge's northern end.

Hwy-331 continues north for 4.5 miles and meets Route 20. Turn left and, shortly ahead at the crossroads town of Freeport, turn right on to the continuation of Hwy-331. For the next 17 miles, the route is intermittently enlivened by small villages. At the junction with I-10, a signposted driveway leads to the **Chautauqua Vineyards** where there are complimentary tastings of some of Florida's finest wines. Continue on Hwy-331 for a mile into **DE FUNIAK SPRINGS** ⑧, following signs for the Historic District which lead to Circle Drive.

Leave De Funiak Springs heading west on Hwy-90 or I-10. After 14 miles is the junction with the southbound Route 285. Take this to return to the coast, crossing Eglin Air Force Base, founded in the 1930s when a golf course was donated as a gunnery and bombing range, and after 18 miles reaching **Niceville**, a dormitory town for air force personnel. Follow signs for Fort Walton Beach, joining Route 85. The entrance to **EGLIN AFB ARMAMENT MUSEUM** ⑨ is 5.7 miles ahead on the left. To rejoin Hwy-98, continue to Fort Walton Beach, 6 miles south.

Also worth exploring

Named after the 16th-century Spaniard who arrived in Florida searching for the Fountain of Youth and was greatly encouraged by the region's plethora of natural springs, the **Ponce de León Springs State Recreation Area**, 12 miles east of De Funiak Springs

4 Florala 153 87 27 4 103 28

85A Laurel Hill 181 Gaskin 179 177 Esto Noma

kman Paxton + Highest point Darlington 2 Graceville

2 85 in Florida Leonia 185 179A Izagora 177 173 77 Jac

189 393 345 2 81 HOLMES 79 273

27 Campton 25 Glendale Prosperity 1

Cannon 393 1084 83 183B 181 179 Bonifay Chip

Town Auburn 1087 Liberty Westville Caryville

Baker Crestview Deerland Shoal De Funiak R 16 16 17 8 18

gan 90 10 8 Springs 280

2 28 13 Mossy R Ponce de Leon

85 Head 2 Ponce Springs S. R. A. 79 277 Falling

285 14 280 11 de Leon 170 278 Waters

OOSA 18 WALTON Eucheeanna 15 Vernon St. Rec.

N A.F.B. 331 284 25 Wausau

Okaloosa 16 Rock Redbay New 279

Co. Air Term. Niceville Hill 20 81 Hope

Rocky Bayou Portland 79 WASHINGTON

alparaiso St. Rec. Area Freeport Bruce Red Head

an City 20 24 10 20 Crystal Lake 20

ht Shalimar Toll Choctawhatchee A Ebro 17 Bennett

9 12 Destin 293 Miramar Bay Choctawhatchee PINE LOG 14

6 Beach Pt. Wash. 11 Eden St ST. FOR. 388

Fort 5 St. For. Gardens Pine 77 2301

Walton 23 Santa Rosa 4 Seaside Log BAY 388 Vicksburg

Beach Henderson Beach 3 79 20 Southport 24

Beach S.R.A. Grayton Seagrove West 231 Bayou

Grayton Beach 30A Bay Lynn Haven

OF MEXICO Beach S.R.A. Sunnyside 36 West Bay Hiland Park

Laguna Beach Cedar Grove

Miracle Strip Amusement Park Springfiel

and Shipwreck Island Panama City Callawa

Panama City Beach 1 2 Parker East

St. Andrews Bay

0 10 miles State Beach TYNDALL

0 10km A.F.B. St. Andrews

Bay

Crooked 98

Island

Mexico Beac

Beaco

St. Joseph P

off Route 181A, is the perfect spot to cool off on a hot day. The major spring here is fed by 14 million gallons of water pumping daily from a deep limestone cavity. With a constant temperature of 68°F, the spring invites a dip and there is a designated swimming area. Picnic tables and a nature trail through pine woods encourage a longer stay.

Ratings

History	●●●●●
Museums	●●●●○
Architecture	●●●○○
Entertainment	●●●○○
Food	●●●○○
Shopping	●●●○○
Scenery	●●○○○
Children	●○○○○

Pensacola

Anyone hankering for history will find Pensacola much to their liking. While the nearby beaches and islands are the main attraction for most visitors, the city itself has done an impressive job of preserving and restoring its past. Entire streets are still lined by the early-1800s buildings whose ethnically diverse occupants laid the foundations of the modern city. Another area retains turn-of-the-century commercial façades, while a third leafy neighbourhood still boasts the sumptuous middle-class homes that set the tone for gracious Pensacola living through the early 1900s.

Adding spice is the fact that while Pensacola now occupies a relatively remote corner of the state, Florida's destiny was shaped by the events that unfolded here. The Spanish and British established forts and challenged each other for supremacy of this important sea base until both were unceremoniously removed by future president Andrew Jackson, who oversaw Florida's admission to the US here.

Sights

1 Pensacola
Convention &
Visitors Information
Center *1401 E Gregory
Street; tel: (850) 343-1234
or (800) 874-1234;
www.visitpensacola.com.
Open Mon–Fri 0800–1700,
Sat 0900–1600, Sun
1100–1600.*

Blount Building
17 Palofax Place.

**Civil War Soldiers
Museum** $ *108 S Palafox
Street; tel: (850) 469-1900;
www.cwmuseum.org. Open
Tue–Sat 1000–1630.*

Blount Building*

Replacing an earlier building destroyed by fire, the 1907 Blount Building turned many heads on the northern approach to the commercial centre of Pensacola. The beaux arts features such as copper cornices and terracotta arches were regarded as daring, while the fire-proof steel-girder construction spared it the fate that befell its predecessor.

Civil War Soldiers Museum**

The Civil War often seems a recent memory throughout the Panhandle, a region more involved than any other part of Florida. Several rooms of maps, uniforms and weapons tell the story of the war that killed 620,000 Americans, while personal items such as letters and photos belonging to soldiers reveal its impact on everyday life.

Particularly striking are the medical exhibits that form part of a reconstructed Confederate field hospital, highlighting the difficulties

Fort George
Junction of Palafox and LaRua streets.

Historic Pensacola Village $ *Includes entry to museums of commerce and industry, Julee Cottage, Dorr and Lavallé houses, and TT Wentworth Museum; part of Seville Historic District; tel: (850) 595-5985; www.historicpensacola.org. Open Mon–Sat 1000–1600.*

encountered by physicians tending the injured. Alongside some crude surgical tools are artificial limbs, crutches and a portable dental chair in which the unfortunate patient would be tethered for an emergency extraction without anaesthetic.

Much less gory is a section on Civil War music, with instruments purpose-made for battle. Alongside drumsticks from the Battle of Gettysburg is a wooden flute that could swiftly be converted into a baton.

Fort George and North Hill*

For 60 years from the 1870s, the well-to-do of Pensacola built homes in North Hill, a 50-block area immediately north of the city's commercial district. Doctors, lawyers and bankers were among those who occupied elegant houses in styles spanning neo-classical, Queen Anne, Tudor Revival and more. Most are excellently preserved and set along the neighbourhood's quiet oak-lined streets. Another well-maintained building is **Christ Episcopal Church**, its Mediterranean Revival form intended to reflect Pensacola's Spanish past, its pebble-dash exterior topped by a 64-ft-high dome.

Although only a plaque and small park marks the spot, it was in North Hill that the British built the largest of their three Pensacola forts, **Fort George**, completed in 1778. Three years later, the Spanish regained control of the city and the fort became Fort San Miguel.

Historic Pensacola Village***

Within the Seville Historic District (*see page 267*), Historic Pensacola Village comprises several small museums and homes and is often roamed by period-attired guides and volunteers re-enacting life in bygone times. Historical orientation is provided by a short video at the visitors' centre.

Inside a 19th-century warehouse, the **Museum of Industry** explores the fishing, lumber and brick-making industries that provided the backbone of the local economy for many years. A brick kiln (local clay proved an ideal raw material) and a re-created sawmill are among the exhibits; others detail the rise of the railways that helped Pensacola flourish as a transportation centre. Next door, the **Museum of Commerce** enjoyably re-creates Pensacola street scenes of times past. A print shop is packed with antique presses, a pharmacy carries vintage medicines and there is more nostalgia to be found within the hardware and toy stores.

Before it joined the US, Florida provided a sanctuary for runaway slaves and allowed Black people to work and prosper in a manner not possible in neighbouring states. The 1804 **Julee Cottage** belonged to a successful Black woman, Julee Canton, and exhibits about her and Black life in Florida occupy the interior.

Museum of Industry $$ *(included in Historic Pensacola Village admission); Zaragoza Street, part of Historic Pensacola Village.*

Museum of Commerce $$ *(included in Historic Pensacola Village admission); Zaragoza Street, part of Historic Pensacola Village.*

Julee Cottage $$ *(included in Historic Pensacola Village admission); Zaragoza Street, part of Historic Pensacola Village.*

Pensacola Historical Museum $ *115 E Zaragoza Street; tel: (850) 433-1559; email: phstaff@pcola.gulf.net; www.pensacolahistory.org. Open Mon–Sat 1000–1630.*

Plaza Ferdinand VII *On Palafox Street between Zaragoza and Government streets.*

Saenger Theater *118 Palafox Place; www.pensacolasaenger.com*

Seville Historic District *Bordered by Tarragona, Florida Blanca and Wright streets, and Bayfront Parkway.*

TT Wentworth Museum $$ *(included in Historic Pensacola Village admission); 330 S Jefferson Street; tel: (850) 595-5985. Open Memorial Day–Labor Day, Mon–Sat 1000–1600, Sun 1300–1600. Closed Sun rest of the year.*

Pensacola Historical Museum✦✦

A better setting for an historical museum is harder to imagine than Old Christ Church, built in 1823 and among Florida's oldest churches. Inside the sturdy redbricked structure, which served as a barracks for Union troops during the Civil War and spent many years as a public library, the exhibits comprehensively trace Pensacola's development from Native American times onwards.

Plaza Ferdinand VII✦

It was in the palm-studded Plaza Ferdinand VII in 1821 that Florida formally became part of the US. A statue of future president and Florida's first territorial governor, Andrew Jackson, who drove the British out of Pensacola stands in the centre of the plaza, which was laid out by the Spanish and used by the British as a drill field.

Saenger Theater✦

Regaining its role as an entertainment venue in the 1980s, the Saenger Theater dates from the era of vaudeville and silent movies: Cecil B De Mille's *The Ten Commandments* was the attraction on opening night in 1925. The Spanish baroque details, inside and out, now make an atmospheric setting for Broadway shows, Pensacola Symphony Orchestra concerts and other cultural events.

Seville Historic District✦✦✦

Still an important cargo terminal, the harbour triggered large-scale settlement of Pensacola. By the late 1700s, the nascent city was a thriving multicultural trading post where French, Spanish, British and freed slaves (some escaping across the border from the US) lived and prospered side by side. On streets laid out by the British but named by the Spanish, the Seville District still has many wood-frame homes of the early days intact, some now housing museums, shops, restaurants and cafés. The district, a strange mixture of Victorian and Creole architecture, includes Historic Pensacola Village (*see page 265*) and the Seville Quarter, a popular nightlife complex.

TT Wentworth Museum✦✦

The three-storey yellow brick creation in Renaissance Revival style that rises in eye-catching manner beside Plaza Ferdinand VII was built in 1908 as Pensacola's City Hall. The building's architecture alone merits viewing, with red-tiled towers, overhanging eaves and a triple-arched entrance, but the contents also warrant closer inspection.

Reflecting the eclectic collecting passions of a local property dealer, TT Wentworth, the museum boasts an amazing array of antlers, shrunken heads, coke machines, car licence plates, telephone paraphernalia and seemingly whatever else Wentworth, who began his collection aged eight with a gold dollar coin in

1906, could lay his hands on. Alongside are strong displays on local history; the top floor is a hands-on educational area intended for children.

Accommodation and food

The accommodation selections below are limited to those in and around Pensacola's historic core, adjacent to the suggested tour. The same applies to restaurants, with those listed all within walking distance of the described route. If neither accommodation nor food appeal it is a simple drive to find many other options, such as those described in the Pensacola area and its beaches route (*see pages 272–81*).

Barracks Street Fish House $–$$ *600 Barracks Street; tel: (850) 470-0003; www.pensacolafishhouse.com.* A good reason to visit the Pensacola docks is this friendly restaurant serving excellent fresh seafood, plus steaks, sandwiches and salads, and freshly made desserts.

Marsh House $$–$$$ *205 Cevallos Street; tel: (850) 433-4866.* Cross the white-painted wraparound veranda and spacious armchair-filled lobby to find several distinctively furnished bed-and-breakfast rooms.

McQuire's Irish Pub $–$$ *600 E Gregory Street; tel: (850) 433-6789; www.mcguiresirishpub.com.* Steaks, seafood and burgers are on the menu of this pseudo-Irish bar serving lunch, dinner and own-brew beers.

Noble Manor $–$$ *110 W Strong Street; tel: (850) 434-9544; email: info2@noblemanor.com; www.noblemanor.com.* Bed and breakfast in a 1905 Tudor Revival house in the elegant North Hill neighbourhood is an excellent way to immerse yourself in Pensacola's past; the gardens invite a stroll.

Pensacola Grand Hotel $$–$$$ *200 E Gregory Street; tel: (850) 433-3336; www.pensacolagrandhotel.com.* Modern high-rise hotel, often hosting conventions, at odds with its historic surrounds but within easy walking distance of the city's attractions, dining and nightlife.

Pensacola Victorian Bed & Breakfast $$–$$$ *203 W Gregory Street; tel: (850) 434-2818 or (800) 370-8354; email: ppcolabedbrk@pcola.gulf.net; www.pensacolavictorian.com.* A Queen Anne home built for a ship's captain who also founded the Pensacola Symphony Orchestra. Private bathrooms, cable TV and home-baked snacks.

Seville Inn $–$$ *223 E Garden Street; tel: (850) 433-8331 or (800) 227-7275; email: info@sevilleinn.com; www.sevilleinn.com.* Hard to better for good-priced accommodation in a central location.

Spanish Quarter *130 E Government Street; tel: (850) 434-6211; www.rosies.com.* Replicating the Church Street Station dining and nightlife complex of Orlando, the Seville Quarter provides a downtown focal point for evening entertainment. Included is the **Palace Oyster Bar $$**, serving seafood and local specialities.

Right
Pensacola's Historic District

Barkley House *410 S Florida Blanca Street.*

Seville Square *Bordered by Zaragoza, Government, Alcaniz and Barracks streets.*

Dorr House $ *(included in Historic Pensacola Village admission), 311 S Adams Street.*

Lavallé House *205 E Church Street, part of Historic Pensacola Village.*

Pensacola Museum of Art *407 S Jefferson Street; tel: (850) 432-6247; www. pensacolamuseumofart.org. Open Tue–Fri 1000–1700, Sat and Sun 1200–1600.*

The 1912 *Pensacola Grand Hotel, 200 E Gregory Street; tel: (850) 433-3336.* Good-quality lunch menu; by night it becomes a slightly more formal and highly rated dinner restaurant.

Suggested tour

Length: Main tour, 0.75 miles; detour 1.5 miles and best undertaken by car.

Duration: 3–4 hours on foot including viewing time; add 30 minutes for the detour.

Links: Pensacola lies within the area described in the Pensacola area and its beaches tour (*see pages 272–81*).

The oldest quarter of the city, the **SEVILLE HISTORIC DISTRICT ❶** makes a good beginning to an exploration of Pensacola. At the foot of Florida Blanca Street, the 1825 **Barkley House ❷**, built for a British merchant, is one of the oldest masonry homes in Florida and still enjoys a splendid view over Pensacola Bay despite the busy highway which runs close by. Walk to Zaragoza Street and turn left, passing more early-1800s homes before reaching **Seville Square ❸**, a block ahead and overlooked by Old Christ Church, which now holds the **PENSACOLA HISTORICAL MUSEUM ❹**. The museum's collections help make sense of the city's turbulent and complicated history.

The next step is to purchase a ticket for the homes and museums of **HISTORIC PENSACOLA VILLAGE ❺** from the visitors' centre, a block ahead at the junction with Barracks Street. The wooden **Julee Cottage ❻** stands directly opposite the visitors' centre; the **Museum of Commerce ❼** and the **Museum of Industry ❽** face each other on Zaragoza Street just across Barracks Street.

Within the village are several former homes with historic exhibits. The most substantial, both viewed by guided tour, are the sumptuously appointed 1871 **Dorr House ❾**, across Church Street facing Seville Square, and the 1805 **Lavallé House ❿**, co-built by a French woman fleeing a slave rebellion in the Caribbean. The latter is a good example of the French Creole architectural style, complete with overhanging porch, while the interior suggests life in 1820s Pensacola.

Continue west along Church Street to reach **PLAZA FERDINAND VII ⓫**, on the east side of which the former City Hall is now taken up by the **TT WENTWORTH MUSEUM ⓬**. Among the museum's exhibits are those describing the archaeological dig which has unearthed parts of the British fort which occupied the Seville area in the 1700s. A still-expanding **trail ⓭**, beginning behind the museum, links several points of interest from the old fort. A block south on Main Street, the

North Hill Historic District *Bordered by Wright, Blount, LaRua and Palafox streets.*

St Michael's Cemetery *Alcaniz Street, opposite junction with Garden Street.*

Pensacola Museum of Art ⓮ is less notable for its exhibitions than its setting: a two-storey Mediterranean Revival structure that formerly held the city jail.

A block west is the 1892 **Bear Block ⓯**, an ornate neo-classical structure marking the southern end of **Palafox Street ⓰**, the commercial core of Pensacola during the booming early 1900s, with many buildings of the time remaining. Walk north along Palafox Street. The 1887 **Escambia County Courthouse ⓱** rises on the left immediately beyond Government Street. Cross Palafox Street to admire the Spanish Revival details of the

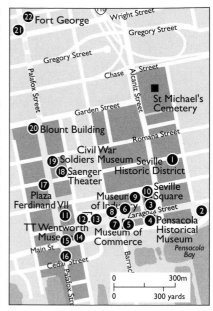

SAENGER THEATER ⓲. On the same block is the **CIVIL WAR SOLDIERS MUSEUM ⓳**. A block north on the corner with Garden Street is the **BLOUNT BUILDING ⓴**.

Detour: Those who grew rich as Pensacola thrived built homes immediately north of the Palafox district in North Hill, which rises steadily away from the bay filling a 50-block area. Although none are open to the public, many of North Hill's historic houses remain in excellent condition and collectively suggest the affluent local lifestyles of the 1870s to the 1930s. Palafox Street continues across Garden Street into North Hill, oak trees decorating its centre. On the junction of Wright Street is the distinctive domed form of **Christ Episcopal Church ㉑**. Two blocks further, near the junction with LaRua Street, is the site of the British-built **Fort George ㉒**.

Also worth exploring

On the northern edge of the Seville Historic District and announced with its name theatrically emblazoned on an iron grille above its entrance, **St Michael's Cemetery** was laid out under the orders of the Spanish in the late 1700s. Among the 3000 internees, many of them in masonry tombs raised above the ground, are slaves, settlers, priests and merchants; a glance at the inscriptions reveals old Pensacola's ethnically diverse make up.

The Pensacola area and its beaches

Intensely white-sand dunes and beaches are a common sight around Pensacola. The local shoreline includes several federally protected untamed expanses between heavily developed sections dominated by the motels, vacation condos and beach supply stores that attest to the popularity of the area. The barrier islands that hold the beaches form a natural shelter for Pensacola harbour, as do the long, thickly-forested peninsulas that jut from the mainland.

On one such peninsula is Gulf Breeze, a name familiar to UFO buffs throughout the world; on another is a vast Naval Air Station which displays the US's foremost collection of naval aircraft. Dotted throughout are historical markers such as Spanish-era forts and the former jail cell that held the famed Native American leader, Geronimo. The combination of beaches, nature and history makes for a varied and interesting route with many spectacular views. Venture inland and the reward is some of Florida's best canoeing.

FORT BARRANCAS✧

ℹ Pensacola Beach Visitors Center
735 Pensacola Beach Boulevard, Pensacola Beach; tel: (850) 932-1500 or (800) 635-4803; www.visitpensacolabeach.com. Open daily 0900–1700.

🏛 Fort Barrancas *in grounds of US Naval Air Station; tel: (850) 455-5167. Open Mar–Oct, daily 0930–1700; rest of the year daily 1030–1600; guided tours daily at 1400.*

Following Florida's acquisition by the US, Pensacola was selected as a naval base. With the aid of 400 slaves, the Spanish-built Fort Barrancas was extended and completed in 1845. The site's strategic importance below a series of bluffs to conceal it from attackers had been noted by early Spanish settlers who raised the first fortification here in 1698 and by the British who, in the 1770s, erected the Royal Naval Redoubt adjacent to the existing fort.

The fort and its interior can be explored though there is little to view, save for the brickwork galleries and the battery from where Spanish cannonballs could be bounced off the sea to strike enemy ships on their waterline.

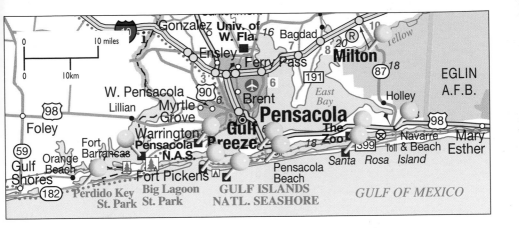

FORT PICKENS❖❖

Fort Pickens National Park $
Western end of Fort Pickens Road, Santa Rosa Island; tel: (850) 934-2635; www.nps.gov/guis/extended/FLA/History/FtPck.htm. Open Mar–Oct, 0930–1700; rest of the year, daily 0830–1600.

Pentagonal-shaped Fort Pickens was completed in 1834, the largest of a group of fortifications designed to protect Pensacola's naval shipyard. With its 40ft-high, 12ft-thick walls, the slave-built fort still has an air of invincibility, even though advances in weaponry rendered it obsolete soon after its completion. A small museum describes the fort's history and construction, and the Gulf Islands National Seashore (*see page 274*) of which it forms a part. A walk around the former storage rooms and along slender passageways to the gun placements overlooking the bay makes for an atmospheric hour.

While the fort saw no action of consequence, it did for two years incarcerate the legendary Native American, Goyahkla, popularly known as Geronimo. Leading Native resistance to enforced resettlement, Geronimo and the other Apache held with him became reluctant tourist attractions in the 1880s, before being moved, eventually to Oklahoma.

GULF BREEZE❖

Barnhill's Country Buffet $ *3075 Gulf Breeze Parkway, Gulf Breeze; tel: (850) 932-0403; www.barnhills.com. Although it can vary in quality, the food is usually good and there is always lots of it at this all-you-can-eat restaurant.*

With its balmy climate, great fishing, affordable homes and much more to lure would-be settlers, Gulf Breeze would be just another comfortable Florida coastal community were it not for the fact that, since the 1980s, it has become one of the world's most celebrated UFO-sighting locations.

Photos of an unidentified craft taken here in 1987 and published by a local newspaper were the start of what quickly escalated into hundreds of eye-witness accounts of unusual aerial activity, sometimes captured by photography and video. While sceptics are quick to point out the proximity of Pensacola's US Naval Air Station and the Eglin Air Force

Base, a short distance east, as an explanation for unusual sightings, some video footage shot here continues to defy rational explanation.

Armed with cameras, camcorders and binoculars, many would-be UFO-spotters regularly gather at **Shoreline Park**, undeterred by the notoriety that seems to bring as many hoaxers as believers.

GULF ISLANDS NATIONAL SEASHORE✦✦✦

Gulf Islands National Seashore
1801 Gulf Breeze Parkway (Headquarters), Hwy-98; tel: (850) 934-2600; www.nps.gov/guis/index.html. Open daily 0800–1730. Separate hours and fees for forts and other areas.

Spanning 135,000 acres of beaches, barrier islands, marshes and bayous (and forts Barrancas and Pickens, *see pages 272–3*) in Florida and Mississippi, the Gulf Islands National Seashore is a federally administered area protecting the natural landscape and providing environmentally friendly recreation facilities. Park ranger-led activities and guided tours, most frequent throughout the summer, are highly recommended.

The headquarters and main visitors' centre for the area is within the 1378-acre **Naval Live Oaks Reservation**. Producing a dense, disease-resistant wood, live oaks were ideal material for shipbuilding and it was here in 1828 that the government acquired a tract of land and started an experimental farm, aiming to cultivate a live oak species tailored to the needs of the navy.

The centre's displays detail the links between live oaks and shipbuilding, and document the natural and human history of the area, a site of prehistoric habitation holding one of Florida's first roads, the Pensacola–St Augustine mail route opened in 1824. A short nature trail loops from the centre through a section of the forest and to several slender beaches lining Santa Rosa Sound.

MILTON✦

Blackwater River State Park $ *Holt, 15 miles northeast of Milton; tel: (850) 623-5363; www.floridastateparks.org/ blackwaterriver. Open daily 0800–sunset.*

Once known as Scratch Ankle for the effect the local scrub had on visitors' legs, Milton has a deserved reputation as a centre for canoeing. With several creeks and the tannin-stained Blackwater River close by, canoe rental outlets are abundant in and around the town. Further north, the Blackwater River flows through **Blackwater River State Park**, forming a section of the excellent Florida Canoe Trail, meandering through forests of oak and cypress and passing sandbanks that invite a picnic stop.

NATIONAL MUSEUM OF NAVAL AVIATION✦✦✦

Opposite
National Museum of Naval Aviation

In 1914, long before the creation of the US Air Force, Pensacola became the country's first naval air station and remains its major training centre for naval pilots. This overwhelming museum fills

National Museum of Naval Aviation
In grounds of US Naval Air Station, signposted from Navy Boulevard; tel: (850) 452-3604; www.naval-air.org. Open daily 0900–1700. Free.

300,000 square feet with the aircraft, spacecraft and various other craft flown by the US Navy and Coast Guard over the years.

A large section is devoted to World War II, including a full-sized reconstruction of an aircraft carrier flight deck, lined by planes of the period with a below-decks area complete with a shop selling 1940s shaving cream and soft drinks. The use of naval pilots in the US space programme is illustrated with the command module from the first skylab mission in 1973, crewed by naval personnel. Among many hands-on exhibits are the cockpit simulators used to train pilots.

Short of being airborne, the best way to experience the thrills and spills of cutting-edge flight is with the ultra-realistic films shown in the IMAX cinema. A more sombre side of naval pilotry is provided by a reconstruction of Hoa Lo Prison, housing captured American pilots during the Vietnam War, the misery of their incarceration suggested with photos and possessions of former inmates.

NAVARRE BEACH*

Narvarre Beach, among the smallest of the area's coastal settlements, has many homes raised on stilts to avoid flooding and a strip of white-sand beach from which extends a busy fishing pier. Sailing, parasailing, water-skiing, jetskiing, scuba-diving, snorkelling, fishing and canoeing are among the activities which can be enjoyed here. Immediately west begins a 17-mile stretch of sand dunes that divides the town from Pensacola Beach.

PENSACOLA BEACH**

The most developed portion of the 20-mile-long Santa Rosa Island (*see page 278*), Pensacola Beach has numerous restaurants, hotels and beach supply outlets. Commercial growth does little to dent its appeal, however, because the beach is superb and easily accessible. Though it may be hard to hear above the sound of the surf, the sand, due to its composition, squeaks as you walk on it.

Accommodation and food in Pensacola Beach

Bobaloos On The Beach $–$$ *699 Pensacola Beach Boulevard; tel: (850) 934-3434; www.bobaloos.com.* Seafood takes pride of place at this beachfront eatery, where crab claws, crawfish tails, scampi, and other marine delights feature.

Clarion Resort & Suites $$ *20 Via de Luna Drive; tel: (850) 932-4300; www.clarionsuitesresort.com.* Kitchen-equipped suites adjacent to the beach and local amenities; free continental breakfast.

Left
Gulf Islands National Seashore

The Dunes \$\$ *333 Fort Pickens Road; tel: (850) 932-3535 or (800) 83DUNES; www.theduneshotel.com.* With two pools, penthouse rooms and a 24-hour café this is one of the area's better-equipped lodgings.

Five Flags Inn \$–\$\$ *299 Fort Pickens Road; tel: (850) 932-3586; email: info@fiveflagsinn.com; www.fiveflagsinn.com.* All the rooms of this good-value motel face the Gulf of Mexico, tempting a pre-breakfast swim.

Flounder's Chowder & Ale House \$\$ *800 Quietwater Beach Road; tel: (850) 932-2003; www.floundershowderhouse.com.* Chargrilled seafood is the speciality of this intentionally rustic eatery which extends on to a patio bar overlooking Santa Rosa Sound.

Hampton Inn Pensacola Beach \$\$ *2 Via De Luna Drive; tel: (850) 932-6800 or (800) 320 8180; www.hamptonbeachresort.com.* Perfect for the beach with clean, comfortable, well-sized rooms and very good off-season rates.

PERDIDO KEY❖❖

🅗 Perdido Key State Recreation Area \$
Perdido Key; tel: (850) 492-1595; www.floridastateparks.org/perdidokey. Open daily 0800–sunset.

🍴 Flora-Bama Lounge \$ *17401 Perdido Key Drive; tel: (850) 492-0611; www.florabama.com.* Live music, drinks and oysters served on the Florida-Alabama border.

Perdido Key is a long, slender barrier island connected by road bridge to Florida in the east and Alabama in the west. It has its share of high-rise condos and holiday homes, but much of its beach is protected within the **Perdido Key State Recreation Area**.

Along the island's most easterly 5 miles, the beaches and sand dunes form part of the Gulf Islands National Seashore (*see page 274*). Here, the short **Johnson Beach Nature Trail** picks a route beside salt marshes supporting a rich variety of birdlife, through maritime forests and over sand hills. Facing the far-better preserved Fort Pickens (*see page 273*) across the bay, the 1830s **Fort McRee**, accessible only by foot or boat, marks Perdido Key's eastern tip.

SANTA ROSA ISLAND❖❖❖

Almost 50 miles long, this narrow finger of land reaches from Fort Walton Beach (*see page 257*) in the east to Fort Pickens (*see page 273*) in the west. Although it holds several beach communities, the largest being Pensacola Beach (*see page 277*), much is undeveloped, providing a matchless setting for sunbathing, swimming and beachcombing. The whiteness of the sands, intensely bright in strong sunshine, is due to the grains being almost pure quartz, lacking the crushed seashell or feldspar that forms darker and less powdery sand.

THE ZOO❖

This manageably sized zoo includes lions, tigers, zebras, giraffes and what is claimed to be the world's largest gorilla. The zoo can be explored from

The Zoo $ *5701 Gulf Breeze Highway, Gulf Breeze; tel: (850) 932-2229; www.the-zoo.com. Open daily 0900–1700.*

atop an elephant or on the **Safari Line**, which carries passengers on a miniature railway through a 30-acre plain where rhinos, hippos, alligators and many other creatures roam comparatively freely. The children's section has a full complement of cuddly, furry creatures available for hugging and stroking.

Suggested tour

**Pensacola
Convention &
Visitors Information
Center** 1401 E Gregory
Street (foot of Three Mile
Bridge), Pensacola; tel: (850)
343-1234 or (800) 874-
1234;
www.visitpensacola.com.
Open Mon–Fri 0800–1700,
Sat 0900–1600, Sun
1100–1600.

Length: Main tour 78 miles; Milton and Blackwater State Park detour 92 miles; Perdido Key detour 37 miles.

Duration: Main tour 2.5 hours; 1 hour for the Perdido Key detour. Detours to Milton and Black Water State Park will add 2 hours' driving time but are only worthwhile if a canoe trip is included, therefore allocate at least half a day.

Links: Crossing the Panhandle (*see pages 254–63*), Pensacola (*see pages 264–71*).

Arriving from the east, Hwy-98 reaches the small bayside community of **Navarre**. Turn left here on to Route 399 which crosses Santa Rosa Bay (toll) to **NAVARRE BEACH ❶** on Santa Rosa Island, consisting of a few shops, a fishing pier and a brilliantly white-sand beach with dunes topped by coarse vegetation. A similar outlook fills the next 17 miles to **PENSACOLA BEACH ❷**, the area's largest beach town. Motels, shops and restaurants become increasingly plentiful along Via de Luna (the local name for Route 399), the heart of the community.

West of the junction with Pensacola Bridge Road, signs of development thin and 2.6 miles ahead is the **Fort Pickens State Park** section of **GULF ISLANDS NATIONAL SEASHORE ❸**. The road picks through 7.5 miles of wooded picnic and camping areas before expiring close to the substantial remains of **FORT PICKENS ❹**, overlooking the seaborne approach to Pensacola.

Return to Pensacola Bridge Road, turning left to cross the bay (toll payable on return) to reach **GULF BREEZE ❺**. On the left immediately after the Hwy-98 junction is Shoreline Drive, which leads quickly to **Shoreline Park**, a popular site for UFO watchers. The entrance to **Naval Live Oaks** is 1.3 miles east on Hwy-98. Also on this route, after passing through the small town of **Oriole Beach**, is **Woodlawn Beach**, 8.5 miles from Gulf Breeze and site of **THE ZOO ❻**.

Some Gulf Breeze UFO sightings may be aircraft belonging to Pensacola's US Naval Air Station, located directly across Pensacola Bay from Gulf Breeze. To reach the station and its excellent **NATIONAL MUSEUM OF NAVAL AVIATION ❼**, head north on Hwy-98 as it crosses Three Mile Bridge above Pensacola Bay and swings west to pass through the city of Pensacola before becoming Navy Boulevard (Route 295) from which the museum is signposted. Signs also indicate the route to **FORT BARRANCAS ❽**, located within the Naval Air Station grounds.

Canoeing

A number of specialist canoe companies operate in and around Milton. Most will provide everything for a canoe trip, including transportation to and from the launch site. Some have guided canoe tours. Two of the longest established are **Adventures Unlimited** tel: (850) 623-6197 or (800) BE-YOUNG; www.adventuresunlimited. com and **Blackwater Canoe Rental** tel: (850) 623-0235 or (800) 623-6789; www. blackwatercanoe.com

Detour: MILTON ❾, the self-styled 'canoe capital of the world', can be reached by taking Route 87, north off Hwy-98 in Navarre. Route 87 weaves through several diminutive communities and crosses the

Big Lagoon State Park $ *12301 Gulf Beach Highway; tel: (850) 492-1595; www.floridastateparks.org/ biglagoon/default.asp. Open daily 0800–sunset.*

eastern section of the Eglin Air Force Base (*see page 257*) before, after 20 miles, passing beneath I-10 and, a few miles ahead, meeting Hwy-90. Milton lies 4.3 miles west on Hwy-90, a route that crosses the Blackwater River. The river is one among many canoe-friendly waterways in the vicinity. There is more canoeing at **Blackwater State Park**, 15 heavily-forested miles north of Milton on Route 191.

Detour: Immediately north of the Naval Air Station, Navy Boulevard crosses Route 292 (Gulf Beach Highway, becoming Sorrento Road). Take this route west, after 10 miles passing the entrance to **Big Lagoon State Park** (*see Also worth exploring below*). Turn left on to Perdido Key Drive which continues to **PERDIDO KEY ❿**. The route continues west, following the shoreline, passing high-rise condos and the undeveloped **Perdido Key State Park**. The even more pristine eastern section of Perdido Key, part of the Gulf Islands National Seashore, is accessed by Johnson Beach Road, off Perdido Key Drive.

Also worth exploring

The swimming and picnicking areas of **Big Lagoon State Park** are a well-guarded secret. Even in summer, when the area's beaches are swamped by sunbathers, this 678-acre park retains much of its natural peace and tranquillity. The park's beaches flank the placid Big Lagoon, popular among anglers for its stocks of mullet and sea trout, and several walking trails pass through woodlands and around wildlife-rich salt marshes. At the east beach, an observation tower provides a panoramic overview of the park and beyond.

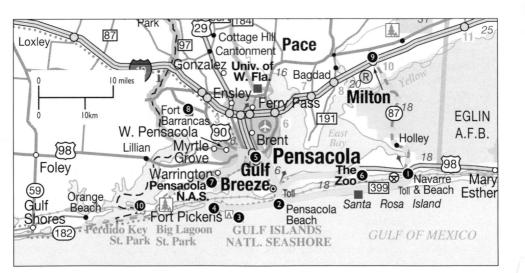

Language

Idioms

Alternate: Means 'alternative', not 'every other'– sometimes a source of confusion when reading timetables.

Bed & Breakfast (or 'B&B'): Overnight lodging in a private home, usually with private facilities and almost always more expensive than nearby hotels and motels.

Brewpub: A tavern that brews its own beer.

Buffalo wings: Chicken wings, usually fried and served with a spicy sauce as an appetiser or as bar food.

California cuisine: Anything the chef wants it to mean, as long as it's expensive, but usually based on fresh, organically grown foods.

Chili dog or chili burger: Hot dog or hamburger disguised with chilli, onions and cheese.

Chimichanga: A pseudo-Mexican concoction of a fried tortilla filled with meat, beans, cheese, tomatoes and lettuce.

Chips: Crisps, usually made from potatoes, but also from corn, taro, cassava, rice or other starches.

Corn dog: Hot dog dipped in corn meal and fried. Usually served hot on a stick.

Dead head: Fans of the band the Grateful Dead; also a term for hippies.

Designer water: Pejorative term for bottled water.

Downtown: City or town centre.

Holiday: A public holiday, such as Labor Day, not a private holiday, which is a vacation.

Lodging: The usual term for accommodation.

Natural ingredients: Food that has been grown, processed and prepared without pesticides or other chemical additives.

Outlet shopping: Shopping at large stores specialising in factory overruns at reduced prices. Sometimes, factory outlets are simply low-priced retail stores selling direct from the factory.

Resort: A fancy hotel which specialises in leisure activities such as golf, tennis and swimming.

Road kill: Literally, animals killed by passing cars, but usually used to describe bad restaurant food.

Floridian driving terms

Big rig: A large lorry, usually a tractor pulling one or more trailers.

Boulevard stop: Slowing at a stop sign, but not stopping.

CNG: Liquified petroleum gas used as fuel.

Crosswalk: Pedestrian crossing.

Connector: A minor road connecting two freeways.

Curve: Bend.

Divided highway: Dual carriageway.

Fender: Bumper.

Freeway: Motorway.

Garage or parking: Garage car park.

Gas(oline): Petrol.

Grade: Gradient, hill.

Highway: Trunk road.

Hood: Bonnet.

Metering lights: Traffic signals controlling access to bridges, freeways, etc.

Motor home: Motor caravan.

Pavement: Road surface. A UK 'pavement' is a US sidewalk.

Ramp: Slip road.

Rent: Hire.

Rubbernecking: Slowing down to peer while driving past the scene of an accident or some unusual event.

RV (recreational vehicle): Motor caravan.

Shift (stick): Gear lever.

Shoulder: Verge.

Sidewalk: Pavement.

Sig-alert: An official warning of unusually heavy traffic, usually broadcast over local radio stations.

Switchback: Serpentine road.

Tow truck: Breakdown lorry.

Traffic cop: Traffic warden.

Truck: Lorry.

Trunk: Boot.

Yield: Give way.

Index

Acknowledgements

Project management: Cambridge Publishing Management Limited
Project editor: Karen Beaulah
Series design: Fox Design
Cover design: Liz Lyons Design
Layout and map work: Concept 5D/Cambridge Publishing Management Limited
Repro and image setting: Z2 Repro; PDQ Digital Media Solutions Ltd/Cambridge Publishing Management Limited
Printed and bound in India by: Replika Press Pvt Ltd

We would like to thank the following photographers and organisations for the photographs used in this book, to whom the copyright in the photographs belongs:

Front cover: Ocean Drive, Miami Beach, Jon Arnold Images/Alamy
Back cover: Lifeguard station, Miami Beach, Angelo Cavalli/Getty Images

Maxine Cass: pages 3, 5, 9, 13, 14, 22, 24, 28, 32, 34, 42, 45, 48, 52, 55, 56, 59, 60, 64, 67, 68, 70, 74, 77, 81, 86, 88, 91, 94, 96, 99, 103, 104, 106, 108, 111, 114, 117, 118, 120, 122, 124, 127, 128, 130, 132, 134, 136, 139, 140, 146, 148, 151, 154, 157, 162, 164, 166, 168, 172, 173, 175, 176, 179, 183, 187, 192, 195, 197, 200, 203, 205, 208, 210, 212, 218A, 218B, 220, 222, 225, 226, 228, 231, 233, 234, 244, 248, 254, 258, 261, 264, 266, 269, 272A, 272B, 275, 276, 279; **Fred Gebhart:** pages 7, 17, 36, 41, 46, 78, 84, 85, 100, 102, 110, 144, 147, 180A, 180B, 184, 189, 191, 206, 214, 247, 251; **Pictures Colour Library:** pages 16 and 20; **Tallahassee Area Convention and Visitors Bureau:** 236A, 236B, 239.

Feedback form

If you enjoyed using this book, or even if you didn't, please help us improve future editions by taking part in our reader survey. Every returned form will be acknowledged, and to show our appreciation we will give you £1 off your next purchase of a Thomas Cook guidebook. Just take a few minutes to complete and return this form to us.

When did you buy this book? ....
....

Where did you buy it? (Please give town/city and, if possible, name of retailer)
....
....

When did you/do you intend to travel in Florida? ....
....

For how long (approx)? ....

How many people in your party? ....

Which cities, national parks and other locations did you/do you intend mainly to visit?
....
....
....
....

Did you/will you:
❏ Make all your travel arrangements independently?
❏ Travel on a fly-drive package?
Please give brief details: ....
....

Did you/do you intend to use this book:
❏ For planning your trip?   ❏ Both?
❏ During the trip itself?

Did you/do you intend also to purchase any of the following travel publications for your trip?
A road map/atlas (please specify) ....
Other guidebooks (please specify) ....

Have you used any other Thomas Cook guidebooks in the past? If so, which?
....
....

Please rate the following features of *Drive Around Florida* for their value to you (circle VU for 'very useful', U for 'useful', NU for 'little or no use'):

The *Travel facts* section on pages 14–25	VU	U	NU
The *Driver's guide* section on pages 26–31	VU	U	NU
The *Highlights* on pages 40–41	VU	U	NU
The recommended driving routes throughout the book	VU	U	NU
Information on towns and cities, National Parks, etc	VU	U	NU
The maps of towns and cities, parks, etc	VU	U	NU

Please use this space to tell us about any features that in your opinion could be changed, improved, or added in future editions of the book, or any other comments you would like to make concerning the book:

....
....
....
....
....
....
....
....

Your age category: ❑ 21–30   ❑ 31–40   ❑ 41–50   ❑ over 50

Your name: Mr/Mrs/Miss/Ms ....
(First name or initials) ....
(Last name) ....

Your full address (please include postal or zip code):

....
....
....
....
....

Your daytime telephone number: ....

Please detach this page and send it to: The Series Editor, Drive Around Guides, Thomas Cook Publishing, PO Box 227, The Thomas Cook Business Park, 15–16 Coningsby Road, Peterborough PE3 8SB.

Alternatively, you can email us at: *books@thomascook.com*

We will be pleased to send you details of how to claim your discount upon receipt of the questionnaire.